DATE DUE

Praise for
City of Dust

"Part chronicle of tragedy and heroism, part detective story, and part legal thriller, this book offers a comprehensive and fearless account of the environmental aftermath of the September 11th attack on the World Trade Center and the public health consequences of the worst environmental disaster in New York City's history."

—**Eric A. Goldstein**, New York City Environment Director for the Natural Resources Defense Council

"*City of Dust* delivers what is so often missing from 9/11 coverage—deep, careful, clear, fair reporting that separates fact from fiction. But DePalma also rouses the reader to indignation over the shortcomings of a system that, nearly a decade after the collapse of the World Trade Center, still hasn't done right by responders and residents whose health was destroyed by the poisons they breathed."

—**Jonathan Alter**, author of *The Promise: President Obama, Year One*

"*City of Dust* is the most complete account of 9/11 and its aftermath yet written. *City of Dust* is a must-read for anyone involved in emergency preparedness and response or in environmental safety and health, for students of government and politics, or for the general reader who wants to understand more about the tragic aftermath of 9/11.

Much has been written about what led up to the World Trade Center terrorist attacks, as well as what happened on the terrible day of September 11th. Until *City of Dust*, though, no writer has told the complete story of the tragic aftermath of 9/11 on the health and well-being of thousands of World Trade Center responders, cleanup workers, and community residents. Finally, a writer has chronicled in detail what these responders and residents have lived with for nearly ten years—the loss of good health, the inability earn a living, the ever-present worry about developing cancer in the future, and the difficulties in obtaining appropriate compensation for what they lost.

Although DePalma's subject is a difficult one, *City of Dust* weaves stories about responders' heroic actions on 9/11, the persisting human health effects caused their response work, government decision-making then and now, medical detective work, and court cases into a very compelling and readable book.

For anyone who thinks that the tragic consequences of 9/11 ended in December of 2001 when the fires at Ground Zero were finally extinguished, I urge them to read *City of Dust* to learn of the continuing story of 9/11."

—**John Howard, M.D.**, Coordinator, World Trade Center Health Program, U.S. Department of Health and Human Services

"For anyone concerned about the long-term health effects of 9/11—or for that matter about the bungled handling of disasters in general—this book is essential. Thoroughly researched, well-written, passionate, it's the final word on what should be done and should not be done."

—**John Darnton**, author of *Black and White and Dead All Over* and *Neanderthal*

"After 9/11, when the truth was shockingly hard to come by, Anthony DePalma never settled. With careful reporting and masterful storytelling, *City of Dust* is the essential guide across the heavily contested terrain of environmental safety and medical care for those who served at Ground Zero. Lies are toxic. This book is the antidote."

—**Jim Dwyer**, author, with Kevin Flynn, of *102 Minutes: The Untold Story of the Fight to Survive Inside the Twin Towers*

CITY OF DUST

CITY OF DUST

ILLNESS, ARROGANCE, AND 9/11

Anthony DePalma

Vice President, Publisher: Tim Moore
Associate Publisher and Director of Marketing: Amy Neidlinger
Acquisitions Editor: Kirk Jensen
Editorial Assistant: Pamela Boland
Operations Manager: Gina Kanouse
Senior Marketing Manager: Julie Phifer
Publicity Manager: Laura Czaja
Assistant Marketing Manager: Megan Colvin
Cover Designer: Alan Clements
Managing Editor: Kristy Hart
Senior Project Editor: Lori Lyons
Copy Editor: Krista Hansing Editorial Services, Inc.
Proofreader: Kay Hoskin
Indexer: Lisa Stumpf
Compositor: Jake McFarland
Manufacturing Buyer: Dan Uhrig

© 2011 by Pearson Education, Inc.
Publishing as FT Press
Upper Saddle River, New Jersey 07458

FT Press offers excellent discounts on this book when ordered in quantity for bulk purchases or special sales. For more information, please contact U.S. Corporate and Government Sales, 1-800-382-3419, corpsales@pearsontechgroup.com. For sales outside the U.S., please contact International Sales at international@pearson.com.

Company and product names mentioned herein are the trademarks or registered trademarks of their respective owners.

Printed in the United States of America

Second Printing October 2010

ISBN-10: 0-13-138566-6
ISBN-13: 978-0-13-138566-5

Pearson Education LTD.
Pearson Education Australia PTY, Limited.
Pearson Education Singapore, Pte. Ltd.
Pearson Education North Asia, Ltd.
Pearson Education Canada, Ltd.
Pearson Educación de Mexico, S.A. de C.V.
Pearson Education—Japan
Pearson Education Malaysia, Pte. Ltd.

Library of Congress Cataloging-in-Publication Data

DePalma, Anthony.
  City of dust : illness, arrogance, and 9/11/ Anthony DePalma. — 1st ed.
      p. cm.
  ISBN 978-0-13-138566-5 (alk. paper)
 1. September 11 Terrorist Attacks, 2001—Health aspects—New York (State)—New York. 2. September 11 Terrorist Attacks, 2001—Environmental aspects—New York (State)—New York. 3. Air quality management—New York (State)—New York. 4. World Trade Center Site (New York, N.Y.) I. Title.
  RA566.D47 2010
  363.739'2097471—dc22
                        2010008389

For Aahren, Leanne, Laura Felice, and Andrés,
That they may always see the truth.

And for all those who responded when
the need was greatest,
That their sacrifice may never be overlooked.

Contents

Acknowledgments

Besides all those whose names appear in this book, I need to acknowledge several individuals without whose help these pages could never have been written. First, Bill Keller and *The New York Times* gave me the opportunity to cover this important story and to keep pursuing the truth. Monsignor Robert Sheeran and Seton Hall University provided the time and space for me to complete this book. I also want to thank Ellen Borakove of the New York City medical examiner's office, Kate O'Brien Ahlers at New York's law department, and Prof. Lester Brickman of the Benjamin N. Cardozo School of Law. Over several years, they provided many answers to my insistent questions. And I owe a substantial debt to Amy Green for her good work in Florida.

I also have complied with the request of those who gave their time and shared their knowledge but asked not to be identified by name. They should know how much I appreciate their assistance. Because of the gargantuan legal proceedings against New York City, many individuals were unable to speak freely. In those instances, I relied on 7,826 pages of written depositions, a mountain of filed memos, and countless other documents. A Freedom of Information request produced important insights into the early days after the 9/11 attacks, and the New York fire department's oral histories proved invaluable. Despite repeated requests, Christie Whitman, Rudy Giuliani, and other important players simply refused to say anything, although their input could have provided valuable insights.

I was aided in the conception of the book by Stuart Krichevsky, my agent, and Kirk Jensen, my editor at FT Press, who threw his full support behind the project. Finally, I need to thank my family, especially Miriam, for bearing with me yet again.

About the Author

Anthony DePalma is the writer-in-residence at Seton Hall University. He spent 22 years as a reporter and foreign correspondent for *The New York Times,* where he reported on environmental issues and served as bureau chief for Mexico and for Canada. In 2009 he received the Maria Moors Cabot Prize for distinguished international journalism. He is also the author of *Here: A Biography of the New American Continent* (Public Affairs, 2001) and *The Man Who Invented Fidel: Castro, Cuba, and Herbert L. Matthews of the New York Times* (Public Affairs, 2006).

"If we are not subject to a kind of ignorance, akin to madness, which often overtakes men in the wretched condition of this life so that they mistake a foe for a friend or a friend for a foe, what is there to console us in this human society full of misunderstandings and calamities except the unfeigned faith and mutual affection of true and good friends?"

—Augustine of Hippo,
City of God (19:8)

Part I

Catastrophe

Introduction

Of all the images of the September 11, 2001, attack on New York, the one that's been hardest for me to shake is not the fiery flash of impact, or the harrowing sight of desperate people leaping to their deaths, or the awesome 10.52 seconds it took for the first tower to buckle and cave in on itself in a maelstrom of concrete and ash, followed incredibly by the second tower falling just as fast, a few yards away. Terrible indeed were those images, but there was also an aspect of cinematic unreality about them that has kept me distant, as though watching a movie or playing a video game. The one picture that has left an indelible scar on my heart is an unlikely photograph that my colleague Eddie Keating took of an elegant tea set he came upon in a vacated apartment near ground zero. The matching teapots, cups, and sugar bowl, perhaps set for breakfast on that achingly clear September morning, were covered with a skintight layer of dust the color of dried bones.

That ghostly tableau has stuck with me in the years since I first saw it, not because it elicits horror or dredges up anger, but because it so strikingly symbolizes the way the event and its aftermath have clung to so many people far beyond the grim arenas of terrorism, war, and the doomed World Trade Center itself. The fancy china had no direct connection to the events of that day before the first plane struck. And yet it had been enveloped in a supple coating of death and destruction that transformed it from a treasured implement of daily life to an artifact of a moment of death. The dust infiltrated thousands of offices and apartments in the same way. It was carried back to thousands more homes by first responders, construction workers, and volunteers who helped in the days and weeks after the attack—at first to find survivors, then sadly to recover the remains of victims and clean up the site to show the terrorists, and the world, that the great city had been hurt but not humbled. It turned New York into a city of dust.

That dust has clung to the city just as surely as it coated the tea set, transforming New York. What happened after the attack is a uniquely American tragedy, triggered by the same virtues of generosity and care that have come to be most associated with the American character. It took only seven days for Wall Street to limp back to business, showing the terrorists that their violence had not undone America. That was the essential message. There was no time for the great city to dwell on what the long-term impact of the dust might be, or even to acknowledge that there could be a lingering danger. The failure to reopen Wall Street quickly would have been a certain disaster. A distant threat that the dust might have poisoned the air and made part of the city unlivable was then not only uncertain, it was unacceptable.

So the ground was set for a tug-of-war between truth and exaggeration, between alarmism and deception, between personal safety and political expediency that turned the worst environmental disaster in New York City history into a test of our science, our laws, our precepts of governance, and even our traditional understanding of the common good. In essence, it became a test of ourselves. Although the attack exposed mortal flaws in the nation's ability to protect itself from terrorists who hoped to die in the attack, reopening Wall Street proved that America had not been defeated. But the very success of that effort, and the quick work that was made of the cleanup and recovery that followed, was laced with tragedy. In ways that would become apparent only over time, our handling of the aftermath of the attack revealed that this nation was not prepared to protect itself from itself.

The problems that arose after 9/11 have been presented as a deliberate attempt by the Bush administration, as well as the city, to cover up the danger, a vast conspiracy to put profit ahead of people's health. But it wasn't that. Many bad decisions clearly were made, but there was no venality, nor was there a conspiracy to hide the enormity of what happened, if that were even possible. Rather, a long sequence of individual decisions—some made in haste, some made with arrogance—favored the recovery of the city over the recovery of its people.

In response to this catastrophe, the men and women of science and medicine tried against enormous odds to piece together a compassionate response and to provide answers for those who desperately needed to know what had happened to them and what they could expect in the future. The word *hero* was thrown around freely, at times used when and where it was not warranted. There were genuine heroes and villains, but they did not confront each other in the direct way this conflict was portrayed once the tabloid press hijacked the disaster. Mayor Rudy Giuliani wasn't the only one who made difficult choices that seemed to put recovery ahead of precaution. Even those who were most experienced at rescue made decisions that ultimately would have tragic consequences. The heroic firefighters who searched for their fallen brethren believed that exposing themselves to hazardous material in order to recover their dead was a justified calculation. In their eyes, the living owed a debt to the dead that made self-interest intolerable.

The defining characteristic of the catastrophe is that from the morning of September 11, the dangers presented by the dust and ash were clear for everyone to see. Billowing gray dust plumes rampaged through city streets like monsters unleashed from hell. Microscopic dust was transformed into a gruesome invader, attacking the most essential of human needs—the need to breathe. It was inescapable, yet the dust became a metaphor for the blindness that descended on the city, obscuring reality and confounding decisions that would later be regretted.

Although millions of people watched in horror as the buildings disintegrated, the dust itself remained a mystery. Even with the most advanced science, we do not yet know what the wicked concoction of dust, ash, and toxic materials did when it landed deep inside the heaving lungs of responders. We don't know how it short-circuited their immune systems or toyed with their genes. And we won't know for years if it combined with other poisons to speed up or exacerbate carcinogenic attacks on the bodies of people who were coated with it, just as the tea set was coated. However, we do know that the doubts sown in the very earliest days have been long lasting. What might have been a sentinel case of emergency response that raised an entire nation from its knees instead became an endless cycle of bickering, mistrust, sickness, and uncertainty as officials tried to deflect blame, responders became crusaders for themselves, lawyers sought to make courtroom history, and emotions that had never before been felt rose to the surface. A wounded city became a diseased city that often refused to recognize its own disabilities.

Now, long after most of the dust itself has been cleared away, many individual stories of true courage and heroism burn through this haze of doubt. There has been no end to the searing accounts of men and women who truly acted like heroes only to be laid low by diseases they cannot explain. There have been stirring examples of men and women of science who have refused to allow politics or public opinion to shade their work, and who have toiled against great odds and in the most challenging of circumstances to continue to provide care in the screening and treatment their patients needed. Heroes have abounded.

Unfortunately, the combination of our darkest traits and our most noble ones made the story of the city of dust more compelling than the truth could justify, and some have succumbed to the temptation to bend the truth to serve their needs. It will take years for the air to clear, if it ever does.

Certainty, in principle and in practice, itself became a victim. The doubters initially used principles of certitude to challenge the notion that the dust made people sick. By denying any danger in the early weeks and months after 9/11, New York City and Washington hesitated to take steps that could have reliably assessed the safety of workers and residents. By not being clear about the risks, the federal and municipal governments—in what has been called a conspiracy of purpose— sacrificed a degree of safety for the quick recovery of Wall Street. Then, by staking out a high moral ground that made it difficult to question survivors' symptoms, advocates made it easier for abuses to take place.

For four years, I covered the environmental and health consequences of ground zero for *The New York Times*. Many of my articles appeared on the front page of *The Times* and were reprinted around the world. I got to know many of the most important people involved, from the earliest attempts to identify the contents of the dust, up to the historic mass litigation that brought thousands of responders to court charging New York City with negligence. At every turn, I encountered people on both extremes of the issue—those who refused to believe that the dust had caused anyone to become sick, and those who refused to accept that the dust was not going to kill everyone it touched. When the head of the federal Environmental Protection Agency said the air was safe to breathe, I, like so many New Yorkers, was relieved because, at that time, in the days just after the attacks, it seemed impossible to have processed more bad news. I believed because I wanted to believe. Later, as I investigated what had happened, I came to view things differently.

The city of New York at one point estimated that more than 500,000 people may have been affected by the dust in some way.[1] In addition, thousands of people from across the country came to New York at that tragic time to work on the pile. Millions watched the towers fall and sympathized with those who were injured while doing their jobs. Under most circumstances, American society celebrates the efforts of those who respond to emergencies. In New York, some of those people have been all but forgotten. The painfully slow physical rebuilding of ground zero receives far more attention than does the health of those who responded to the disaster. Even as the ranks of the sick grow, they fade farther into the background. And not just the responders were touched by the dust. Residents, workers, scientists, doctors, lawyers, and politicians all felt the dust in some way. This story of the victims of the aftermath of 9/11, told through the personal experiences of the individuals whose lives have never been the same since that day, represents an overlooked chapter of one of the most extraordinary events of our time.

The scientific, medical, political, and legal scope of the disaster has never been looked at in this comprehensive way. Because of the massive litigation against the city, many of the individuals most intimately involved in the cleanup and its aftermath have declined to speak out publicly, leaving their court testimony to speak for them. Everything about the disaster is monumental, except for the dust itself. But only when the small decisions and the individual acts of arrogance, ignorance, and courage are examined will a telling sense of the tragedy come through. In the end, it is a story of fear and a story of hope. The people of the city, like the city itself, were laid low but were not broken. And we, as a society, will not be prepared to handle the next disaster unless we fully understand what we did right—and wrong—the last time.

Endnotes

[1]"Assessing the Health Impacts of 9-11," Report of the World Trade Center Health Panel, February 13, 2007: 50.

1

All that we hold dear

Stowed among the beakers and boxes in the cold room of the Central New Jersey lab are several jars filled with elemental material that, if the need arose, could be categorized as catastrophe. The jars—standard chem-lab bottles in amber or clear glass—are labeled only with the dates September 16 and September 17. Those are the days in 2001 when Dr. Paul J. Lioy, a leading scientist at New Jersey's Environmental & Occupational Health Sciences Institute, made his way to New York City to sample fallout from the most devastating attack on American soil and the worst environmental disaster in the city's history. If the terrible calamity of the destruction of the World Trade Center could be reduced to its essence and bottled, this is what it would look like. Held at a constant 39°F since 2001, the dust now looks so benign. But at its moment of creation, it roared out of the base of the collapsing towers with uncontrolled fury. Tens of thousands of people touched it, breathed it in, swallowed it, rubbed it out of their eyes, wiped it off their clothes, and tried to brush it off their carpets and drapes, their sofas and teacups, even the teddy bears that their children hugged to sleep at night. Breathing is the most elemental yet essential part of life. Our lungs are especially sensitive to contaminants because they come in direct contact with the environment, as if the body were turned inside out. Lioy was determined to find out what that dust was made of and how dangerous it might be.

When he arrived at the confusion of Lower Manhattan early on September 16, a pretty Sunday morning tainted by the inescapable sense of dread, Lioy already had an inkling of what he was going to find. As each 110-story paragon of modern architecture and unbridled capitalism had disassembled in ten transfixing, confounding seconds, he had been at the quirky 120-year-old Victorian home that he and his wife, Jeanie, lovingly restored in suburban Cranford, New Jersey, watching spellbound on TV. With his years of experience studying environmental contamination, Lioy was certain the doomed buildings contained a long list of dangerous chemicals and harmful elements that would be blown far and wide by even the gentlest breeze. He also was quite familiar with the complicated grid of Lower Manhattan that had been blanketed by the dust. He'd grown up across the Hudson from New York and had watched the towers being built. Lioy's spine had stiffened as the television screen filled with images of first one and then, 29 minutes later, a second angry thunderhead of dust roaring through the streets like a bloated tornado, blotting out the sun while engulfing everything—and everyone—in its path.

In the world of environmental health science, what looks bad often ends up being bad for people unlucky enough to live or work around the suspected hazard. That's the easy part of the science, which has existed only since the world became sensitive to environmental issues in the 1970s. The hard part is getting anyone to do anything to eliminate the hazards, or even control them. In the past, factories, shipyards, mines, and the towns around them were routinely contaminated by industrial processes, but little or nothing was done to correct things. People got sick. Many died. Even when a link between working conditions and disease was suspected, few thought anything could be changed. Fewer still were willing to do what it took to make a difference.

Environmental health had not always been Lioy's passion. He had never worked in a factory, and big industry was not a part of his family background. But it was a part of the environment in which he was raised. His father, Nicholas, an Italian immigrant, was part owner of a building in the gray industrial town of Passaic that housed a combination delicatessen and liquor store. As a teenager, Paul often worked in the deli and came to prefer being there—or playing sandlot baseball—to wasting time in the classroom. He was an indifferent student, too smart for school, too lazy or distracted to strike out on his own. His report card was regularly marked "L.A." in behavior—it stood for "lousy attitude."

But then Lioy discovered science, particularly chemistry. More important, he found out that he was good at it. He saw a problem and was challenged by the mechanics of trying to figure out the answer. And the beauty of the answers, the intricate structures of the physical world and the way elements stacked atop one another, linked in curious ways according to intractable rules, intrigued him. He studied physics and applied mathematics, and in 1975 earned his PhD in environmental science at Rutgers. One of his first jobs after graduating was a safe bureaucratic one as an engineer with the Interstate Sanitation Commission that served New York and New Jersey. One of the first projects he was thrown into there was testing a theory advanced by a colleague that ozone in the atmosphere was not produced locally, but was being transported in the air from Midwestern states. Elaborate testing gear was set up on the highest spots around, including the roof of the recently completed World Trade Center. Lioy collected and analyzed the data, eventually coming up with an answer (much of the ozone turned out not to be produced locally, but came from faraway states).

Thirty years later, Lioy was sent back to the trade center by the National Institute of Environmental Health Sciences, an arm of the federal Department of Health and Human Services. In the fear and confusion of those first days after the planes smashed into the towers, officials at the institute ignored pronouncements by Mayor Rudy Giuliani and the Environmental Protection Agency about conditions in Lower Manhattan. They were thinking about the fallout and the potential danger it represented for the people who lived and worked there, including the rapidly expanding horde of workers scraping through the top layer of the monstrous debris pile for survivors. As deputy director of the environmental institute in New Jersey (which is sponsored jointly by Rutgers and the University of Medicine and Dentistry of New Jersey), a member of the faculty at the Robert Wood Johnson Medical School, and a nationally recognized expert on air exposure, Lioy was a natural choice to lead the investigation. Lioy had excused Giuliani's optimistic outlook about the dust as political necessity, but it struck him as strange that Christie Whitman, the head of the Environmental Protection Agency and former Republican governor of New Jersey, had sounded no warning about any contaminants other than asbestos. Just two days after the attack, Whitman's agency stated that monitoring and sampling for asbestos was "very reassuring about potential exposure of rescue crews and the public to environmental contaminants."[1]

For the firefighters and police officers working on the pile; for the news cameramen breathing in noxious gases as they flew over the superhot debris in helicopters; for the first ironworkers who scrambled over the still-smoking mound to begin the massive job of removing more than 1.5 million tons of mangled steel; and for the volunteers, office workers, and residents who all gulped the tainted air into their frightened lungs, there would be only speculation, not hard scientific facts, about what they had actually been exposed to in those first hours and days after the buildings fell.

Lioy left home before sunrise that Sunday morning, steering his black Lincoln Mark VIII up the Garden State Parkway toward the George Washington Bridge. It was hardly an emergency vehicle, or even a sensible one for such a mission. The only outward sign that this wasn't just a weekend drive was the copy of an American flag from a local newspaper that Lioy had taped to his back window. In those first hyper-patriotic days after the attacks, so many people felt the urge to fly the flag that supplies ran out. Newspapers printed their own. Lioy's aging Lincoln wasn't the only car to have sprouted one.

That weekend, the bridge was the only way to get a private car like Lioy's across the Hudson River from New Jersey to the city. The Lincoln and Holland tunnels both had been closed to most traffic since the 11th, and all the ferries and trains into the city had been cancelled. On his way north, Lioy stopped to pick up a colleague, Dr. Clifford Weisel, who was deputy director of Rutgers' exposure science division. Once over the bridge, they headed downtown to Canal Street, the edge of the restricted zone. There they steered east, hoping to find a way past the police barriers and into the hot zone. The closer they got, the more chaotic everything became. Police were out in force. Dazed residents wandered around, looking for a way into or out of the restricted zone. Normal routines were disrupted; the unexpected suddenly became unexceptional. Finally, Lioy pulled over to a police barricade. He showed his Rutgers ID and took out the letter he had received from the National Institute asking him to investigate conditions at the site. With his voice of calm reason, Lioy explained his mission, then held his breath as the duty cop turned a suspicious eye toward the Lincoln. The big black coupe with the flag in the back window must have given the policeman pause, but he waved them in.

Lioy drove slowly through the familiar streets that now looked like a scene from *The Twilight Zone*. Most people had been evacuated, and nothing was moving but emergency vehicles. Cruising the abandoned streets in the Mark VIII might have seemed theatrical, even farcical, but Lioy wasn't thinking about that. From the moment he had watched the towers fall, he had been at turns angry and confused. He recognized that he was reacting emotionally, seeing things as an American who had benefited greatly from the opportunity that the nation offered and that the terrorists deplored, not as the dispassionate scientist he was trained to be. The days since that awful Tuesday morning had been interminable. Everyone who had watched the towers come apart wanted to be able to do something in response. Now Lioy had his chance to pitch in. Now he could matter.

He parked the car at the edge of the East River near the Manhattan Bridge and walked in from there, knowing that security would get tighter the nearer he and Weisel got to the debris pile. They had packed the trunk with essentials—they did not expect to find electricity for any sophisticated monitoring device. Besides, they figured that carrying around anything that looked technical might seem suspicious and get them detained, or worse. All they brought with them were notebook-sized sample bags, labels, plastic Fisher Scientific shovels, and a small camera.

It didn't take long to find what they had come for. They walked less than five minutes before they saw a light blue Chevrolet Lumina sedan parked near a cyclone fence. It clearly hadn't been moved or touched since 9/11, and an overhanging tree had shielded it from the rain on September 14. The car was about four-tenths of a mile east of ground zero, in the path of the initial dust plume as it blew over the East River into Brooklyn on the morning of the attacks. The windshield was blanketed with a thick layer, 4 to 6 inches deep, of light gray dust; the car looked like it had been left untouched after a snowstorm. With just one swipe of the Fisher shovel, Lioy filled a sample bag with nearly a pound of material. He was surprised at how light and fluffy it seemed, given its origin. He didn't yet know what the dust contained, but he knew that it wasn't merely dust. It should have been classified as remains, the essence of bustling commerce and life itself—thousands of snuffed-out personal lives. In seconds, it all had been reduced to this most elemental form. He marked the sample bag with the time, 8:20 a.m., and the place, Cherry Street in Lower Manhattan. The date was September 16.

After sealing the first sample bag, Lioy and Weisel pressed on. A few yards away, they found more undisturbed dust, which they also bagged and recorded. They then turned back to the car and loaded the samples in the trunk without getting close enough to see ground zero for themselves. Lioy later regretted that decision and wished he had ventured into the inner circle of hell that morning. But he was a scientist, and his mission—to collect dust samples—was accomplished.

He also knew that he would be returning the next day, September 17, when Wall Street was scheduled to reopen. He had a second assignment, this one from the Port Authority of New York and New Jersey, the large bi-state agency that had built the trade center and owned the ground on which it stood. The Port Authority had asked Lioy's colleague Mark Robson to pull together a team to do an initial analysis of the environment at the 16-acre site. This time, Lioy left the Lincoln at home and drove up in a rented van with four other scientists.

With Port Authority officials escorting them, the Rutgers team easily crossed the security barriers at Canal Street and entered the restricted zone, which extended from the destroyed trade center to a ring of commercial and residential buildings that had also been damaged, some severely, in the attack. The scientists were brought to a prep station, where each was given a hard hat, white haz-mat overalls, boots, gloves, and a half-face respirator. They spent much of the rest of the day at the heart of ground zero, getting close enough to feel the infernos beneath the debris. The air around the pile was the most contaminated in the city; Lioy and the others wore their respirator masks and were puzzled to see firefighters and construction workers in the same area without theirs. As the group walked along Cortlandt Street, one block east of the trade center's foundations, Lioy grabbed another sample from a protected ledge. Because the dust did not appear to have been diluted by rain, he figured it could reveal what had been in the air in those primal moments just after the towers came down.

At the time Lioy began his investigation, the dust was not considered a priority. With Wall Street reopening and the reeling nation trying to get back on its feet, most people were desperate to hear some positive news. And while most took nervous comfort in official pronouncements that the air seemed safe, men like Lioy knew from experience that heavy exposure to such a broad range of contaminants would likely harm the respiratory systems of the men and women who worked there. As someone who had already spent years studying environmental exposures, Lioy was aware that the twin towers, built in the early 1970s, contained tons of asbestos fireproofing that had probably been ripped from the steel beams it was intended to protect. Once loose, the asbestos fibers had spread over Lower Manhattan in the towering dust plume.

"The first order of business was to test for asbestos, but in retrospect, I think it was a mistake," Lioy recalled. "We had a situation where people swallowed gobs and gobs of this stuff. We should have been thinking about ways to characterize it so we could look for acute respiratory disease"—that is, the kinds of reactions that would befall responders within days, not the decades that asbestos can take to do its work. But since asbestos was the hazard that every New Yorker knew about, "at that moment, people just grabbed for asbestos."

Within days of the attacks, nearly all of the city's firefighters, and many other men and women working on the pile, started to cough. Some of them took time away from the desperate search to see their own doctors and complain that, since 9/11, they couldn't stop coughing and had not felt themselves. Most kept searching.

Millions had watched New York's tallest buildings disintegrate, and then, from different angles and perspectives shown on television, they saw them come apart again and again in the days following the attacks. What people didn't know then was what engineers subsequently determined about exactly what happened to bring down the towers that had once seemed indestructible. The jets had smashed into each building at around 500 miles per hour, severing steel columns designed to work together to hold up the colossal structures.

The remaining columns were strong enough to support the weight of the floors above for a short time after the impacts. But as fires fueled by the thousands of gallons of jet fuel raged, the high-strength steel began to weaken and eventually buckle on the floors nearest the impact zone. Stirrups holding the lightweight floor trusses to the exterior skeleton were deformed by the heat and soon pulled apart. The entire block of upper floors above the area where the planes had smashed into the buildings twisted almost imperceptibly, then tilted and collapsed with tremendous force, as though one building were dropped on top of another. What happened next was unprecedented. Engineers who studied the collapse extensively believe the first collapsing floor traveled the 3.7-meter distance from ceiling to floor in 0.87 seconds. Subsequent floors fell even faster,. The ocean of air in the building was compressed by the collapsing floors and had nowhere else to go but downward, then out. The dust cloud unleashed by the destruction was powerful enough to blow responders who weren't killed immediately right off their feet. The collapses poured an estimated 100,000 micrograms of particles into every cubic meter of air,[2] a whirlwind of dust so dense that it nearly solidified the air and turned it into a blinding black curtain for several minutes. Years later, when workmen undertook the laborious task of tearing down the badly damaged Deutsche Bank Building on Liberty Street, at the southern end of ground zero, they found that the pulverized construction material had been blown into the building with such force that it raced through the elevator shafts and then blew out through the narrow spaces around the closed doors on each floor, leaving halos of dust.

Although Americans were deluged with the sobering images of destruction, little was known with certainty about the composition of the dust and the effect it might have on those who were breathing it. Even less was known about the extremely toxic smoke and gases rising from the burning pile in those first days. No air monitors capable of capturing the toxic emissions were functioning, nor could they be brought to Lower Manhattan quickly enough to record the crucial data.

Common sense would dictate that there was danger. Common sense would say that there had to be asbestos in the dust because the trade center was one of the last buildings in New York to have asbestos fireproofing. Common sense would make it clear that anyone working on or near the pile would be exposed to an immense amount of dust and other health hazards. But emotions ruled those days, not common sense, and it was widely accepted that wearing a dust mask when thousands of victims could have been lying beneath the rubble was not only unnecessary, it was unpatriotic.

Lioy did not wear a dust mask when he collected his first samples. But he did have one on the following day when he participated in the Port Authority task force. Still, even he didn't keep the respirator on all day—it was just too hot, too uncomfortable and too difficult to communicate while wearing it. He wore it religiously anywhere near the pile, even though few of the firefighters and responders did so. For the rest of the time, it was just hanging around his neck.

For days after he returned to the laboratories at Rutgers' Piscataway campus, those days stretching into weeks and months and, eventually, years, Lioy and his colleagues delved into the intimate makeup of the dust, studying the tiniest particles as they tried to understand this almost unfathomable event. They began by dividing the big plastic bags of dust into smaller samples, putting some in chem-lab jars and keeping the rest in plastic pouches.

The dust was deceptively normal—what it mostly looked like was the inside of a vacuum cleaner bag, fluffy and gray, the color of dirty New York snow. At first the dust had an odd pinkish tint, a blush that was as curious as it was repulsive because it suggested blood and human remains. It was probably caused by some chemical reaction, and it did not last long. Eventually, the dust took on the more neutral color of dry bone. When Lioy and his colleagues put the dust under a scanning electron microscope or subjected it to polarized light microscopy, it began to reveal some of its secrets. They could see the awesome destructive force of the collapse. It was as though the buildings and everything they contained had been put through a gigantic wood chipper, and then those remnants passed through a coffee grinder, were thrown into a gigantic mortar, and were smashed with a pestle until all that was left were indistinguishable particles, a powder of the past. Lioy theorizes that the initial plume that was released as the towers came crashing to the ground was made up of larger, lighter, material that traveled farther. People caught in the plume described it as being swallowed by night.

Much of the dust was composed of cement particles, the minute remnants of the towers' 110 floors—each the size of a football field and 4 inches thick. In seconds, the hardened concrete had been ground into bits smaller than any controlled demolition ever created. Because of the way the floors had crashed on top of each other in rapid succession, the concrete had literally been pulverized. When the scientists subjected it to chemical analysis, they found that the dust had a surprisingly high pH value because of the cement dust, which made it very alkaline and caustic, significantly increasing its ability to harm the delicate nasal passages and throats of workers on the pile. Cement is ubiquitous in cities, but its standard form is solid. After the twin towers came apart, an extraordinary transformation took place. The rock-solid concrete in the towers was turned into windborne specks. The air above and around ground zero was literally filled with cement. Lioy found that the pH was highest in the coarse particles, which the body generally can filter out before they travel too deeply into the respiratory system. The smaller particles, which can easily slip in and, therefore, are more dangerous, were not so caustic because acid particles in the smoke, with their low pH values, acted to neutralize them. Two researchers at New York University, George Thurston and Lung Chi Chen, came to a similar conclusion about different pH values for coarse and fine particles after analyzing dust samples that had been collected around ground zero. They predicted that health effects caused by the dust would be severe in the short run because the dust was so caustic, but that the body's natural defenses would trap most of the material before it could reach deeply into the lungs, minimizing long-term impacts. Their thesis would be severely tested in the coming months.

To determine how irritating the dust was, Stephen H. Gavett, a scientist at the EPA's National Health and Environmental Effects Research Laboratory in North Carolina, exposed mice to it.[3] Gavett isolated the fine particles of less than 2.5 micrometers in the dust and blew them into the lungs of the mice at high concentrations, equivalent to what might have been in the air right after the towers came down. The dust caused mild to moderate lung inflammation, but importantly, it left the mice hypersensitive to things that could trigger asthmalike restrictions in the lungs. For most people with the same level of sensitivity, cold air and cigarette smoke can trigger an asthmatic attack. Lioy worked with scientists at the National Toxicology Program on a test to replicate the effects of the dust, exposing lab animals to both fine and large particles. They came up with similar results that persisted in the lab animals somewhat longer than they had in the EPA study. But the scientific journal they sent the results to found fault with the study, and it was never published. The experience showed Lioy that national health authorities might not be as interested in the fallout from 9/11 as he was. Even so, it was becoming increasingly clear to him that ground zero dust did not conform to the typical pattern with which aerosols move into and out of human lungs. The dust was full of surprises.

Lioy first presented some of his findings to residents of Lower Manhattan on October 18, 2001, at a meeting on NYU's Washington Square campus that was organized by the scientific community. But the data on the caustic nature of the dust was largely overlooked because the hundreds of residents of Lower Manhattan who attended the meeting were fixated on other elements that seemed scarier—namely, lead and asbestos. Mixed in with the caustic particles of cement were the asbestos fibers that Lioy had feared he would find.

Asbestos is an incredible mineral, made up of long, thin strands that can withstand heat and pressure. Man has used asbestos for thousands of years, and it became widely industrialized in the latter half of the nineteenth century. Asbestos becomes most dangerous when the fibers break loose and can be breathed in. They can become lodged in lower airways, where they cause irritation that can lead to debilitating diseases like asbestosis, as well as fatal ailments like lung cancer and a rare disease of the thin lining of the lungs called mesothelioma. The asbestos fibers are normally long, tough, and thin—so thin that 100 of them laid side by side are no wider than a single strand of human hair. Once they get inside the lungs, they are almost impossible to get out. Although considered nearly indestructible, the asbestos fibers in the trade center dust had broken into smaller pieces because of the force of the collapse. Some had attached to fibrous mats of other elements and compounds, making them even more insidious.

The actual amount of asbestos in two of Lioy's dust samples was relatively small—.8 percent chrysotile asbestos—but still significant. The dust he had scooped up on Market Street contained 3 percent asbestos. Even small amounts can cause lasting damage after many years, but asbestos could not account for the cough workers had started experiencing almost immediately.

Lioy, who had investigated toxic exposures for over 30 years, had never seen anything like the trade center dust. Neither had anyone else. It contained an unprecedented variety of materials, a tragic mixture whose toxicity was yet unknown. In time, he and his colleagues identified more than 150 different elements and compounds in the dust. They found common construction debris that included particles of plaster, glass, synthetic foam, vermiculite, and charred wood. They identified dead skin cells, the type typically found in household or office dust. They also found plenty of exotic elements, including titanium, from the white paint used in the towers' offices. Most worrisome were the benzene, lead, and dioxin that were released when miles of PVC pipe in the twin towers went up in flames. Lioy classified the ground zero disaster as a "dual nature event," the first phase being the collapse of both towers and the second the fires that raged at over 1,000° for days and then smoldered at lower temperatures for months, leading to incomplete combustion that released dangerous soot. Using transmission electron microscopy, the scientists found polycyclic aromatic hydrocarbons and were able to isolate individual fibers of asbestos. When they tested for inorganics, they found gold, lead, and the mercury from thousands of fluorescent light bulbs.

The list would have contained much more than the 150 elements and compounds if the scientists had continued to classify the material that appeared in ever smaller quantities. Had they carried on this work, they would eventually have had to list human DNA from the vaporized victims, although in infinitesimally small amounts (1 in one sextillion, or 10 to the minus 20) because even 3,000 human souls made up only a miniscule percentage of the overall mass of the trade center. The New York City fireman who had shouted "We're breathing dead people" was correct, in a scientific sense. But Lioy knew that even if he had continued to categorize the dust into smaller and smaller amounts that could separate out human DNA, he would not have come up with enough to link the genetic material to any of the victims, at least not with currently available methods and equipment.

Though the Institute's scientists could not carry their investigation that far, they did find strands of what they easily identified as human hair. The super-hard concrete of the buildings' floors had been ground to dust, but the hairs had survived intact. Lioy was not prepared to subject these remains to DNA analysis, either. He believed the hair probably came from the carpets of the office towers, the accumulated human detritus of 40 years of daily commerce. The hair and cells caught in the carpets could have come from the thousands of victims. Or they could have come from anyone—including him—who had ever worked in the buildings or visited long enough to drop a single strand of hair. Perhaps in decades to come science would be able to reliably match DNA from such samples. But not now.

Even without the genetic stamping, the material in Lioy's lab jars clearly constituted the sum of countless individual lives and the passage of those lives inside the walls of the doomed buildings. The minute particles of gold Lioy found might have started as a wedding band or an earring given as a birthday gift. The tiny strands of black polyester may have come from the back cover of a picture frame that once held the photo of a beloved parent or a childhood friend. And some of the ubiquitous cellulose in the dust may have originated in the desks where men and women whiled away countless hours in their high-rise offices. Or it may have come from the memos those people wrote while they were daydreaming of the beach, or from the pages of the calendars on which they noted the ordinary milestones of daily living—the dentist appointments, birthdays, and special anniversaries that could not be missed.

Lioy spent as much time studying the dust as anyone in the scientific community. His growing intimacy with the material eventually led him to see it not just in scientific terms, but in a humanistic way as well. Those two sides of his personality had been wrestling since September 11, and occasionally the personal side burned through without him being aware. At a 2005 conference, Lioy summed up the tragedy before an audience of students and faculty at Montclair State University in New Jersey. He narrated a short list of the chemicals, minerals, and compounds that had been detected in the dust, making clear that the entire list was extremely long and all-inclusive. Finally, he abandoned the language of the laboratory all together. "The trade center dust contains everything we hold dear." The words were uncharacteristically emotive for a traditional scientist like Lioy, who hadn't even realized what he'd said until it was brought to his attention. It astonished him to think that he had dropped his professional detachment so fully. But it's clear that those sentiments must have come from a deep emotional well that usually is off-limits in his scientific work.

This time emotion prevailed, at least temporarily.

On the same day that Lioy and Weisel collected their dust samples with shovels and plastic bags, the U.S. Geological Survey (USGS) sent one of its most sophisticated imaging spectrometers over ground zero.[4] Mounted on a Canadian-built de Havilland Twin Otter airplane, the Airborne Visible/Infrared Imaging Spectrometer (AVIRIS) is capable of detecting heat and identifying chemical bonds in molecules based on how they absorb infrared light. The spectrum of colors in the resulting images can reveal the presence of different minerals, including asbestos. As the AVIRIS flew over ground zero, it picked up more than three dozen hot spots. Some measured 800°F; a couple were a blistering 1,300°F. (Most were gone or greatly reduced by September 23, when the AVIRIS again flew over the area.) The imaging also picked up trace amounts of what was believed to be asbestos. On Monday, September 17, a two-person USGS ground crew began gathering dust samples. They collected material from 35 different spots within half a mile of ground zero and managed to get much closer to the debris pile than Lioy had on his first expedition. They took two samples from the coating on steel beams that had just been removed from the pile. Two other samples came from indoor spaces that presumably had not been diluted by rain. It took the crew two days to grab everything. All the samples were sent to USGS laboratories in Denver, where they went through a battery of tests. The results were in line with what Lioy's team was finding. Trace amounts of asbestos showed up in most of the outdoor samples. But the material taken from the steel beams confirmed that asbestos that had been used as insulation on at least some portions of the buildings was still there on 9/11. These samples were laden with asbestos fibers—as much as 20 percent chrysotile asbestos, a known carcinogen.

The Denver lab also found that the calcium sulfate in the concrete made the dust highly alkaline. As with Lioy's samples, the USGS discovered pH values as high as 10, which made it as strong as ammonia. The pH of indoor samples that had not been diluted by the September 14 rain were even higher, hovering around 12. At that level, the dust was about as caustic as drain cleaner. This crucial information was posted September 27 on a USGS website that was accessible only to the EPA and other government agencies. Even though Lioy and the NYU researchers had independently come to the same conclusion about the corrosive nature of the dust, many clinicians and ground zero workers didn't find out about it until an out-of-town newspaper reported the results, along with startling headlines, five months later.[5]

At the Institute, Lioy and his colleagues continued their multifaceted investigation. One group studied the dust plumes and created a computer simulation of their movements.[6] Using motion graphics like those on TV weather reports, the physicists showed that the ominous clouds rose on updrafts caused by warm temperatures and then were buffeted by September winds. Over several days, the winds pushed the plume around so that it snaked across the metropolitan region, slashing over Brooklyn, twisting back again over Manhattan north of Canal Street, and then sweeping across the Hudson to New Jersey before blanketing the harbor again. The animation indicated that a broad swathe of the metropolitan area, not just Manhattan's financial district, had been touched by the airborne dust, which eventually settled in those areas as well, although less densely because of the distance from ground zero.

As the energy that carried the plume up and out eventually dissipated, the dust drifted back down to Earth, coming to rest on hundreds of buildings, seeping underneath thousands of windows, sucked into countless air-conditioning ducts, and infiltrating every surface. Much of it would quickly be washed away, mopped up, or swept into the trash. But the tiniest of particles would remain for years and would rise like unwelcome ghosts every time something disturbed them.

Since 2001, Paul Lioy has given away over half of the dust he collected to scientists from all over the world who have asked to study
the material. He finally stopped sharing it when he feared that the
composition of the dust had changed so much with time that testing
would no longer produce reliable results.

Still, requests come in, and Lioy sometimes makes the long walk
from his office down the hallway of the Institute, around a corner,
and into the cold room.

"Like a police evidence room," he says, pulling open the heavy
metal door. The refrigerated chamber, about 12 feet by 12 feet, is
lined with five open metal shelves that go from floor to ceiling, front
to back. On a shelf on the left side of the room is a pair of ordinary
plastic storage bins, clear with blue lids. They are marked "Dr. Lioy's
WTC samples—Please do not touch." No one does.

Lioy hauls one bin back to his office. As time has passed, he's
moved on to other issues and eventually immersed himself in a huge
national children's study with Dr. Philip J. Landrigan of the Mount
Sinai Medical Center. But he can never get far from the dust. He has
written more than a dozen scientific papers about his investigations
into the exposure risks at ground zero, and he is often asked to weigh
in on issues involving health and environmental issues related to the
disaster. In 2009, the National Society of the Daughters of the American Revolution gave him a patriotism award for his work on 9/11
dust. On a bookcase in his office he keeps the hard hat, respirator,
and gloves he wore at ground zero. And on the wall is a photograph
he took while he was there. The debris pile looms over several workers who are pitching in with the rescue and recovery operation. One
of them wears a respirator mask. One has a mask hanging around his
neck. A third doesn't wear any respiratory protection at all. It is a pre-
view of an unfolding disaster.

Since those first bleak days after 9/11, Lioy has confronted the
same kind of intricate, many-layered problem that originally drew
him into science. How does everything fit together? How does one
element affect others? What was there to fear—the dust itself, or the
pattern of exposure, or the way the government responded to the disaster, or the responders' own failure to protect themselves? Would
emerging fears turn out to be overblown or underestimated? Who

was telling the truth? Who was shading the truth? Could anything be known with certainty?

Lioy was determined to be guided by science, not emotion. He had felt himself slip over from cold analysis to the warm emotions of anger, fear, and awe, and he did not want to be there again. His instruments and graphs would tell the story. He feared that the frenzy over asbestos was overshadowing the dust's more immediate threats. Moreover, no one knew what was in the gasses and smoke that belched from the pile in the first few days of utter chaos. And that worried him, because he believed that all the responders who were exposed to that material immediately after the collapses probably breathed in a dangerous combination of toxins that could interact in ways that might not be clear for decades. People who had been exposed were frightened and wanted answers, and they wanted them right away.

Through it all, Lioy harbored a painful over-riding doubt. He knew better than most that certainty about the real danger of the dust may not come for a long time. Some workers who were exposed to asbestos mixed with the gases from the burning rubble might not become ill until 30 years after they left ground zero. But many are already sick, far sicker than the results of tests of lab animals would have suggested. Something else clearly was going on, but what? Certainty won't come for decades, but if the dust—combined with the gases and smoke—truly was toxic, waiting that long could cost lives. If the threat that the dust could cause cancer and other fatal diseases could not be discounted outright, waiting could cause tremendous pain and endless anguish. Uncertainty and fear could make victims of those who escaped becoming victims on 9/11.

Clearly, there wasn't time to wait, especially not after so many men and women started complaining of respiratory problems they shouldn't have had if the air had truly been safe to breathe. Nor was there an easy explanation for why the workers who were digging in the rubble for remains weren't wearing the masks that would have kept them from being hurt by the air that so obviously was filled with danger. There was a troubling disconnect between what was expected and what was actually happening. Even after the dust plumes had started to dissipate, it was as if the dust continued to cling to the air, blinding reason, obscuring truth, and distorting belief.

Endnotes

[1]EPA press release, 13 September 2001.

[2]Lioy, Paul J., "Characterization of the Dust/Smoke Aerosol That Settled East of the World Trade Center (WTC) in Lower Manhattan After the Collapse of the WTC 11 September 2001," *Environmental Health Perspectives* 110, no. 7 (July 2002). Available at http://ehp.niehs.nih.gov/members/2002/110p703-714lioy/lioy-full.html.

[3]Gavett, Stephen H., "Toxicological Effects of Particulate Matter Derived from the Destruction of the World Trade Center," abstract presented at the American Association for Aerosol Research, 7–11 October 2002. Available at http://cfpub.epa.gov/si/si_public_record_Report.cfm?dirEntryId=62264&CFID=8344117&CFTOKEN=48481859&jsessionid=203074134a7808465f213c42524179398054.

[4]USGS, "Environmental Studies of the World Trade Center Area After the September 11, 2001, Attack," 27 November 2001. Available at http://pubs.usgs.gov/of/2001/ofr-01-0429/.

[5]Andrew Schneider, "Caustic Dust Blankets World Trade Center Area," *St. Louis Post-Dispatch*, 9 February 2002, p. 1. See www.stltoday.com/stltoday/news/special/asbestos.nsf/0/8DC49C62C3BDFD2186256CAD0076A1ED?OpenDocument.

[6]Lioy, Paul, and Panos Georgopoulos, "The Anatomy of the Exposures That Occurred Around the World Trade Center Site," *Annals of the New York Academy of Sciences* 1076 (2006). Accessed at www.nycosh.org/environment_wtc/WTC/WTCexposures_Lioy_Georgopoulos.pdf.

2

Optimism or arrogance?

Planning for catastrophe is like planning for war. The overriding goal is to anticipate possible outcomes and engineer responses that are most likely to ensure victory. All too often, however, in both war and disaster, almost nothing turns out the way it is supposed to. What was expected does not happen as imagined. And the well thought-out plan, the coordinated attack, the deliberate response falls apart when it is needed most.

After the bombing of the World Trade Center in 1993, New York City officials understood that the city had become a prime terror target and that there could be another attempt sometime in the future. To be better prepared for the next time, Mayor Giuliani wanted a new emergency command center built where he could manage a coordinated response. He wanted a big space where all his key people could work shoulder to shoulder as he deployed forces. And he wanted the new control room to be within walking distance of City Hall. Several sites were considered, but in the end, against the advice of some, he located his emergency bunker on the 23rd floor of 7 World Trade Center, one block north of the towers that had been targeted in 1993. He spent $13 million on a Noah's Ark response center that was designed to survive any calamity. It was self-sufficient and equipped with the most up-to-date electronics, along with its own huge reservoir of diesel fuel to run emergency generators in the event the power grid stopped functioning. The building where Giuliani's Armageddon room took shape was connected by walkways and ramps to the rest of the trade center complex and had exceptionally large floors. Drexel Burnham Lambert, the big investment banking firm that was supposed to have rented the entire building, had backed out of the deal in 1990, leaving loads of vacant space that the city gladly took over.

On the morning of September 11, 2001, Giuliani was just leaving a business breakfast in midtown when he took a call notifying him that a plane had smashed into the twin towers. As he was being driven downtown, Giuliani could not have imagined the scene that awaited him. He arrived at the trade center shortly after the second jet plowed into the towers, making it painfully clear this was no accident. The car did not drop him off at the command bunker, which was being pelted with debris from the burning towers. The building was being evacuated, and Giuliani's aides decided that it wasn't safe for him to be anywhere near it. Instead, he was whisked to a temporary police command post that had been set up at Church and Vesey Streets. There he met up with police commissioner Bernard Kerik. Fire department commanders had established their own command post two blocks away, on West Street. When Giuliani, who knew of the sometimes poisonous rivalry between the two groups of uniformed responders, needed to talk to the fire officials, he and Kerik walked over. Giuliani conferred briefly with Chief of Department Peter Ganci as the situation around them grew more urgent. Desperate people trapped on the upper floors had started jumping or falling from the towers. Fires raged on many floors, and huge chunks of the building rained down around them. Giuliani, Kerik, and other city officials decided to head north, seeking a safe haven where they could set up a command and communication post. Kerik took Giuliani to an office building at 75 Barclay Street, a block north of the towers, where he believed he could commandeer a working land line to the White House and to the governor's office. With cellphone service overloaded or knocked out completely, working telephones were essential for the mayor to receive up-to-date information and to get messages out to the people of his stunned city.

Giuliani's team—which by then included Neal L. Cohen, the city's health commissioner—took over the ground-floor office space on Barclay Street and got to work. But then the South Tower came down, breaking the large plate-glass windows on street level and shooting debris, dust, and ash into the temporary headquarters, forcing another hasty and unplanned escape. The police led Giuliani down to the safety of the Barclay Street building's basement and then eventually into an adjoining building and back out onto the street.[1]

With horror unfolding around him, Giuliani marched up Church Street, looking for a way to take control. Until he did, no one was in charge. To the frightened New Yorkers he passed, Giuliani shouted, "Just keep going north." The dust plume from the first collapse continued to roil the streets of Lower Manhattan, blanketing everything and everyone in its way. People who were caught in the cloud described it in various ways, but they all had in common the darkening of the sky until it became nearly impossible to see anything; a brutally strong wind that rushed out as the 110-story tower was flattened; the flurry of office papers rising and falling like flocks of gray pigeons; and the thick wave of choking material from the pulverized building that they waded through, breathed in, and swallowed as they tried to survive. And then, after the roar of the man-made mountains being torn apart, an eerie quiet that was broken by the dulled wail of an alarm from a car buried beneath the debris.

Giuliani stumbled in the darkness for about ten blocks until he reached an empty firehouse at Houston Street and Avenue of the Americas, only to find the doors locked. The crew had responded to the unfolding emergency. The city's top officials then tried to break into the building by smashing the combination lock on the front door. Before they could get it open, someone reached fire headquarters and took down the combination. For the next few hours, Giuliani and the others used the firehouse as a temporary command post while they took stock of what had happened and tried to figure out how to react.

Once he finally got settled into a command post hours later at the Police Academy on East 20th Street, Giuliani provided a steady hand and a sober demeanor that calmed the city and showed a stiff-lipped, even defiant, face to the world. In many ways, the city's survival depended on the projection of that kind of determination and grit.

With emergency response plans torn up, and the top hierarchy of the fire department (including Chief Ganci) killed in the collapse, municipal government could have been paralyzed. Giuliani knew that in such a situation, people desperately seek out information, and if they can't find it, they quickly replace truth with rumor, potentially making a bad situation worse. Perhaps Giuliani's greatest accomplishment that day was in the way he presented a face of steely control at the first news conference, even when he was asked the question that everyone who had ever been inside the towers wanted to ask: How many people died? Around 50,000 people worked at the trade center. No one knew with certainty how many had made it out before the buildings fell down, but the worst was feared. Giuliani's immediate response was as emotional as it was restrained, a pitch-perfect answer to a tough question at a critical moment. "I don't think we want to speculate about that," Giuliani cautioned the reporters gathered around him at a press conference just after 2:30 that first afternoon. Here he was the broad-shouldered father offering sober advice to a frightened child: "The number of casualties will be more than any of us can bear, ultimately."

Giuliani was speaking honestly and from the heart; the impact was resounding. He leveled with New Yorkers and the rest of the world about the extent of the hurt that had been visited upon the city. He brought everyone up to speed on what he knew about the people who worked in the towers, as well as what he didn't know about the extent to which the actions of the fire and police departments had managed to clear the towers before they imploded. His statement undoubtedly had the unintended effect of adding to the fears of those who had only voices on home answering machines to hang on to as they hoped for a miracle. The mayor's blunt and open-ended assessment of the tragedy inflated horror with uncertainty. But at the very least, he prepared people for the worst.

Lamentably, Giuliani did not continue to level with New Yorkers in the same way over the following weeks. What he did was not outright subterfuge, nor deliberate distortion of the facts. Rather, as he helped his city get back on its feet and he showed the world New York's (and his own) toughest face, he released information in a way that suggested the gravest danger had already passed and there was little to continue to worry about. That attitude squared with instructions coming out of the Bush White House. Limited information was put out, and unrealistic assumptions were made without the support of sound science. When taken together with flawed information from other official sources, the communications led to an overriding impression that was in line with the reality most people favored, despite their best instincts otherwise.

"The air quality is not dangerous," Giuliani said in one of his first public statements about the environment at ground zero, early on the

morning of September 12.[2] Fires were raging, infernos of heat and
smoke feeding off the tattered ruins of the two towers and the 91,000
liters of fuel that had spilled out of the transcontinental jets. Giuliani
was worried that television viewers around the world would get the
wrong impression if they glimpsed uniformed responders wearing
flimsy dust masks or, rarely, a half-face respirator. So much is now
known about the events of that day and their aftermath that it can be
difficult to recall the extent of the uncertainty that existed then. September 11 was rife with recurring rumors that other planes were
headed toward more targets in New York City or elsewhere. Some
feared that more than 600 firefighters had died (twice the actual number) and 10,000 people in the towers had been killed. And, assuming
the worst, there were great concerns that the planes had carried biological weapons or that the trade center rubble was emitting deadly chemicals that forced some responders to wear masks.

"The reason that everybody is wearing masks, which I know people see it on television, and they think there must be a chemical agent
or biological agent or ... the reason they're wearing masks is, if you
expose your eyes and you inhale too much of the dust, it's going to
irritate you and that can become serious," Giuliani told New Yorkers
on September 12. In a television interview the next day, Giuliani said
that although asbestos tests were negative, there was plenty of dust in
the air and that might give people with asthma and health conditions
some trouble. "But for others," he said, "it's not gonna be a major
problem."[3] The bottom line, according to Giuliani, was that there was
hardly anything to worry about except getting back to work.

In the months and years ahead, and especially when he ran for
the Republican nomination for president, Giuliani would return to
these same primal moments. Over time, the uncoordinated wandering and other less dramatic aspects of that morning would blur and be
replaced by vivid images of him taking charge of his wounded city,
calmly and soberly urging his people to go about their normal business. His early actions would come to have far-reaching negative consequences, but they would always have to be weighed against the
good he did. If what the terrorists had aimed for by flying passenger
jets into the tallest buildings in the heart of the most important financial district in the Western world, if what they had hoped the death

and destruction would do was bring to the surface the worst traits of the culture they despised—envy, greed, and self-interest—then Rudy Giuliani's lock-jaw performance denied them that satisfaction and kept the city from panicking. Yet decisions that Giuliani and his team made in the immediate aftermath would contribute to a climate of suspicion, mistrust, and, ultimately, fear that would linger far into the future.

On Broadway, several blocks north and east of ground zero, a formidable 32-story building—clad in Deer Isle granite with just the slightest tint of salmon that shows through in certain light—houses several federal departments and agencies, including the Region 2 headquarters of the Environmental Protection Agency. The EPA's role in responding to the disaster had been made clear in several executive orders, the most recent being Presidential Decision Directive #62, issued by Bill Clinton three years before the trade center was destroyed. The directive laid out a plan for federal responses to a terrorist attack and assigned the EPA lead responsibility for decontaminating areas that had been targeted. Some of the EPA's air quality specialists and environmental watchdogs were within walking distance of the disaster site. It seemed like a small silver lining in the gloomiest of days.

But just as Giuliani's emergency command post failed at a crucial moment, the EPA found that its response plan worked better on paper than it did in real life. It was apparent right from the start that this was no ordinary hazardous waste spill, nor was ground zero anything like the worst Superfund toxic waste sites in the nation. A few blocks from EPA headquarters lay a hellish scene that scientists later agreed represented the largest environmental disaster in New York City history.[4] But it was also a raging all-alarm fire, an extremely dangerous rescue operation of as yet undetermined scale, and a crime scene where thousands of people had been murdered.

Before any rational response could be effectively implemented, the question of who was in charge of the site had to be answered. At first, it was clear that the EPA was not the lead agency. New York had marshaled its municipal resources almost immediately. By the end of the first day, some 20,000 police officers had responded to the call for help. The fire department had called in nearly all 14,000 firefighters, including those who were off duty. Other city employees mobilized quickly—thousands of transit workers came out with their heavy equipment, and sanitation workers, health officers, building inspectors, and others took their places in a massive response. At the helm of it all was Giuliani, who, after nearly eight years as mayor, operated as though he owned the city.

The EPA saw the dust plume and knew, just as Paul Lioy had immediately recognized, that it couldn't be good. The dust was so thick that the agency's own satellite phones couldn't work properly. Electricity was knocked out in parts of Lower Manhattan, further restricting the agency's capabilities because many monitors ran on electricity. Still, it managed to collect dust samples within two hours of the buildings' collapse. An environmental response crew was sent from the agency's offices in Edison, NJ, about 40 miles south of Manhattan, to sample the dust and the air as best they could under the circumstances. Because that there wasn't a lot of sampling equipment on hand that day, the rapid response team went to a local store and bought Ziploc bags.[5]

After the New York City police set up a security perimeter around the debris site, it became far more difficult for the EPA to get inside. The closest the Edison crew could get was Liberty State Park in Jersey City, opposite Lower Manhattan, and Brooklyn, where they took air samples. By the following day, the first analysis of the dust samples from ground zero was complete. Reporters had already asked about the amount of asbestos in the air and how dangerous it might be. The EPA's tests showed a range of results, from a reassuring finding of no asbestos particles of detectible size, to worrisome samples that contained as much as 4.5 percent asbestos.

Officials also knew there were going to be other concerns. The burning jet fuel that had torched the remains of the towers and its contents—the carpets and wooden desks, the plastic computer casings and the synthetic ceiling tiles—would be emitting volatile organic compounds and dangerous chemicals. The thousands of fluorescent bulbs containing mercury, the computer monitors containing lead, the splintered glass, the shredded fiberglass and the tons of reinforced concrete that had been turned to dust—all these and a hundred more had been discharged by the tremendous force of the collapsing buildings and saturated the air in Lower Manhattan to an extent that could only be guessed at until more tests were done.

Sensible caution now struggled against spirited resistance and a commitment to normalcy that carried great consequence. Signs of danger were obvious. This was no factory worksite where exposures and dosages could be carefully measured. This was the nightmare scenario of one of the busiest and most crowded places on Earth being exposed to an unprecedented mix of known and suspected hazards. Hundreds of thousands of people potentially could be affected. They were office workers and residents, schoolchildren and tourists, service employees and municipal workers in Manhattan and across the rivers in Brooklyn, New Jersey, and the rest of New York. All were exposed to a mixture of contaminants whose toxicity was unknown. In a setting fraught with so much danger, the only proper response was caution.

But there were other interests to consider besides science and public health policy. And these factors were seen as equally important at that time. The terrorists hoped to incite panic in the streets. They wanted people to refuse to go back to work on Wall Street. They wanted to see a population on the run, people unwilling to put aside their own interests for any greater good. In such a poisoned atmosphere, a stout heart and firm resolve become weapons of counterterrorism. And that is the message that filtered out of both City Hall and the White House. It became a matter of utmost importance to get the city back on its feet as quickly as possible, and the first step toward achieving that was reopening Wall Street.

That need for normalcy helped set up a struggle between common sense and patriotism, between reasonable caution and willful optimism, between respecting the science and exploiting the science. What ensued was not criminal, nor was it triggered by venality, despite what critics have said. The only conspiracy involved was a conspiracy of purpose. And that purpose was to show those who had supported the terrorists on the jumbo jets that the city, that this country, would not allow the space that had been occupied by the towers to be filled with fear.

For much of the time, that essential message was conveyed by the EPA and its head, Christine Todd Whitman. Whitman was well known to New Yorkers. The former governor had been tapped by

President George W. Bush to head the EPA at the beginning of his administration, although in time she would find herself out of step with the hard-core conservatives surrounding Bush. At first Whitman was friendly enough with the Bush family to have given the president and Laura Bush their black Scottish Terrier, Barney. But as Bush moved farther to the right on environmental issues, a gap opened between them. Early in Bush's first term, Whitman had traveled all over the world representing what she thought was the president's position on climate control and the Kyoto Treaty, which American business leaders strongly opposed. By the time she returned home, Bush had come out strongly against it. That experience led Colin Powell to refer to Whitman as the administration's "wind dummy," a military reference to the way air troopers test the direction of the wind before a jump by throwing a dummy out of the moving plane.[6]

As the EPA faced its biggest test at ground zero, Whitman was out front, personally releasing some of the test results to the public. She had always been effective on camera, able to cover her political ambition with a patina of honest sincerity. But two major issues would stand in the way of full and honest disclosure: the inadequacy of environmental measurements and the politics of presentation.

The EPA was monitoring the disaster, but it was doing so in an unprecedented vacuum. There were no outdoor standards for airborne asbestos exposure. For as long as asbestos has been considered dangerous, exposure levels were set for indoor spaces, such as factories or school buildings, where breathing in asbestos posed the highest risk. Asbestos fibers resist fire and can hold together plaster or cement in an almost miraculous way. But they are so thin that when they are released into the air, they can be breathed deep into the lungs. Once they get lodged there, they can lead to irritation, inflammation, and, eventually, a range of diseases, including cancer.

Initially, the EPA didn't know which asbestos safety standards to apply. Confusion even arose over how measurements ought to be taken. Existing regulations were designed for industrial settings, where exposure was intense and lasted for an eight-hour shift or longer. No health-based standards covered the number of asbestos strands in the outside air that would be safe to breathe for days, weeks, or months at a time. The first dust samples analyzed by the

EPA showed varying amounts of asbestos, and it was becoming clear that hot spots within the 16 acres of ground zero were more contaminated than others. The agency used standard phase-contrast microscopy, which it had relied on for years. The EPA said that it also utilized more advanced technology—transmission electron microscopy—which can detect much smaller particles with a higher degree of accuracy.

The federal government has established strict workplace standards for asbestos workers exposed to the mineral over a working lifetime. The government also has standards that are used when asbestos-laden insulation is removed from school buildings. In those instances, air samples inside the remediated schools must contain no more than 70 asbestos particles per square millimeter before children are allowed back in. Another standard is in place for determining when asbestos is present in a building and has to be removed. Insulation, floor tiles, and other products that contain at least 1 percent asbestos is officially considered asbestos-containing material and has to be handled as though it is hazardous. Coming in below the 1 percent standard does not indicate that the material is safe. The EPA has long held the position that there is no safe level of exposure to asbestos.

None of the existing asbestos exposure standards fit the particular situation that existed at ground zero. But they were all the agency had. And as asbestos continued to be a priority concern in New York, the EPA turned to these standards to help determine the level of risk. Thus, twice each day, the agency collected samples from more than 20 air-monitoring stations at ground zero and the surrounding area. Of more than 9,500 samples analyzed, 21 exceeded the school-safety standard of 70 asbestos particles per square millimeter.[7] When the EPA reported on the level of contamination at ground zero, it said that all but a handful of the thousands of samples met the standard for asbestos exposure, even though the agency knew that it had applied a standard that had not been designed for such circumstances.

Still, that is the benchmark against which the air samples had been compared when Whitman stated on September 13, "[The] EPA is greatly relieved to have learned there appears to be no significant levels of asbestos dust in the air in New York City." Applying the same asbestos standards over the ensuing days, Whitman continually reassured New Yorkers that they needn't worry too much about the air they were breathing. She did say that the rescue workers who were searching for survivors on the pile itself needed to take precautions because the conditions there were far more dangerous. Sampling taken from directly above the debris showed several hazardous chemicals, including benzene, at relatively high levels. But a short distance away from the rubble, those levels dropped dramatically. Rescue workers were told to wear respirator masks to protect themselves. The EPA had no data on PCBs, small particulate matter or polycyclic aromatic hydrocarbons that were being emitted by the fires, nor had the agency yet studied the synergistic ways those contaminants might act when mixed with asbestos and other toxic materials. But the main thrust of Whitman's statements, and the message most people got out of them, was that there was nothing to worry about.

After what New York and the nation had been through since the morning of September 11, news that the air was safe was a relief. I can recall being in the newsroom of *The New York Times* and hearing the reassuring statements about asbestos. Knowing what I know about such contaminants, I found the results difficult to accept. Yet at that moment I was comforted by what I heard because it made moving forward so much easier. I suppose it is like hearing an overly optimistic diagnosis of a loved one who is very sick. It can be clear that the doctor is putting absolutely the best face on the crisis and wouldn't attest to any of it in court, but he is saying what relatives want to hear, no matter how illogical it seems. As they looked for their dead, New Yorkers did not want to worry about danger in the air.

For many reasons, America's strongest response to the terror attack was to reopen Wall Street as quickly as possible. That was the priority when President Bush told senior members of his staff that he wanted to see the New York Stock Exchange back in operation by Thursday morning, September 13. But Treasury Secretary Paul O'Neill convinced him that the worst outcome of all would be to open the doors of the exchange prematurely, allowing a technical problem to crash the system and creating more havoc while diminishing confidence. At a tense National Security Council meeting on the morning of September 13, O'Neill told Bush that the earliest the exchange could safely and reasonably be reopened would be the following

Monday, after a closure of just four working days, including the day of the attack. The president reluctantly agreed to wait.[8]

To prepare for the reopening, the EPA sent a fleet of specially equipped vacuum trucks to Wall Street to begin the massive job of cleaning up. Rain on Friday, September 14, had already washed away some of the dust. Over the weekend, the vacuum trucks swept the asphalt. But officials were horrified to discover that the contractor who operated the trucks was running them without the high-efficiency HEPA filters needed to pick up the super fine strands of asbestos. The trucks were actually doing more harm than good by disturbing the settled dust and blowing it back into the air. Once the mistake was discovered, the operator was ordered to redo the streets, this time with the proper filters installed. (The company later was suspended from further government work.)

The New York Stock Exchange reopened at its normal time on Monday, September 17. A handful of the employees who reported to work that day wore light dust masks. Most had nothing. To wear a respirator mask while firefighters desperately clawed through the rubble looking for survivors a few yards away struck most people as either selfish or inappropriate, like applying hand sanitizer before responding to a forest fire. But some people in Lower Manhattan did anyway. One of them was Suzanne Mattei, then the head of the New York City office of the Sierra Club. Because of her work, she knew how hazardous the contaminated air could be. And because of previous run-ins with the government, she also believed the EPA's test results were probably inaccurate or misleading. As she walked to her downtown office wearing a half-face respirator, Mattei could feel the harsh stares of passersby, and eventually they made her feel strangely unpatriotic for taking personal precautions at a time of national tragedy.

The day after Wall Street reopened, Whitman's office released the most definitive statement yet about environmental conditions in New York. "We are very encouraged that the results from our monitoring of air quality and drinking water conditions in both New York and the Pentagon show that the public in these areas is not being exposed to excessive levels of asbestos or other harmful substances," Whitman was quoted in a press release put out by EPA. She then took her reassuring tone even further. "Given the scope of the tragedy from last week, I am glad to reassure the people of New York and

Washington, D.C., that their air is safe to breathe and their water is safe to drink." The word *public* in the statement was the only direct attempt to bifurcate the message by suggesting that there was a significant difference between the public and the rescue workers, who would be mentioned only in the last paragraph of the two-page release. There the agency boasted that it had "assisted efforts to provide dust masks to rescue workers to minimize inhalation of dust." But it did not say that the dust was laced with hazardous chemicals. The agency did recommend wetting down the debris pile to reduce the dust, and it provided wash stations for workers to clean off before they went home. The responders also were encouraged to wash contaminated clothing separately from "normal household wash."

It all sounded so domesticated and unthreatening that the overall impact was to simply repeat what Giuliani and Whitman had been saying since the beginning: Most people had almost nothing to worry about. Whitman has said she wanted to keep her message simple. But the way it came across was contradictory, confusing, and so vaguely worded that it was open to many interpretations—and most people clearly wanted it to mean there was no danger. It would be hard for officials to argue that such an ambiguous message was unintended. The EPA is sophisticated at communicating hazards and conveying environmental information. It was especially so in the Bush administration, which tried to control messages about pollution, energy consumption, and global warming. Whitman's September 18 statement, and all the press releases issued by the EPA during the initial cleanup, were scrubbed by the White House and the Council on Environmental Quality before they were released. In some instances, the Bush White House made subtle word changes that effectively repackaged the message, slimming down the risks while puffing up what the agency said it knew but, in fact, could not have known at that time because it did not yet have the scientific data on which to base those statements. In one of the earliest releases, the EPA's original wording that it "considers asbestos hazardous in this situation" was changed slightly, but the meaning of the statement was altered substantially. In place of the original, the statement that was released to the public said that the EPA "is greatly relieved to have learned there appears to be no significant levels of asbestos dust in the air in New York City."[9]

In an earlier instance, the EPA had initially planned to report on September 16 that some asbestos had been found: "Recent samples of dust gathered by OSHA (the Occupational Safety and Health Administration) on Water Street show higher levels of asbestos in EPA tests." Apparently believing that this frank statement of fact would be too difficult for traumatized New Yorkers to bear on the day before many were supposed to return to work in the financial district, the Council on Environmental Quality made several edits that rendered it far less frightening and much more reassuring:

> The new samples confirm previous reports that ambient air quality meets OSHA standards and consequently is not a cause for public concern. New OSHA data also indicates that indoor air quality in downtown buildings will meet standards. EPA has found variable asbestos levels in bulk debris and dust on the ground, but EPA continues to believe that there is no significant health risk to the general public in the coming days. Appropriate steps are being taken to clean up this dust and debris.[10]

Although the EPA had been kept out of ground zero for security reasons for 48 hours, and many of the tests Whitman would have needed to see before she could characterize conditions in any reliable way had not been completed by September 18, she nonetheless declared the air safe to breathe. The agency later insisted that Whitman's statement addressed only long-term health effects, not acute problems like coughs that arose almost immediately. She claimed that her evaluation referred to outdoor air only, not the air inside apartments, offices, and schools. It was not meant to apply to children, the elderly, or anyone who was not healthy, and it referred to asbestos only, not other hazards that might be contained in the dust. For an agency with decades of experience in carefully outlining the environmental hazards of toxic spills and hazardous waste sites, Whitman's statement was appallingly vague and unclear. A health alert on a high smog day would be more specific than were these pronouncements about one of the nation's most serious environmental calamities.

A scathing report by the office of the Inspector General for the EPA[11] later concluded that Whitman and her agency, their hands forced by the Bush White House, had unrelentingly pushed the overly optimistic message that "the public did not need to be concerned about airborne contaminants caused by the World Trade Center collapse. The reassurances appeared to apply to both indoor and outdoor air." The report concluded that neither Whitman nor the agency she ran had enough data to support such an upbeat view. The report also found that the White House had tinkered with the final message to address interests that competed with public health, namely national security and the push to reopen the financial houses of Wall Street.

As part of this all-out mission to restore calm to the city and get New York back on its feet, the words and sentiments that Whitman and Giuliani conveyed were absolutely essential. But they sometimes strayed from the truth, and in the months and years to come, they would prove to be consequential for untold thousands of people who took their imprecise message of hope to heart. Critics would come to portray them as outright falsehoods and deliberate lies, the product of political ambition and malicious interference. By March 2002, seven out of every ten New Yorkers who responded to a telephone poll did not believe the agency's statements.[12] A 2003 survey of more than a thousand residents of Lower Manhattan found that despite the EPA's reassuring words, a majority still worried about the health effects of indoor and outdoor air contaminated by trade center dust.[13] If the air over New York had been tainted by the dust storms of 9/11, then the atmosphere in the city at the time was tainted by the urge to exaggerate and mold perception, to use the tragedy as one side or the other saw fit, regardless of the truth.

What ensued was a tug-of-war between policy and pragmatism Emergency response plans and scientific analysis called for restraint, control, and sober study. But the calamity of 9/11 was so great that the plans were almost immediately abandoned or chipped away until they barely resembled themselves. Speed became more important than study, conjecture replaced analysis, hope trumped caution. The city needed to be rebuilt, and quickly. If doing so meant something needed to be sacrificed—time, money, the delicate bond of trust between a government and its citizens—then the pragmatists who were in charge were willing to make that sacrifice to ensure the short-term gain, regardless of the long-term cost.

Endnotes

[1]Barrett, Wayne, and Dan Collins, Grand Illusion (New York: Harper Collins, 2006); and Pérez-Peña, Richard, "Trying to Command an Emergency When the Emergency Command Center Is Gone," The New York Times, 12 September 2001, p. 7, accessed at www.nytimes.com/2001/09/12/us/day-terror-government-trying-command-emergency-when-emergency-command-center.html?scp=1&sq=Pérez-Pena%20and%20September%2012,%202001&st=cse.

[2]Press briefing with Gov. George Pataki, Hillary Clinton, Charles Schumer, and other elected officials.

[3]CBS News transcripts, The Early Show, 13 September 2001, interview by Jane Clayson.

[4]Landrigan, Philip J., et al., "Health and Environmental Consequences of the World Trade Center Disaster," Environmental Health Perspectives 112, no. 6 (May 2004): 731-739.

[5]Solecki, Mike, "What It Was Like to Be an On-Scene Coordinator at Ground Zero," www.epa.gov/superfund/accomp/news/wtcstory.htm.

[6]Seelye, Katharine Q., "Whitman Quits as E.P.A. Chief," The New York Times, 22 May 2003, p. 1, accessed at www.nytimes.com/2003/05/22/politics/22WHIT.html?scp=1&sq=.

[7]"EPA Response to September 11, Region 2," available at www.epa.gov/wtc/stories/yearreview.htm.

[8]Suskind, Ron, The Price of Loyalty (New York: Simon & Schuster, 2004).

[9]U.S. Environmental Protection Agency, Office of Inspector General, "EPA's Response to the World Trade Center Collapse: Challenges, Successes, and Areas for Improvement," 21 August 2003: 17.

[10]Ibid., p. 16.

[11]Ibid.

[12]Ibid., p. 42.

[13]U.S. Environmental Protection Agency, Office of Inspector General, "Survey of Air Quality Information Related to the World Trade Center Collapse" (Report No. 2003-P-00014), 26 September 2003.

3 ———————————————————

Significant chaos

As the air began to clear over Lower Manhattan that first morning, and the heaviest dust from the choking plumes started to lift, weak September sunlight revealed the terrorists' shocking achievement: a ten-story pile of twisted steel and blasted concrete festering like a tumor on the heart of America's most critical financial district. Hopelessly entangled and incredibly complex, it was like nothing that had even been seen outside of a war zone. This is the oldest part of the city, and four centuries of commerce and growth had been wiped out—right down to the primordial bedrock. It is difficult to imagine any municipal government being in a position to take charge in such a chaotic moment. History has shown time and again how governments can be practically paralyzed by disaster. After the 1985 earthquake that devastated Mexico City, local officials were so slow to act, and their tepid response—eventually taken over and run insensitively by the federal government—was so inept that residents quickly concluded that they were on their own. They then began to organize neighborhood action groups to provide emergency shelter, food, and water. And from those self-help groups sprouted Mexico's fledgling democracy movement. Still, all that civic spirit wasn't enough to bring the city back. Buildings that had been flattened in the quake—and buried occupants inside the ruined structures—festered untouched for years.

New York City's response to the 9/11 terrorist attack began with more blind pragmatism than plan, as Giuliani's wandering that morning showed. But the effort was not held back by any lack of confidence about the city's ability to handle whatever it confronted. From the very first moments, even as the mayor and his top police officials wandered through the dusty streets searching for a place to set up emergency operations, the legion of New York's municipal bureau-crats—hardened from years of experience in running the devilishly complex city, with all its different groups and competing interests, while handling unique emergencies nearly every day—responded in a prac-ticed, matter-of-fact way to the biggest disaster any of them had seen.

What they had in their favor was the accumulated experience of keeping New York City going, and that, in itself, represented a formi-dable degree of expertise. The ordinary functions of a municipal gov-ernment had mutated in New York so that the ordinary became exceptional. The most mundane became singular. The city's building code must be comprehensive enough to cover the construction of backyard decks as well as the exigencies of erecting some of the world's tallest buildings; the bedrock of Manhattan is tunneled with the country's most extensive underground transportation system along with the city's telecommunications network—the busiest and most complex in the country. Even such simple municipal duties as providing water are colossal undertakings. The deep underground tunnels for the city's water works had to be drilled through the Man-hattan schist bedrock on such a scale that they carried more than a billion gallons of fresh drinking water a day from as far as 120 miles away.

On September 11, those who were in charge of the ordinary had to respond to the unthinkable. One of the men who would eventually play a key role in the recovery operations was Michael Burton, execu-tive deputy commissioner of the Department of Design and Con-struction, a low-profile city agency that had responsibility for all municipal construction projects except for schools and sewage treat-ment plants. His day began like any other. Burton was attending a regularly scheduled meeting at City Hall in downtown Manhattan when the first plane struck a few blocks away.[1] A deputy mayor, Tony Coles, initially took it in stride, recalling, as many New Yorkers did, the black-and-white photos of a B-25 bomber that had crashed into the Empire State Building in a thick fog in 1945. As a precaution, City Hall was evacuated and Coles asked Burton to look for the Office of Emergency Management's command bus, hoping to find Mayor Giu-liani there. With phone lines almost immediately overloaded, Burton walked four or five blocks south on Broadway, hoping to find the bus. But no such luck. Burton was thinking ahead, knowing that, with or without the command bus, once the fire department had put out the blaze, there might still be broken glass and other debris falling from the World Trade Center, threatening pedestrians. Burton reached out to the construction companies he knew and arranged to have one of the big scaffolding contractors load their trucks and stand by, ready to assemble protective coverings over the trade center plaza and on nearby sidewalks so passersby wouldn't get hurt. So far, it was just another day in the big apple.

Then the second plane hit the South Tower, and 57 minutes later that building came down. Burton's boss, Kenneth Holden, was well aware that the trade center site was owned by the Port Authority, which still kept its executive offices there.[2] Holden tried to get through to someone at the agency, but the phones were dead. With the legal owner out of pocket and the lessee of the building, developer Larry Silverstein (who had just taken out a long-term lease on the huge complex a few weeks earlier), not in a position to handle what needed to be done next, Holden took it upon his own department, which had the best contacts with the private construction industry, to step in. The badly hurt fire department—which at that time knew only that it had lost its top commanders and an unbearable number of firefighters—needed help moving the steel and concrete to rescue survivors. Deputy Mayor Rudy Washington had tried to find someone with equipment and expertise but struck out.

Holden, and particularly Burton, had better luck. In a few hours, they had sent out police vans to pick up the executives of four construction companies and rush them to ground zero. Three were very big contractors that regularly worked on the city's most complex projects, usually employing dozens of smaller subcontractors and hundreds of workers. The fourth was a local construction company that already had some heavy equipment nearby because it was just finishing a long-term project on the West Side Highway. The trade center site was hastily divided into quadrants, and each company took control of a section in an initial attempt to bring order to ground zero.

When the contractors joined the city officials at what had hours before been the World Trade Center, they saw for themselves the overwhelming scale of the calamity. Fires raged, the air was still opaque with dust, and firefighters and cops crawled over portions of the pile, looking as small as ants. "For the first week, and probably more than the first week, there was significant chaos," Burton said later. Indeed, the chaos generated by the cataclysm in Lower Manhattan, along with the city's robust though admittedly imperfect response, would become critical factors in what transpired later. For despite the city's heroic efforts, the actions taken in the early days established a pattern of unintended consequences, missed opportunities, crossed signals, and lack of coordination that would undermine later attempts to set things right.

In the confusion of those early hours, other city agencies moved just as quickly as Burton's own department. The city's veteran chief medical examiner, Dr. Charles S. Hirsch, rushed down to the trade center within minutes of the first plane hitting the north tower. He and one of his staff investigators, Diane Crisci, were on the West Side Highway, scouting places to set up a temporary morgue, when the South Tower came crashing down. Hirsch was cut and bruised and had sprained an ankle. Crisci's leg was broken. The air had turned so dark that Hirsch was convinced he had been buried by debris, and rumors spread that he had been killed. After a few minutes, he shook off the debris. When the air started to clear, he and Crisci made their way toward an unusual light. As they drew nearer the light, they felt heat and realized the light was actually a burning car. They later stumbled upon an emergency medical services team that took care of them. Another rumor spread that Hirsch had sewn together a gash on his own arm, but that also turned out to be false. He was treated at the New York University Hospital and then walked next door to the medical examiner's office, where he prepared for what he knew would be the grim task ahead.

Kelly McKinney, the city health department's associate commissioner for environmental health, was just coming out of the #1 subway at Chambers Street and West Broadway that morning and heading to work when he ran into a group of people pointing in the air.[3] He turned and saw the jagged gash where American Airlines Flight 11, which had left Boston's Logan Airport bound for California, had ripped through the North Tower a few minutes earlier. He stood at the corner trying to figure out what had happened. Nobody there knew any more than he did. He then walked several blocks to the health department offices on Worth Street and stopped to talk to members of his staff. As they pieced together their own experiences that morning, the second plane, United Airlines Flight 175, smashed through the South Tower in a ball of flame. McKinney rushed everyone into the building and put them to work.

"The main things we did that morning were to put up a 24-hour operation and begin to put a surveillance system into place to try to figure out what health issues were going to transpire," McKinney later recalled. "We weren't down there, but we knew there was dust." Before that first day ended, McKinney and the department had issued a self-evident advisory recommending that any workers on the pile wear steel-capped boots, hard hats, protective goggles, and an N95 white paper dust mask to protect them from the large dust particles suspended in the air.

The next morning, some of city government's most powerful officials squeezed themselves into grade school desks at Public School/Intermediate School 89 in Lower Manhattan as they tried to figure out the best way to proceed. McKinney had some important information to share. He had met separately with representatives of Consolidated Edison, the big New York utility that had lost two gigantic substations in the base of Number 7 World Trade Center when that building, damaged by fire and debris from the twin towers across the street, had fallen down. The Con Ed workers showed McKinney the results of some early environmental testing that indicated there could be asbestos in the air. Con Ed had a troubled relationship with asbestos and was exceptionally careful about disclosing possible contamination. The company had suffered a blow to its reputation in 1989 when steam pipes near Gramercy Park exploded, killing three people and sending mud and asbestos flying into the air. It was later revealed that Con Ed had withheld information about the presence of asbestos for three days, even as residents of the neighborhood returned to their homes. This time, Con Ed officials were quick to share data with the city. A company employee had walked around ground zero on September 11 wearing a personal air monitor that had picked up a small number of samples with slightly elevated asbestos levels, but not enough to incite panic. Still, McKinney felt it should be taken into account.

"The one thing we thought about in our minds was that there were hundreds and maybe thousands of people that were still trapped in the rubble," he recalled. "So when I saw the data, I said to myself, does this mean we have to recommend a P100 respirator?" With its tight-fitting straps and changeable filter cartridges, the P100 respirator offered protection against asbestos and many other contaminants that the N95 masks McKinney had recommended did not. If he decided to upgrade his recommendation, should he make it an official advisory or recommend that the health commissioner issue a formal order, which carried far more weight? "Does that mean that I go to the incident commander at ground zero and tell him to pull his fire-fighters off and tell him to pull the construction people off until we can fit them with half-face dual cartridge respirators?" he wondered.

Slowing down the rescue operation at that moment was unthinkable. So McKinney walked to the office of the city's purchasing agent and ordered 10,000 P100 respirators to be delivered to the site as quickly as possible. He did not recommend shutting down the site or holding up operations until every worker was properly fitted with a mask and given detailed instructions on how to use it. The masks would be made available, and workers would be advised—and, in some instances, ordered—to wear them. It was a faint sense of security, certainly not the kind of assurance that McKinney or any other health official would have wanted in an ideal world.

The Con Ed data had shown a slight elevation in asbestos fibers, but McKinney, more than most, was aware that a densely packed city like New York is loaded with potential sources of contaminants like asbestos and lead. Had the data come back with a definitive answer about significantly elevated levels of asbestos in the air, he would have had all the evidence he needed to tell the incident commanders what was required. McKinney knew a lot about how dangerous asbestos could be. Before joining the health department, he had worked as an environmental engineer for the Port Authority, designing asbestos-abatement and lead-abatement projects at the agency's airports and terminals and the trade center itself.

McKinney needed more data, but the department's ability to take samples was severely limited. He formally asked the EPA to conduct comprehensive testing for asbestos, metals, PCBs, and volatile organic compounds, but he didn't know how long the federal agency would take to come up with answers. Then he discovered something about the catastrophe unfolding around him. He could petition just about anyone in city government for just about anything he needed and expect to receive it right away. He could even ignore the city's normally rigid requisitioning procedures. McKinney called a friend from the New York City School Construction Authority, where he once worked, and requisitioned five environmental consultants from the authority's preapproved list. Each consulting company sent three technicians with personal air monitors to take samples. McKinney also talked fire department officials into allowing him to put personal air-monitoring equipment on 15 fire department battalion chiefs.

By September 13, the EPA was beginning to report its data, which coincided with the early Con Ed information. But McKinney was dismayed that the EPA, with all its resources, had not set up the comprehensive network of sampling stations he had asked for and was not analyzing the samples for other contaminants. "[The] EPA was not noticeably quick in implementing any of the decisions that we had come to in terms of what samples needed to be taken," McKinney recalled.

As that first week ended, samples began to show higher asbestos levels in some locations away from the debris pile. This prodded McKinney to change the department's advisory yet again. He upgraded his safety recommendation to P100 OVAG respirators, a more protective mask with cartridges that could block out organic vapors and acid gases, along with the asbestos fibers and other contaminants that a regular P100 could block. The health department advised everyone who was working on the pile and within a 50-foot radius around the pile to wear the respirators and to change the filter cartridges regularly. McKinney tried to keep the message simple because he believed that was the only way to make it effective. He feared that trying to draw too fine of a line about where and when the masks should be used would muffle the message and cause confusion, without leading to compliance. "If we were going to be anywhere near effective with communications," he remarked, "we had to make the message extremely simple."

Even without Giuliani's emergency command center, the city's agencies continued to step up to the plate. Samuel Benson, Director of Health and Medical Planning and Preparedness at the Office of Emergency Management, had been in the 7 World Trade Center bunker when the first plane hit.[4] He and others who were on duty early that

morning began to activate the city's emergency plan. Benson notified
the Greater New York Hospital Association and the state Emergency
Management Office before being evacuated from the bunker at
around 9:30. He lingered in the building's lobby for half an hour, but
when the first tower came down, he and other workers were forced out.
They later regrouped, this time in the street. When the second tower
fell, Benson took shelter in a restaurant on West Broadway. He found a
working telephone inside and called the United States Public Health
Service. He spoke to the director of the Office of Emergency
Response, apprising him of what was unfolding on the ground in New
York. Two hours later, after he had joined the rest of the emergency
management team at the police academy, Benson called the Centers
for Disease Control in Atlanta and requested deployment of the
national pharmaceutical stockpile, preparing for the worst. City health
department officials were worried that the planes might have carried a
secret nuclear device that could spread deadly radioactivity around the
area. They also checked for blood-borne pathogens and other potential
bioterrorism agents, and were quickly able to determine with a degree
of certainty that neither posed a threat. Still, the department had to
check.

The city agencies were moving with remarkable speed, but it was
the uniformed services—police, firefighter, and emergency medical
teams—that were on the front line. The police department secured
the perimeter of the site and used all its officers to protect the rest of
the city from further attack. A few detectives were sent out to secure
private ice skating rinks that could be used as makeshift morgues for
the large number of bodies that were expected to be recovered. Uniformed volunteers from all over the country backed up the city's own
forces. Armed National Guard troops patrolled the streets around
ground zero, and an army of federal agencies soon began to arrive.

But the fire department handled the bulk of the work in the early
days. The trade center was a working fire (and would be for months),
and the fire department brass were designated incident commanders,
which put them in charge of the sprawling operation. Several of the
department's top officials had been killed in the collapse, and a
makeshift command had to be quickly put in place. A handful of firefighters continued to battle the subsurface blazes, pouring thousands
of gallons of water on the pile. Most others focused on the rescue.

The water itself kept hope alive that, deep down in the six stories below ground that had once made up the parking decks and the concourse, lined with cafes, restaurants, and stores, pockets of water, food, and air might be keeping survivors alive.

Using shovels, pickaxes, and often no more than their own hands, firefighters inched onto the shifting rubble, listening for cries of help and clawing through smoking debris when someone spotted a bit of clothing or anything else that looked hopeful. The air tanks that were standard issue for New York City firefighters were useless because they carried only about half an hour of compressed air. Some firefighters wrapped pieces of clothing around their mouths and noses on the first day, and later some picked up dust masks, if they could find them. Most worked unprotected, and nearly all thought little about their own safety while the possibility of rescuing survivors was still considered real.

Deputy Chief Peter Hayden had arrived four minutes after the first plane hit and set up a command center in the lobby of Number One World Trade Center (or World One, as some knew the North Tower) until it came down. In the disturbing aftermath of the collapses, Hayden and other fire officials scrambled to regroup. New York firefighters are bound by deep tradition and fierce loyalty. They attracted a huge amount of public sympathy when the devastating losses became known, and those who survived were treated as wounded heroes. The rest of the city vowed not to get in their way as they searched for fathers, brothers, and sons. Even the volunteers who flew in to offer their help didn't know quite how to approach the department. Several days after the attacks, a man came up to Chief Hayden and announced, "I'm here to help you."[5] Hayden turned around and looked at the stranger as though he were seeing a mirage. The man wore a T-Shirt from the U.S. Forest Service Incident Command Team. How was Smokey the Bear going to help when two of the biggest buildings in the world had been turned into dust? But his offer actually made sense. The Southwest Forestry Service had sent a 35-member incident command team to help the department deal with a blaze like none the city firefighters had ever encountered but that, in some ways, the rangers could recognize. Whereas most urban fires can be brought under control within an hour (which is why tanks containing 30–45 minutes of compressed air were usually sufficient), open-range fires in the Southwest can last for weeks. The rangers had developed a command structure that brought together logistics, performance review, and a daily update that kept a multifaceted response under administrative control for long periods of time.

The forest service rangers helped Hayden establish incident-management teams and provided the backup to augment the daily incident action plans that were distributed to all agencies at morning meetings. The plans listed available resources, the number of police personnel and firefighters on-site, the accomplishments of the previous 24 hours, and a plan of action for the next one to three days. They also included a daily safety message reminding everyone to use personal protective equipment, including the recommended respirators.

But Hayden and the other fire officials decided not to discipline firefighters who failed to heed warnings about respirators. Although the firefighters were taught to follow orders and to be more than cautious about safety, this was an extremely emotional issue. The experienced brass were no more insulated from the tragedy than were the freshest newbies, and in deciding how to proceed in this unprecedented emergency, they took into account all the information they had available and acknowledged the personal intangibles of sorrow, loss, and hope. The environmental reports they received showed that levels were generally acceptable, although there were hot spots and spikes. However, the need to shout orders and steer clear of the bent steel, busted concrete, and mammoth machines was constant, and respirators simply got in the way. Putting all those needs together, Hayden voiced the sentiment that many felt, acknowledging that some firefighters had lost family and friends but continued working under perilous conditions. "I don't think it would have been appropriate to discipline any of them because they failed to wear a respirator," he recounted.[6]

Besides, many of the men on the pile didn't have any compelling reason to take such precautions. The word at daily safety meetings was that air samples did not continue to show any increased risk. All the federal, state, and city agencies said the same thing: The air was safe. The testing did show occasional hot spots above the pile, but they were considered anomalies instead of justification for changing the requirements for respirator equipment. Officials were looking for consistently high readings that made a strong case for taking further steps, and those readings did not materialize.

When the private construction companies began to show up with their heavy equipment, some temporary confusion arose over what the site had actually become: Was it still a working fire, or had it morphed into a crime scene or, worse, an urban junkyard? Now cops and firefighters were working side by side with crane operators and construction laborers in a vast and complex zone of labor. Sorting it all out while still responding to the tremendous emotional pressure to recover bodies and restore normalcy to the financial district was an unprecedented challenge that led to some ad hoc decisions, with severe consequences.

One of the most important decisions was how to handle workplace safety rules. The agency normally charged with ensuring that workers do not face unwarranted hazards on the job is the Occupational Safety and Health Administration. OSHA's own offices in Number 6 World Trade Center had been crushed by debris falling from the twin towers. The agency's employees had escaped unharmed well before the towers came down, but they had lost their desks and their files. Within a few days, they were ready to go back to work, but as the magnitude of the recovery operation became apparent, they were stymied. The dangers of the site were many. In fact, there may have been no more dangerous workplace in the country at that time than ground zero. The debris pile was unstable, undercut by jagged steel and raging fires. The trade center complex housed hundreds of offices and businesses, with an almost infinite number of potential dangers, from the freon of the complex's huge air-conditioning system to the guns and ammunition held in the offices of the U.S. Customs Service. To get through the mountain of debris, the construction companies rolled in their big equipment: 300-ton, 400-ton, 700-ton, even gigantic 1,000-ton cranes and heavy-duty grapplers that could pick through the jackstraw tangle of steel to look for survivors.

When the heavy equipment moved in, firefighters needed to be stationed close by to signal the crane operators when a body was found. Instead of establishing a 50-foot radius around the machines that normally was a no-enter zone for workers on foot, firefighters stood within 6 feet of the biggest equipment. Some of the cranes and grapplers were designed for huge open-pit mines, not city streets, and were so heavy that officials feared they might collapse the honey-combed streets. After the overlaying debris was cleared from an area, ironworkers with acetylene cutting torches sliced through the mangled remains so the biggest girders could be quickly moved out of the way.

OSHA was well aware of the dangers. The agency also recognized that this was no ordinary worksite. It was still under the control of the fire department and still considered not only a working fire, but a crime scene where thousands had been murdered. Workplace safety regulations were not suspended, but the agency couldn't impose its normal method of enforcing those regulations—issuing fines for noncompliance—as long as it was a rescue operation. Strict adherence to the rules would have essentially halted the work, as Kelly McKinney of the health department had initially feared. Each worker would have to be fitted with a respirator, instructed in its use, and given a physical examination to determine whether using the restricted breathing of the respirator could lead to other health issues. If inspectors then found workers without respirators, they would issue warnings first, then fines.

Besides slowing down operations, OSHA believed fines would have had minimal impact because the contractors were working on a time-and-materials basis, charging the city as they went along. The fines would go to the employers, who would merely roll them into other charges, in effect fining the city itself. Even labor union leaders were skeptical of the power of fines to improve safety because they could merely be written into contracts and their relative value was nothing compared to the cost of time and production. Perhaps most significantly, the culture at OSHA had changed under the Bush administration. Strict enforcement of regulations had given way to an idealistic cooperation between regulators and management, which sped up production. New York City officials did not insist that OSHA strictly enforce its rules, but rather asked the agency to remain in an advisory role. OSHA would not have had authority over the police and firefighters anyway. Eventually, the city, the contractors, and OSHA entered into a voluntary agreement: the contractors themselves would enforce employee compliance with safety rules while OSHA agreed to monitor the site but not issue fines. OSHA had found this kind of voluntary arrangement effective in other instances. Given all the complex operations going on at ground zero and the apparent need to move ahead quickly, it seemed like a workable solution.

One other city agency that had responded quickly to the disaster was an unlikely one, the Department of Sanitation. Collecting garbage is a Herculean task in New York City, which generates 25,000 tons of residential and commercial garbage every day. The unique logistics of the waterbound city make getting rid of the trash a complicated choreography involving trucks, cranes, trains, and sometimes even barges. At different times over the last century, the city had tried burning its trash in incinerators, dumping it into the ocean, and finally burying it in the world's largest landfill, called Fresh Kills, on Staten Island. Community opposition in the city's most suburban and conservative borough had led Giuliani to agree to close down Fresh Kills, even though he hadn't come up with a permanent alternative. The last loads of garbage were dumped on the towering mounds in March 2001. But in the days after the 9/11 attacks, the department mobilized some of its heavy equipment, and the Giuliani administration determined that the most efficient way to clear the debris from ground zero was to reopen Fresh Kills on an emergency basis.

The sanitation department quickly mobilized pieces of heavy equipment, and the first material to be taken out of the pile was loaded onto New York City Housing Authority dump trucks and transported over the Verrazano Narrows Bridge. A 175-acre section of Fresh Kills was reopened, and a huge sorting and disposal operation was established there under the command of one tough New York City cop, Deputy Inspector James Luongo. It started small, but in no time, as many as 1,300 people a day were sorting through the material for human remains and any items that could help identify the victims. By the time Army Corps of Engineers debris-removal specialists showed up, Luongo had established such an efficient operation that they stood down, offering whatever help they could but gladly allowing the local officials to run the show.

Almost from the beginning, Luongo strictly enforced personal protective equipment rules.[7] Believing that the material handled there contained asbestos, silica, and other harmful materials, he ordered everyone working in several "hot zones" to wear respirators.

He also issued Tyvek suits, although he said it was mostly to protect his officers' clothing. His message to wear protective equipment came across loud and clear, and through most of the operation compliance rates hovered above 90 percent (compared to compliance at ground zero, where rates dipped below 30 percent). However, police officers and detectives outside the designated hot zones often worked without protection.

Luongo later said getting his people to watch out for their own health wasn't difficult. "You stood up at roll call, you said what was expected, and it was complied with," he recalled. Of course, there were substantial differences between Fresh Kills and ground zero. Although it's part of New York City, Staten Island is far removed in both miles and attitude from the hustle of the financial district. The mostly treeless mounds of garbage at Fresh Kills tower over the island and feel like a moonscape, save for the gulls that hover out of habit. Access to the site was strictly controlled, and it was so remote that people who didn't belong there stayed away. Ground zero, on the other hand, was a bizarre world unto itself, a construction site moving backward in time disassembling the once-mighty towers before hordes of onlookers. There the President of the United States embraced workers without wearing a respirator. Congressional delegations and international dignitaries tramped through without wearing protection. Workers, residents, and tourists came by in an unending stream, day after day, most without masks. Armed National Guardsmen watched high-heeled starlets gawk at the pile, unprotected by any kind of respirator.

Conflicts over how best to proceed inevitably arose. The city health department wanted trucks carrying debris from ground zero to be thoroughly washed down before leaving the site, to limit contamination on city streets. But the FBI objected, arguing that the operation would wash away important evidence. The agency reversed itself when it learned that water could trigger the locators on the airplanes' black boxes, which had not yet been found. As the cleanup continued, a more efficient way of moving the twisted steel girders had to be found. A loading dock was proposed for the Hudson River so that workers could transfer the debris to barges, but once it began operation, neighborhood residents objected. They believed the dock was spewing contaminants in the air. Parents also complained that the dock was too close to a nearby school. But the city held that the environmental monitoring of the site did not warrant such concerns. Clearly, operating a loading dock near thousands of school children was not an ideal solution, but as in so many instances in the recovery operation, it was a matter of balancing interests and selecting among imperfect alternatives. The dock remained in operation.

After more than two full weeks of frantic digging on the pile and nonstop attempts to get the city back on its feet, Mayor Giuliani made the announcement that everyone knew needed to be made but that no one wanted to hear. He said that, difficult as it was to face, there was no chance of finding any more survivors. That meant the frenzied rescue part of the operation was over. Most people had given up any real hope long before, and only the pursuit of a miracle delayed the official declaration until the end of the month. By then, what remained was recovery—recovery of the remains of the victims, including the 343 firefighters and medics, and recovery of the city itself.

The fire department's daily incident action plan, the coordinating document that the forest fire service had helped craft and that fire officials have acknowledged was of significant assistance, reflected the change in the status of the operation. The earliest of the daily plans stated that steel cutting and debris removal should move "at the most rapid pace possible" and that although ironworkers would assist the department, "keep in mind—this is a rescue operation." The same words were repeated in every day's rundown of planned actions and operating instructions. But in the plan that was released on the morning of September 28, the admonition to remember the rescue nature of the operation was dropped, although most activities remained unchanged. There was no slowdown, no evident switch in tactics, no directive to increase the use of personal protective equipment despite the low compliance rate. Each day's action plan continued to stress safety: Wearing gloves, safety shoes, and respirators with filters was mandatory. The overall objectives for the work included "health, safety, and welfare of all personnel working in and around the incident." Most often, the safety admonitions included personal messages directed at the firefighters themselves. One said, "Take time to protect yourself. The life you save may be your own."

That was on paper. Out on the street, the city was intent on moving the cleanup ahead as quickly as possible. On October 22, Burton sent out a memo repeating the city's position that the worksite was safe. In part, the memo said "all D.D.C. personnel should feel confident that they're not being exposed to unhealthy levels of chemicals and that the air quality at the WTC is generally good."

The unique demands of building in Manhattan had long before 9/11 created a subculture of construction companies that was hard for outsiders to break into. The four prime contractors at ground zero all had long resumes of building in the city. But their experience with environmental cleanups did not compare to that of Bechtel, a large engineering company with ties to the Bush White House. Bechtel had successfully put out the Kuwait oil field fires in the first Gulf War and helped with the cleanup at the nuclear power plant at Chernobyl. The company had arrived in New York almost immediately after the towers fell. Although Bechtel hadn't been part of Michael Burton's contractor outreach, it had started work on a health and safety plan for the overall site. (For good measure, the company also told Mayor Giuliani that it had contributed $100,000 to a fund for fallen rescue workers.) Bechtel hoped to secure all or at least part of the recovery project. For the California company, this was a chance to break into the New York market. Within days, the company was sending teams of demolition experts and construction safety managers to New York. Bechtel had the resources and experience to handle the job, although it did not understand how New York worked. One of its safety specialists, David Ausmus, arrived in New York on September 26 from Oak Ridge, Tenn., where Bechtel handles environmental cleanup for the U.S. Department of Energy. Ausmus immediately noted that most workers on the pile weren't bothering to wear hardhats, safety glasses, or respirators. "Our job is to assess the situation, install safety procedures, and assist the rescuers and workforce with a safety mindset," Ausmus noted at the end of that first day. "In other words, we are to restore some semblance of safety order."[8] The city allowed Bechtel to submit a bid for the overall project, but then it asked the four companies it was already dealing with—AMEC, Bovis Lend-Lease, Turner Construction, and Tully, the local company working on the West Side Highway—to resubmit their bids. There was no way they were going to let the big job go to an outside company, no matter who Bechtel knew. Bechtel determined that if it was going to be limited to just the safety role, it wasn't worth staying.

On October 17 Ausmus found out that Bechtel was not going to get the comprehensive contract it wanted. The company pulled out its entire staff and handed over its work-safety plan to Liberty Mutual Insurance Company, which had written additional liability coverage when the city—which was self-insured—tried to buy more coverage on the open market. Liberty Mutual then helped develop a health and safety plan in consultation with the city health department, contractors, and other agencies.

The issue of who should wear respirators where and when was a constant topic of discussion at the twice-daily meetings run by the city. It was becoming clear that many workers were ignoring the advisories. The fire department's incident action plans indicated that many firefighters were flouting the rules, the Operating Engineers Union watched the site through binoculars and found unsatisfactory compliance, and the Department of Design and Construction—which Giuliani had declared co-incident commander along with the fire department when the rescue phase ended—had its own proof that the message was falling on deaf ears. One of the first things Kenneth Holden had done when he was named commissioner in 1999 was purchase a dozen digital cameras to monitor construction sites. Violations could be recorded and quickly posted. Now at ground zero, his cameras were coming back with images of workers on the pile without masks. Even those who had masks often wore them around their necks. Besides making workers sweaty and uncomfortable, the respirators came with filters that clogged quickly in the heavy dust that hovered over the pile, and replacements weren't always readily available. Wearing a respirator with clogged filters can feel like suffocating, and the first impulse is to tear it off.

Firefighters were particularly lax about wearing their respirators, and the contractors, who were being hounded by OSHA, complained, "What about them?" When the safety director for one of the construction companies pointed out the lack of compliance to one of the fire department chiefs, the officer thanked him but then snapped "you are out of bounds,"[9] meaning that the intensely proud and independent uniformed services would not take instructions from civilians.

The inspectors had more leverage with construction company supervisors, but after a while, they demanded to know why they were being picked on when the cops and firemen were so clearly violating the rules. James Abadie, a senior vice president with Bovis, said his construction workers were upset because they were being hectored by inspectors for not wearing their respirators, yet they saw most firefighters on the pile and police on the perimeter without theirs. The signs, advisories, and warnings were being widely ignored, and Abadie, who was used to the roughneck attitudes that prevailed on many construction sites, knew that the men simply were not going to take precautions to protect themselves by wearing masks "unless [they had] their mother there to tell them to do it"—even then, he doubted they'd comply.

Across the board, workers being pestered about respirators kept asking the same question: Why should I wear one of those damn things if everybody keeps saying the air is safe? Some men said it was too much of a hassle to wear one; others claimed they hadn't been given anything to wear or couldn't find replacements. Compliance rates dropped; resentment increased. Eventually, Holden was forced to take back the digital cameras and call off the visual inspections— construction workers resented being spied on and caught on camera.

Many people thought it odd to have Holden's department assume control of the cleanup. For the first weeks, Holden himself kept looking over his shoulder, half expecting that the Federal Emergency Management Agency (FEMA) or some other government entity would step in, thank him kindly for all his hard work, and tell him to go home because they were taking over. But it didn't happen. Giuliani didn't ask for help, and the federal agencies didn't insist on giving it. So the work proceeded in the same hectic way it had begun: balancing the desire for speed against the potential slowdowns that would come with precautions. Leo DiRubbo, a senior vice president for AMEC, was one of the construction officials escorted to ground zero in a police van just a few hours after the towers imploded. He worked every day through January except for Thanksgiving, Christmas, and the day his father died. It seemed to him that the city's demand for speed was relentless. "This job was driven by schedule, not by safety," he noted. "We were told machines do not stop—they work 24 hours, 7 days a week, and nothing could stop this job. That was the driving schedule; it was schedule driven. We were actually threatened at meetings: If you are not done for the first of the year, you will not be here on the second."[10]

The construction companies were working so fast that they had not been able to negotiate a full written contract. Working on a time-and-materials basis gave the city incentive for keeping things moving forward quickly. The project was so big that the city had started handing out $10 million checks to the companies before the first week was over, assuming that the billing would come later. There wasn't even time for the contractors to secure sufficient liability insurance to protect themselves under the precarious conditions of working on a shifting pile of red-hot rubble. Yet they continued to work without stopping, understanding that this was no ordinary job and these were no ordinary times. They tried to get additional insurance on the open market, and they raised their concerns with the city several times. They were told it would be taken care of.

For the first two months, ground zero was in continuous motion, stopping only when the air horn blasted three times, indicating that another body had been found. Then if the body belonged to a firefighter, a somber procession moved over the debris as the remains were ceremoniously brought to the surface to be identified and laid to rest. The work was a constant reminder of death, sacrifice, and mission. These funerals later came to symbolize the futility of keeping the rescuers working long hours on the pile without protection, putting themselves at risk and inviting suffering and disease in order to honor the dead, a sacrifice that no one would publicly question.

This was the most dangerous workplace most of the thousands of responders had ever known. It was more complex than any construction site they had ever been involved with. It was a more confounding fire than any they had ever fought. It was the most sampled place in the nation, but widespread confusion still circulated over what the risks were and how dangerous working there might be. But each day the pile grew smaller, each day more remains were uncovered, each day the city took another step toward recovery—and each day countless people were exposed to the dust that would cling to them and change their lives.

What had ground zero become?

- A fire without visible flame
- The scene of a mass murder, witnessed by millions but with few bodies left as evidence

- A rescue without anyone to rescue
- An extensively analyzed and picked-over 16 acres, yet a void filled with lingering uncertainty about what was safe and what was not
- Significant chaos

Endnotes

[1]Deposition of Michael Burton, 8 September 2005.

[2]Deposition of Kenneth Holden, 10–11 August 2005.

[3]Deposition of Kelly McKinney, 19 October 2005.

[4]Deposition of Samuel Benson, 8 September 2005.

[5]Deposition of Salvatore Cassano, 30 September 2005.

[6]Deposition of Peter Hayden, 19 September 2005.

[7]Deposition of James Luongo, 21 September 2005.

[8]Ausmus, David *In the Midst of Chaos: My Thirty Days at Ground Zero* Victoria, B.C.: Trafford, 2004).

[9]Deposition of William Ryan, Tully Corporate Safety Director, 2 August 2005.

[10]Deposition of Leo DiRubbo, Senior Vice President of AMEC and licensed safety manager, 5 December 2005.

Part II

Disease

4

Raising doubts

Not far from the EPA's formidable granite headquarters on Broadway, another office focuses single-mindedly on environmental issues and the frightening impacts those situations can have on the people who live and work near them. Their similarities, however, end there. After 9/11, these two offices became locked in a battle over science and fact, largely because of a rumpled hobbit named Joel Kupferman. Kupferman is the crusading attorney who heads the New York Environmental Law & Justice Project, an in-your-face legal hit squad that isn't afraid to be called radical. Its offices, on the fourth floor of an old Broadway commercial building, are a world apart from the federal building's grand formality and impressive architecture. The ancient elevator rises as slowly as fog on a spring morning, and the crowded floor offers just enough space to squeeze through sideways to get to Kupferman's rat's nest of an office. This is the epicenter of Kupferman's world, the place where he keeps his files in boxes and daunting piles of dog-eared papers. Two laptop computers are always open, and several phones ring at once. Regulars know that if he doesn't pick up, they'll have to try again, because the message box is almost always full. Past the discarded electronics and the coffee-ringed papers is a dirty window that looks out over his beloved Broadway.

Kupferman's mind is organized along the same unorthodox lines as his office. Thoughts are piled on top of each other, seemingly at random, and at times several come spilling out in an avalanche of words that overwhelms anything in its way. But just as he can usually find the documents he is looking for in that junk heap of an office, he follows through on his ideas and concerns about environmental safety. Many of those ideas share the same origin, and that is the gutter smell of social justice in the big city. And because he considers this city—particularly this oldest, most crowded part downtown—to be his own, he was especially on guard after 9/11 when officials consistently said everything was all right.

Kupferman has been a fixture in Lower Manhattan for a long time. He had already spent decades on these streets by the time the federal building that houses the EPA's regional office was constructed in the early 1990s. In a way, he grew up downtown because of the family business, which was not law, but leather—specifically, the leather used to make the soles of shoes. Kupferman's grandfather Harry started Worth Street Leather, later just Worth Leather, right before the great stock market crash in 1929. Harry passed it down to Kupferman's own father, Saul, before Joel came to inherit it. Worth Leather was part of an industry that for centuries had thrived in an area known as the swamp, near City Hall on the Manhattan side of the Brooklyn Bridge (where Pace University came to be built). Kupferman's parents were New York Jewish liberals. His mother, Mollie, had volunteered for the American Labor Party and her father, Bernard, had been a member of the Industrial Workers of the World (the Wobblies). Although the family had lived in relative comfort in Roosevelt, Long Island, his father had firmly believed in workers' rights, and he'd passed along a rigid sense of social justice that took root in his four sons.

Joel Kupferman was the only one of the four interested in keeping the leather business going, more out of a nod to tradition than to any thought that it could provide a living wage. When he entered the State University of New York at Stony Brook, Long Island, he was already launched on a career in social justice. Kupferman studied human-scale economics and development, and in time he gravitated toward environmental challenges such as curbing water pollution and protecting forestry resources. One of the most controversial issues on Long Island at that time was construction of the Shoreham nuclear power plant. Kupferman dived headlong into the anti-nuke protests, which eventually prevented the plant from ever operating commercially.

Kupferman helped run the leather business, but it had changed substantially. As the shoe part of its business declined during the 1960s, Worth Leather had expanded into crafts, supplying the leather straps and metal buckles that counter-culture entrepreneurs used to fashion hippie couture. Kupferman took to the road, sometimes with his father, calling on craft shops throughout the Northeast. He discovered that nearly every one of the shops also functioned quite effectively as a local campaign headquarters for liberal presidential candidate George McGovern. Over time, Kupferman developed a special rapport with grass-roots organizers, and he continued to nurture the relationship after graduating from Stony Brook in 1978.

Working at Worth Leather a couple days a week provided a modest living, while also allowing him to devote his energies to advocacy. Then came one of those defining moments when, without warning, something happens and suddenly the world seems clearer. He was invited to a dinner party at the home of a liberal friend on Long Island. While casually passing a plate at the dinner table, the host asked his wife, who worked at the Brookhaven National Laboratory near Stony Brook, about rumors of a hazardous material spill at the lab. "Oh yes," the woman said, there had been a spill, but when reporters called Brookhaven, officials had denied it because, she said, "the people of Long Island wouldn't know how to handle the information." For Kupferman, it was as though a bowl of hot soup had spilled in his lap. He realized that everyone at the dinner table portrayed themselves as environmentally sensitive and committed to the right side of things. Yet they seemed all too willing to withhold or distort information, and that realization transformed him in significant ways that shaped his future. "It made me realize that I had to have a healthy skepticism whenever there's an announcement that something is safe," he said.

By 1986, Kupferman decided that he had reached the limit of his effectiveness as a socially aware small businessman and probably could have a greater impact as a lawyer, especially if he practiced public interest law. He brought his admission application right to the Touro Law Center in New York, an accredited law school that advocated studies in social justice and is closed on Friday evening and all day Saturday in observance of the Jewish Sabbath. It was the very last day applications could be filed, and before he left the admissions office, he asked to see its director. Kupferman had been arrested eight times already during civil disobedience marches, and he needed to know whether that record would hurt his chances of being accepted to law school and to the bar. He wasn't sure what to think when the admissions director pulled him into the office and closed the door. "I was at Seabrook, were you?" she asked him, referring to demonstrations at the construction site of the Seabrook Nuclear Plant in New Hampshire in 1977. Kupferman acknowledged that he had been there, and at Shoreham, too. With that, they established a special bond. The admissions officer not only told him not to worry, but she gave him details about a dean's fellowship for public advocacy law and encouraged him to apply for it.

It took Kupferman four years to complete his degree. He attended classes at night while still running Worth Leather during the day. In 1991, Kupferman had his law degree—and his passion. With fellow students from Touro, he hung out his shingle as the New York Environmental Law & Justice Project. He had no foundation grants, no outside supporters. His practice was done literally on a shoestring: Kupferman took some of the proceeds out of Worth Leather, which for years had supplied shoelaces to bowling alleys all over the Northeast. The business was in steep decline and, by the mid-1990s, closed its doors. But Mollie and Saul Kupferman's lasting legacy would be the social activism that the humble workshop had instilled in their son. Kupferman never forgot what it was like to work with men who wouldn't eat the edges of their lunch sandwiches because they couldn't wash the work stains from their fingers. The years he spent handling the heavily processed materials at Worth Leather taught him about the environment and the grave consequences business can have on water and land. He embraced the concept of social justice, and he developed the ability to recognize when it was threatened.

Kupferman first set up his legal SWAT team on Long Island, but by 1997, he had moved to the city, back to the old neighborhood downtown. He occupied a tiny space, an office within an office, and was still located there when the planes struck on September 11. Kupferman had continued his broad interest in social justice issues. Besides fighting cover-ups of toxic spills and developments that destroyed wetlands, he helped immigrants in trouble. On the morning of September 11, he was due in an Elizabeth, New Jersey, courtroom to defend an Eritrean immigrant threatened with deportation. As he boarded a train at Penn Station that morning, Kupferman heard a brief news report about the first trade center tower being on fire. He wasn't sure what it meant, and he had desperate people waiting for him, so he didn't turn around. By the time he got to the Elizabeth courthouse, the second tower had come down. The court session was cancelled, and all transportation into the city had been cut off. Kupferman was stranded in New Jersey. He had to spend several days with relatives before he could make his way back to New York.

When he finally returned, Kupferman walked in a daze through the streets he had known since he was a child. "It looked like Kansas after a dust storm," he said. He talked to the people he passed on the streets and, instinctively, worried about what they were breathing. His answering machine was filled with frantic messages from people who hadn't been able to reach him for days and feared he was dead.

A few days after he got back, he received a troubling telephone call from Tommy Barnett, a New York City police officer and Patrolman's Benevolent Association (PBA) delegate. They had met over an earlier environmental threat. It had been late summer, and the city had been spraying for West Nile Virus mosquitoes in a way that exposed on-duty police officers to the toxic chemicals, despite assurances from Mayor Giuliani that there was no danger. Barnett had asked Kupferman for help and together they had managed to get the city to substantially change its spraying schedule and flight patterns so that on-duty cops weren't overly exposed to the pesticides.

After the twin towers caved in on themselves, Barnett told Kupferman that some police officers had gotten sick after working just a brief time at ground zero. "I've got guys who are spitting up blood," Barnett said. Some officers had pulled a number of 12-hour shifts guarding the perimeter of the debris pile without any respiratory protection. Kupferman knew that he had to get into ground zero to see for himself, but he also knew there was no way he would be allowed past security. Barnett understood and offered to meet him at the PBA offices on Fulton Street, a quick walk from the trade center, on September 19, two days after Paul Lioy had gathered his dust samples. Barnett gave Kupferman a PBA shirt and cap, along with a dust mask, and walked him to ground zero. Accompanying them was Columbia Fiero, Kupferman's partner and the project's photographer. Now they were face-to-face with the unreal scenes they had been watching on television. The dust was still quite thick. Kupferman took a blue plastic spoon and Ziploc bags and grabbed as much of the material as he could from a building on Church Street, one block north of the trade center. When he had scooped the dust into the bags, he looked up and saw that he was in front of the big downtown post office, the same post office where he used to mail out packages from Worth Leather.

After Kupferman left the restricted zone, his head was filled with questions. He had heard Giuliani reassuring the people of New York that the air downtown was safe, and he had seen Christie Whitman give her homey assessments of the risk on television. But what he experienced at ground zero—the gray haze in the air, the ashen dust piled up everywhere, the air tinged with the rank aroma of death— reminded him of the fancy dinner on Long Island years before when the hostess had assured everyone there was nothing to worry about.

Kupferman sent the samples of dust he'd collected to two independent labs, one in New York City and the other in Virginia. The city and the EPA had said there were no serious problems in most locations, but he wanted the dust he'd collected with his own hands to be tested and analyzed by labs whose reputation he knew and trusted. He did it for the people who lived and worked downtown, and he did it to hold officials accountable. That had been the mission of his Environmental Law & Justice Project from the beginning. But Kupferman had one more reason, a personal one. This was his neighborhood, the place that had shaped him from the time he was a child. Seeing it damaged that way made him angry. But the thought that someone might be withholding the truth made him angrier still.

The labs sent back the results quickly, and they were frightening. The first four dust samples tested by ATC Associates of New York, a lab that regularly did work for the New York City Board of Education, contained twice as much asbestos as some of the EPA samples, and as much as 15 percent fiberglass. The samples tested by ETI Laboratory in Fairfax found a range of chrysotile asbestos that went from a trace to 5 percent. Working with Monona Rossol, an industrial hygienist, Kupferman put the findings into flyers and distributed them to downtown residents and the men and women working in the debris of the trade center. In the flyers, he came to a basic conclusion: "Health officials may think they are doing people a favor by withholding infor-mation, but there is no reason to assume that New Yorkers will not be just as courageous in dealing with air quality issues as they have been in dealing with the disaster. Failing to provide this information can cause people to take needless risks." He felt the area should have been declared a federal Superfund site. Instead, people were being encouraged to come back to live and work there.

Part of the work that a lawyer such as Kupferman does goes beyond law and public policy and enters the realm of public relations. Kupferman needed to make his findings known, to create pressure on officials. Doing so, a pint-sized legal outfit such as his can multiply its impact many times. Taking an issue to the media often is quicker and, in some ways, more effective than going to court. Lawsuits are an expensive and time-consuming last resort, but talking to a reporter costs nothing. Kupferman also had another reason for going public with his findings. The question of how toxic the 9/11 dust might be was already being played out in public, with Giuliani and Whitman's opti-mistic statements abetting the burning desire of a wounded city to believe that the thick dust was not a problem, despite evidence to the contrary.

Kupferman called Juan Gonzalez, a long-time columnist for the *New York Daily News* who often writes about social justice issues. The two men had met during the West Nile Virus spraying when Kupferman was interviewed about his work with the police depart-ment. The two made an odd couple. Since starting as a columnist at the *Daily News* in 1987, Gonzalez had become one of the most noticeable people in New York media circles. Besides writing the newspaper column, his ability to concisely sum up complicated issues and dig down to the heart of tangled political struggles had made him a star of radio and television, where he dressed elegantly in pin-striped suits and flashy ties. *Elegant* is the least appropriate word used to describe Kupferman, with his wrinkled slacks, long gray hair, and shapeless baseball cap. Most reporters in New York knew that Kupferman tended to ramble, too. But Gonzalez had learned that Kupferman had a way of getting his hands on damning information. He had used his friends and sources to get the facts about the true impact of the West Nile spraying, and Gonzalez had woven the data into columns that made front-page news, angering City Hall. Now

Kupferman was on the phone with him again, this time with information backing up what any thinking person who saw the dust would have concluded. In late September, Kupferman told Gonzalez about the independent lab tests and showed him how different those results were from the optimistic reports coming from the EPA and City Hall.

Like Kupferman, Gonzalez had found it hard to swallow the explanations offered by Giuliani and Whitman. He had done a substantial amount of reporting on exposures to hazardous chemicals when he had worked for the *Philadelphia Inquirer* before coming to New York. In Philadelphia, he had taken on the oil-refining companies and chemical producers, and had traced cancer rates for people living nearby. He also had learned that private companies and government offices weren't the most reliable places to go to for information about incidents involving hazardous materials.

Gonzalez had rushed down to ground zero the first day, and as soon as he got there, the chemicals in the air had reminded him of the refineries in Philadelphia. The fact that he could smell the chemicals made him suspect that whatever was coming from the rubble could harm anyone exposed to it. But he'd hesitated writing anything that contradicted the official line about safety until he had solid information. After Kupferman showed him the independent labs' test results, Gonzalez felt he had enough to go on. His September 28 column was headlined "Health Hazards in Air Worry Trade Center Workers." It was the first public airing of doubts about the official explanation for what was happening at ground zero.

When construction workers at ground zero read Gonzalez's column, they shoved copies of it in the face of David Ausmus, the Bechtel safety supervisor who spent a month on the pile, and demanded to know if what the reporter said about the air was true. Ausmus checked with his bosses, who told him to say that they couldn't confirm that the independent testing company even existed and that Kupferman's group was just trying to stir up trouble lay the groundwork for future lawsuits. "Despicable bastards trying to profit from a national tragedy and scare the workers in the process," Ausmus had commented.[1] He went back to the workers and assured them that everything was okay. If it wasn't, he insisted, he would let them know right away, because he was out there, too, exposed to whatever was in the air just as they were.

Going against official sources wasn't easy for either Kupferman or Gonzalez. The columnist considered the test results and their frightening implications and wrote several more columns warning that something was not right downtown. At that time, the other newspapers and electronic media in New York were focused on the recovery operations; they dutifully repeated the official assurances that the air was safe. Eventually, a round of journalistic sniping began among the competing newspapers. As the *Daily News* moved more strongly into claiming that the air was not safe, despite official assurances, *The New York Times* urged residents to just clean up the dust in their apartments themselves because government tests showed there was nothing for most people to worry about unless they were working directly on the pile.[2]

But recovery workers weren't the only ones who were worried. Thousands of office workers had been told to return to their desks in the financial district starting September 17. Government workers had also been ordered back to the job. And thousands of residents made their way back home clinging to the EPA's optimistic reassurances that everything was safe, only to find thick layers of dust coating everything in their apartments. They found dust on their coffee cups and breakfast dishes, dust on the carpets and in the drapes, dust on the furniture and in the air conditioner, dust under the beds and behind bookcases, and dust in the drawers holding their children's clothes. Unlike Kupferman, most residents had not started out being overtly suspicious of official pronouncements about safety. In their own way, they were willing to support the city's primary goal of getting back to normal to prove that New York had not been bowed.

In the immediate wake of the attack, most New Yorkers felt that questioning the government's response or its sunny outlook was unpatriotic. This had been an attack on America, and New Yorkers would lead the counterattack by proving that the country could shake off the devastating blow and get on with life. In some ways, survivors' guilt compelled New Yorkers to pull together to make it seem that nothing had changed. The example set by the firefighters—both those who had died charging up the staircases of the doomed towers and those who had survived and now were picking at the gargantuan ruins of the two towers—set a tone of selflessness that, for a time, permeated the city. In that atmosphere of self-denial, the act of wearing respiratory gear was perceived as unduly focusing on one's self at a moment when selflessness and patriotism abounded. Even when all hope of finding anyone alive had faded and the operation was converted to a recovery, the pile workers did not take the time or make the effort to protect themselves.

They should have known better. And their employers all the way down the line had a responsibility to tell them point blank after the rescue phase of the operation had ended that it made no sense for them to continue exposing themselves to a menacing mixture of dust, ash, and smoke to recover the remains of friends, brothers, and colleagues who had already died. "It seems as if their attitude is that to wear them is a sign of weakness," Bechtel's Ausmus observed. "I talked to several people that had tears in their eyes from the biting smoke and they still would not put a respirator on, as I suggested, or move out of the area. None of our safety crew has had much success yet in getting them to wear the proper equipment. Some listen and make an effort; however, the majority seem to think we are a nuisance to be avoided."[3] Emotions ran extremely high, and it would have taken a firm voice with respected authority to change their routines. But the underlying message should have been clear: Wear the right mask or risk becoming yet another victim of the terrorists. Ironically, while the city and the White House were determined to send a message that the terrorists had not won, the officials did not make sure this important message about protective gear came across to the people who most needed to hear and believe it. Not wrestling it to the ground at this early stage guaranteed that fear and worry would prowl the streets far into the future—in effect, the terrorists' dream realized.

Ground zero workers were getting what they perceived as mixed signals. Was the air safe or wasn't it? If it wasn't safe, why were the firefighters working without masks? Why, when dignitaries came to look at the devastation, were they given only paper dust masks or nothing at all? How unsafe could it have been to be there when celebrities like Martha Stewart and boxing promoter Don King were parading around without protective gear?

By the time Juan Gonzalez's columns on ground zero were appearing regularly in the *Daily News*, most New Yorkers couldn't tell who was right about their safety. The easiest path for most to follow was to simply accept the fact that the air was safe because officials had said so. Believing was easier than not believing, given the times. And that made getting the negative warning across even harder. Firefighters and construction workers kept coughing, and they knew instinctively that what the officials said bore faint resemblance to what they were feeling. Some complained to Kupferman, who saw their complaints as confirmation of his suspicions about what was wrong.

Once Kupferman sank his teeth into the ankles of the EPA, he didn't know how to let go. Although the EPA was publishing some of the results of its tests and analyses on its web page, Kupferman filed a freedom of information request on September 21 for the results of all of the agency's test results—the actual numbers, not some bureaucrat's generalized observation—going back to the first samples taken on September 12. The agency responded relatively quickly, and by October 19, Kupferman was able to pick up more than 600 pages of testing results. He found that, besides asbestos, which the agency had reported on, tests had shown levels of such deadly chemicals as benzene, lead, PCBs, and dioxin, about which little had been said. He unloaded the data on Gonzalez on a Friday afternoon and urged him to get the story into the paper right away. Gonzalez skimmed the data, looking for things he knew best—levels of benzene, lead, and chromium. Even a cursory look made it clear that a lot of nasty chemicals were present in and around ground zero, but Gonzalez didn't know how to interpret the technical readings. He took the material to the newspaper's metro editor, Richard Pienciak, whom he figured knew more because he had covered the Three Mile Island accident and had written about chemical exposures. Pienciak shared Gonzalez's belief that, in big crises, "the last people to tell the truth are the people in charge."

Gonzalez wanted time to comb through the data more carefully and to reach out to experts who could help interpret it. But early the following week, Kupferman was on the phone again, agitating for the story to run right away. Gonzalez was working with the data, trying to get his mind around the subtleties so he could interpret the results correctly. Kupferman was impatient and threatened to take the 600 pages to another newspaper if Gonzalez didn't write something soon.

Gonzalez published a sensational front-page column that spelled out the fears of many New Yorkers since 9/11. The tabloid headline was "A Toxic Nightmare at Disaster Site," and the article pulled no punches, laying out a horrific scenario while implicating the EPA for deliberately withholding vital information from the public. The headline, and some parts of the article, clearly went beyond what was outlined in the documents, but the overall effect was to change overnight many people's perceptions of ground zero. Mistrust replaced confidence, and anger took the place of relief.

The EPA was quick to respond to Gonzalez's most sensational conclusions, conceding that the toxins had been detected directly above the pile—where fires still burned—but insisting that they were not present just a few yards away. The elevated findings were considered temporary spikes, perhaps caused by the shifting debris. Gonzalez said that ignoring the spikes was deceptive and sent the wrong message. Whitman's office said that focusing on the spikes was misleading and would frighten New Yorkers unnecessarily. The agency remained steadfast in its conclusion that nothing in the dust posed a long-term threat to the health of most New Yorkers.

The same day the "toxic nightmare" column appeared, Giuliani held a news conference challenging Gonzalez's findings. The city's business leaders jumped on the bandwagon, calling Gonzalez an alarmist.[4] Whitman got in touch with the publisher of the *Daily News* to complain. A letter she wrote defending her actions and responding to Gonzalez's accusations was later published on the op-ed page of the *Daily News*. The complaints had their desired effect. The newsroom at the *Daily News* began to feel pressure to lighten up its coverage. Pienciak, the metropolitan editor, had tried to pull together an investigative team to track down the truth of the story of the dust. But within a week of Gonzalez's story, he was no longer metropolitan editor and the investigative team was temporarily disbanded.

None of this stopped either Gonzalez or Kupferman. The columnist continued to write about the unsafe air, even if the newspaper refused to publish some of his pieces. And Kupferman continued to press authorities to fully disclose what they knew—and didn't know—about the environmental fallout. When he had tried to get his hands on state and city health records, the state initially refused to provide any data, saying that the information he wanted was part of an ongoing criminal investigation. Kupferman appealed and eventually got what he was looking for.

By then it was mid-November and thousands of people had already been intensively exposed to dust. The official records showed that, in some of the samples the New York State Department of Environmental Conservation tested, the particles of dust in the air were so thick that they had overloaded air-monitoring machines. The DEC should have recalibrated the monitors to redo the tests, but it didn't. The New York City Department of Health also had trouble testing the heavy concentration of thick particles in the air after the towers fell. With passage of the Clean Air Act, it had been decades since such heavy amounts of contamination had tainted the air over any American city. Testing equipment had long since been recalibrated to detect much finer particles of pollution. The heavy dust from the trade center had quickly overloaded the monitors. Instead of resetting the instruments and repeating the tests, the city's health department had simply listed those test results as "ND," which stands for "No Detect." The department cited them as evidence that there was nothing to worry about. This incensed Kupferman, who felt the results had been deliberately slanted to give a falsely positive view. The samples could have been loaded with asbestos fibers and a host of other toxins, he said, but because the analyzer had clogged, there was no way to count anything. It didn't mean the sample was safe at all. The department contended that the clogged samples represented only a small portion of all the testing that had been done and didn't skew the results.

While Gonzalez and Kupferman continued to challenge the official line about the safety of the air at ground zero, some midlevel bureaucrats were quietly raising their own voices to question whether adequate precautions were being taken to ensure the safety of New Yorkers. On October 5, three weeks after the planes had brought down the towers, an official with the federal EPA wrote to one of the city's top health officials to express his worries about ground zero.

"Health and safety concerns for workers at the World Trade Center site has been a concern from the beginning of the response," Bruce Sprague wrote in a letter to Kelly McKinney, the health department's associate commissioner. Sprague, who was head of the EPA's Response and Prevention Bureau in Edison, said the controlled

chaos of the site threatened the safety of the workers, who were surrounded by tangled beams and monstrous machines. But that wasn't
all. "This site also poses threats to workers related to potential exposure to hazardous substances," Sprague wrote. He explained that the
EPA's position had been to require all workers to wear respiratory
protection (the portion of Whitman's statements that had received
little attention and was being routinely ignored). Despite that
requirement, Sprague said, "[W]e have observed very inconsistent
compliance." Sprague pointed out that the EPA had workplace safety
jurisdiction only over its own employees.

In a memo the next day, McKinney, angry that the EPA had complained to him about conditions that he had been bringing to the
agency's attention for weeks, laid out in three pages an overview of
safety at ground zero—and started a festering dispute over who was
in charge. McKinney unwittingly echoed some of Kupferman's complaints, noting that the EPA had been slow to release the results of
some of its tests and had not sufficiently informed the public of the
real dangers in the air above ground zero. He also raised the issue of
whether the EPA's methods of analyzing air samples had been adequate and whether the process had left the city without sufficient
information to determine the level of safety downtown. Finally, the
McKinney memo opened a window on the real dynamics that were
pushing many of the city's decisions at that time: "The Mayor's office
is under pressure from building owners and business owners in the
red zone to open more of the city to occupancy," referring to the zone
around the trade center site. McKinney then mentioned a discrepancy within city government. Although the Office of Emergency
Management believed that several more blocks north and south of
ground zero could be reopened, the city's Department of Environmental Protection believed that "the air quality [was] not yet suitable
for reoccupancy."

Kupferman and his Broadway office quickly became the headquarters of New Yorkers who no longer trusted their government. Residents worried about contamination in their apartments came to him
for help. So did office workers who feared their cubicles had not been
cleaned properly. Firefighters assigned to trucks that had been coated
with dust asked Kupferman whether it was safe to use the equipment

after it had been cleaned. He did not hesitate to let anyone who would listen know that he did not think it was wise to bring children back to downtown schools within weeks of the attacks. Nor did he believe it was safe for residents in the blocks around ground zero to return to their apartments. Despite such warnings, Kupferman had gone back to work in his own office on Broadway while the EPA headquarters building nearby was still closed for extensive cleaning. As he continued to hound officials to reveal the truth about what was in the air, he could hear the hostess of the fancy dinner party on Long Island casually explaining the willful deception about the spill at Brookhaven Lab decades before. And when he was called an alarmist and accused of distorting the data, he couldn't shake the image of the crusts of sandwich bread imprinted with the dark fingerprints of Worth Leather's employees. Kupferman knew that for Mollie and Saul Kupferman's sake, he would continue to confront the people who were supposed to be in charge of cleaning up this disaster. If there were uncomfortable questions to be asked, and if the authorities had to face the full force of the law before they would reveal the scope of the danger, even when most people would have preferred to just get on with things, he would do whatever had to be done to clear the air.

Endnotes

[1]Ausmus, David W., *In the Midst of Chaos: My Thirty Days at Ground Zero* (Victoria, B.C.: Trafford, 2004).

[2]Revkin, Andrew C., "Monitors Say Health Risk from Smoke Is Very Small," *The New York Times*, 14 September 2001, p. 10.

[3]*In the Midst of Chaos*.

[4]Gonzalez, Juan, *Fallout: The Environmental Consequences of the World Trade Center Collapse* (New York: The New Press, 2002).

5

A gathering storm

Before it came to be known as ground zero, before it stood for a time and a place that made the world look on New York with a mixture of sympathy and admiration, before it symbolized the most vicious attack on American soil in U.S. history, the 16 acres where the World Trade Center stood—and fell—on September 11 was a working fire, and thus was under the command of the Fire Department of the City of New York. That clear, crisp late summer morning, after the first jetliner smashed into the North Tower at 8:46 a.m., a third alarm went out and firefighters from all over the city were mustered to Lower Manhattan. They continued to treat the unfolding disaster as a fire and rescue even after the second jet struck its target and flames leaped from both towers far above the reaches of their longest ladders. The incident quickly escalated to a fifth alarm as hundreds rushed into the doomed buildings with their firefighting and rescue gear, climbing the endless stairs even as the towers themselves came crashing down on them.

The death toll of 343 firefighters was a savage blow to the department of 14,000 firefighters and emergency medical service workers. But in the early hours after the collapse, when the air was still saturated with dust and laced with choking smoke from burning jet fuel and charred furniture, communications went dead and it was impossible to account for everyone. In the chaos that followed the disintegration of the towers, the department's loss was feared to be even greater than the awful tally of 343.

Those who survived the collapse, driven by feelings of loyalty to those who were lost, and undoubtedly haunted by some gnawing sense of survivors' guilt, threw themselves onto the pile with little regard for their own safety. In that hellish scene, literally working atop a raging inferno, they abandoned their sophisticated equipment and scraped through the debris with shovels and buckets until they nearly dropped from exhaustion. In the first 24 hours after the collapse, 240 firefighters needed emergency medical treatment. Twenty-eight were hospitalized with various injuries. Fifty received emergency treatment because, after being enveloped in the dust cloud, they were gasping for breath.

Reports of the condition of the responders went to Dr. David J. Prezant, then deputy chief medical officer of the department and a pulmonologist at Albert Einstein School of Medicine in the Bronx. Prezant, a wiry baby boomer and self-professed techie, and his boss at the fire department, Dr. Kerry Kelly, were on the scene in the very first moments and were immediately immersed in the disaster. In the following weeks, as Joel Kupferman and Juan Gonzalez were busy raising questions about what was in the air, Prezant and Kelly got a head start on providing the grim answers. Firefighters were most exposed to the dust and smoke, and most likely to suffer from all the hazards they contained. The results of the first medical tests on the firefighters were inconclusive, but they contradicted the optimism of the EPA and city officials who had sought to reassure people about the safety of the air. Initial blood tests showed little evidence for elevated toxins, but many firefighters complained of severe respiratory and sinus symptoms. Acid reflux complaints also were unusually high, and pulmonary function tests were beginning to show declines in the firefighters' lung capacity.

As a trained pulmonologist, Prezant had serious concerns that the dust would cause immediate breathing problems. And it didn't take long for those problems to appear. Nearly every firefighter developed a severe cough in the first few days at ground zero. After it rained that Friday, and then again on September 25, washing away much of the settled dust on the streets and scrubbing lingering particles from the air, things should have improved. But most of the firefighters continued hacking and coughing. For some, it seemed constant. Others were spitting up grayish mucus, sometimes laced with solid particles of grit that shocked even veterans who'd been through many bad fires but had never seen anything like that. They complained that they couldn't catch their breath. A few were wheezing; some had chest pains; and most had badly irritated sore throats, nasal congestion, runny noses, and acid reflux so bad that they could barely stand straight without pain. Nearly all the firefighters were feeling these symptoms for the first time. For those few with prior histories, the symptoms were significantly worse than before.

When the coughing became unbearable, some of the firefighters reluctantly left the pile and made their way to see Kelly and her medical team at fire headquarters in the Metrotech complex in downtown Brooklyn, where Prezant examined them. After 15 years taking care of firefighters, Prezant knew how difficult it was for most of them to concede that something was wrong. They were men (and, lately, women as well) who were defined by their work. They knew that if they were sick, they wouldn't be allowed back to the job, so they stayed away from the medical department if at all possible. Prezant did not take their complaints lightly. Right away, the similarity of their symptoms made an impression on him. Concurrence across a broad range of people often is, in itself, confirmation that something is wrong. He knew from experience that after a big fire, it was not unusual for firefighters to complain of a cough, but it almost always lasted a few days and then cleared up. In the weeks after 9/11, not just a few firefighters complained—an overwhelming majority did, and their cough persisted far longer than just a couple days.

Firefighters came to see Prezant with sinus passages so inflamed they were a deeper red than the trucks they drove. Some complained of severe heartburn, which turned out to be gastroesophageal reflux disease, something that is fairly common in the Northeast because of diet but that Prezant was not accustomed to seeing linked to fires. Something else haunted Prezant as he tried to work through the individual cases. Every one of the firefighters who came to see him told the same story, no matter how many years they had on the job. This one, they said, was different. The smoke, the smell, even the taste of the air around ground zero was not like any fire they had been exposed to. They told him, "Doc, this smells different. It tastes different than any fire I've been in." For Prezant, a scientist at heart, this was not hard data, but he had learned never to ignore subjective signs that something was wrong, especially when they came from many different sources. At the same time, Dr. Michael Weiden, a pulmonologist at the fire department, was finding the same pattern of symptoms.

Prezant had another set of clues to help him decipher what was going on. He was experiencing many of the same symptoms as the firefighters he was treating. He had been coping with the same dry, hacking cough from the moment he had emerged from the debris of the first collapse, which had buried him and left him wondering if he had died.

As he did paperwork at home in the Bronx on the morning of September 11, 2001, David Prezant had no inkling that the history of the United States and his unruly hometown was being rewritten by men with box cutters. It was one of the rare days when he planned to stay home, catching up on his work. Besides his position as the fire department's number-two medical officer, he continued to teach at Albert Einstein and to see regular patients at Montefiore Hospital. It was early, and his wife, Laura, was watching television when news of the first hijacked plane hitting the trade center came across. Prezant got revved up, preparing to respond to the emergency just as he was certain many firefighters were already rushing to the scene. But as he prepped, a special insight kept him from thinking immediately that it was a terrorist attack. A few years earlier, he and Laura had taken a trip abroad. On the return flight, their jetliner had hit severe turbulence as they neared New York and had been thrown off course. He had looked out the window and seen that they were headed in the direction of the twin towers. He couldn't tell how close they actually had come to brushing the towers, but from inside that plane, it had looked like a collision was inevitable. Passengers had panicked. He'd heard the two people in the seat behind him vomit. The pilot had regained control and, of course, avoided a collision. But the incident was fresh in his mind as September 11 unfolded. He was just about to leave home when Laura told him a second plane had hit. Now he knew it was an attack.

As deputy chief medical officer, Prezant responded to every major incident. There was no telling what he would find downtown or what he would do when he got there. He just needed to go. He kissed Laura goodbye, got into his unmarked blue fire department Chevrolet, and raced down the West Side Highway as quickly as he could navigate through traffic. When he was unable to drive farther, he parked the car and walked four or five blocks to the temporary command center that had been set up opposite the North Tower on West Street, which is what the West Side Highway is called as it squeezes through the canyon formed by the bulk of the trade center on the east and the chunky modern towers of the World Financial Center and Battery Park City on the west, nearer to the Hudson River.

When he arrived at the unfolding disaster, Prezant reported to the fire department command center. There was such chaos that no one paid him much attention. No firefighters had been injured yet, and although both towers were on fire, no one worried about them coming down. Prezant wanted to do something, to help someone, but there was nothing for him to do. His pent-up nervous energy made it almost impossible for him to just stand around and watch. He hated doing nothing, especially when people were in need. In the back of his mind that day was a particular image that made him more restless still. He had heard about a doctor who, in the 1993 bombing, ran into the smoking trade center to help evacuate the injured, including one very pregnant woman. Prezant didn't know whether the story was true, but the idea of a physician rushing into a burning building to help people in need was the kind of heroic act he hoped to be able to perform if called upon that morning.

He pestered the fire chiefs for an assignment, and they finally gave him one. The plan was for him to set up a triage area on West Street right outside the South Tower. When he was established there, the chiefs would order Emergency Medical Service personnel to bring over anyone who needed help. Because of the scale of the buildings and the fire department's all-out effort, they believed they would need an orderly system of prioritizing care based on the severity of injuries. At last he had something to do — not nearly as dramatic as running into a burning building, but he would be helping. As he rushed toward the South Tower, accompanied by a fire marshal, he heard what he thought was debris falling from the shattered floors of the towers.

"Hear that?" the marshal asked him. "That's people, the noise that people make when they hit the sidewalk."

That brought Prezant into the gruesome reality of what was happening around him. Until that moment, he had been responding as though it were an ordinary fire, albeit a big one. But the sound of the bodies exploding on the sidewalk near him focused his attention. He had entered an entirely new world of danger. He saw one body hit the sidewalk, and then another. There was nothing he or anyone else could do for those people. So he kept moving until he was practically beneath the South Tower. The EMS chief assigned to this post, Charlie Wells, thought the area was too dangerous and wanted to shift the triage to the middle of West Street. He directed Prezant and several EMS personnel to move immediately. The technicians from six ambulance crews gathered their equipment, but suddenly Prezant saw them running away from the tower, toward the river. He knew that some of the ambulances had come from private hospitals or were manned by volunteers who weren't used to the terrifying scope of a New York City fire. "What a bunch of wimps," he thought as he watched them run. It was extremely noisy, with sirens blaring and debris dropping from both towers. Dismayed by what was happening to the triage operation, Prezant nonetheless found himself starting to run along with everyone else. It was a natural reaction—running because others were running, the way New Yorkers rush downstairs to a subway platform if someone in front of them is taking the stairs two at a time, even though there turns out not to be a train pulling into the station.

As he darted across West Street, Prezant was pelted by debris from the tower that was collapsing right behind him. He got hit again and again. On his head. His back. His legs. His knees. He ran faster, heading toward one of the pedestrian bridges that spanned West Street. He was then blown under the bridge, with falling concrete and rubble engulfing him. He lay flat on the asphalt as more debris fell, and he began to worry that it would become his tomb. For a while, it was difficult to move. But he did realize the futility of his efforts. He had come down to help, perhaps to be a hero. Yet he was about to die without having done so much as put a bandage on anyone. "What a f***ing waste!" he thought. No one would know what had happened to him. There wasn't even anyone who could notify his wife that he had died there beneath the rubble that had once been New York City's shining achievement. No achievement now, just wasted breath.

As these grim thoughts ran through his mind, he suddenly came to the kind of conclusion that only a doctor could reach in such a situation. For someone who was buried and suffocating, he thought, he was taking an awfully long time to die. He was no firefighter, but he'd been to many fires. Rescuers had often told him that the secret to staying alive in a collapse was to find a pocket of air. Anticipating that he would be completely buried by debris, he struggled to his hands and knees to create what he imagined to be a reservoir of air. The pulverized contents of the building kept falling as he struggled to protect his life-saving air pocket. The air around him had turned thick with dust. It coated his eyes and nearly blinded him. He breathed in jagged particles that burned his throat. He coughed so hard he thought he would suffocate. His mouth was filled with the remains of the pulverized building that just seconds before had towered over him.

Then it was quiet. He tried to move, and when he did, he felt something strangely solid over him. Two pieces of paneling from the destroyed offices had fallen near him, creating a lean-to that deflected debris. He pushed off the boards and took stock of his condition. His head hurt. So did his right leg. His back felt like he had been worked over with a tire iron. But what bothered him most was not the pain. It was pitch black, and he couldn't see a thing.

Prezant feared that he had injured his eyes. He knew it was morning, but he couldn't see the sky at all. The air was thick with material, like a charcoal paste, he later remembered it. He thought he might be buried inside a crevasse beneath a much larger mound of debris. Or perhaps the falling material had created a tunnel around him, blocking out the light but somehow miraculously keeping him alive. He tried to orient himself, retracing where he had been when he'd been knocked down. Remembering that he had been heading toward the river, he tried to move in that direction, out of the tunnel and into the light.

Later Prezant would watch videotapes of the dust cloud roiling through the streets of lower Manhattan. As a lung specialist, he knew that the unusual nature of the dust that he—and all the firefighters—had been exposed to carried risks. What they inhaled and, because of the extraordinary density of material in the air, what they had swallowed, how it tasted, how it made breathing nearly impossible and triggered a choking cough—all were factors he would take into account as he tried to figure out what effect the dust would have on firefighters. And he knew firsthand what it had been like, because he had been there with them.

✹ ✹ ✹

Kelly also had avoided death. She had been caught in the dust cloud just as a firefighter had pushed her into the protective cover of a building entrance. Her eyes had burned horribly, but her cough was minimal. Unlike Prezant, who had no personal connection to the department and had grown up with no passion for firefighting except childhood curiosity (his mother told him the two places he'd always ask to be brought to as a child were the Bronx Zoo and the neighborhood firehouse), Kelly descended from a long line of firefighters. Her grandfather had been a chief, her father was a retired lieutenant, her brother was a dispatcher, and other relatives were still on the job working as firefighters. Because of her sensitive nature and her obvious care for their well-being, firefighters fondly referred to her as Mother Theresa. She, too, had noticed the extreme density of debris in the air and had worried about its impact on firefighters. To her, it seemed like a blizzard, when the air is so thick with snow that all the light and sound is absorbed and all that's left is an opaque, muffled undertone. Near-silent and near-dark, the air suffocated her. The dust blinded her. The silence confounded her.

In the smoky aftermath of the collapses, the two physicians managed to meet up near the Staten Island Ferry Station just south of the trade center. They joined a handful of fire officials and worked their way back uptown. As they trudged north, they ran into a straggling army of dust people, office workers in ties or smart skirts, completely dusted with chalky powder from head to toe. Dazed, some were in shock; most were silent. The doctors could do nothing for them, so they kept moving north. They passed a Korean grocery store that had not closed. The shopkeeper was tending his shelves as though nothing extraordinary had happened. Kelly took the hose he used to water flowers and washed out her eyes. They then headed north again, quickly coming to an open hardware store where Kelly found a working telephone. She reached her mother and asked her to phone her husband and Laura Prezant to tell them that, despite what they were watching on television, both of them had somehow survived. They continued up Broadway to an office building opposite City Hall Park, where they set up a makeshift triage and urgent care center in the lobby and supplied it with medicine and bandages from an adjoining drug store. Several hours later, a fire department official urged them to move somewhere safer. The chiefs were increasingly concerned about 7 World Trade Center collapsing. Prezant resisted. He'd already relocated once. But the medical team was eventually convinced that it wouldn't be safe to stay there. They moved the medical equipment across the park to the main building at Pace University, near the Brooklyn Bridge (the location of the original swamp that was home to the leather industry in New York, including Joel Kupferman's Worth Leather). When 7 World Trade Center came down, the dust plume quickly spread through lower Manhattan, crossed the gently curving paths of historic City Hall park, and reached the steps of Pace.

Prezant had set up his triage center inside, anticipating a long line of severely wounded who never came. The medical team worked for long hours, treating many survivors with irritated eyes, persistent cough, and some with mild wheezing. By early evening, the doctors and nurses had completed countless eye washes but had not treated more serious injuries. At 9:30 p.m., Prezant and Kelly ordered the lights out and the doors shut.

That was just the start of their long medical mission. When the cough Prezant developed that first day did not go away, he suspected something was not right. The human body has built-in defenses that protect it from airborne contaminants. Under most circumstances, those systems function well. But on September 11, the staggering amount of dust in the air overwhelmed those natural filters just as they had clogged air monitors around the site. People were forced to breathe through their mouths, but as they gulped for precious air, they swallowed the swill floating around them. Large particles normally are trapped in the upper airways, where they can do short-term harm before being expelled. But this was different. The tremendous concentration of foreign material in the air and the all-out effort by the rescuers meant that, as they breathed hard, they pulled the larger particles deeper into their lungs and, for some, into their stomachs.

At the end of that first chaotic day, Prezant was disappointed. Unlike the unnamed hero doctor of 1993, he had not rescued anyone. But his time would come. Being buried by debris and engulfed by dust gave him invaluable insights. "I thought I had done nothing, but by being there, I had experienced the fear and the stress, but also the inhalation, [that the firefighters themselves had lived through]." He had a glimpse of what it was like for them, and now, like them, he had a deep, stubborn cough that was lasting far longer than expected.

Knowing that exposure to such an intense burst of contamination could lead to trouble, Prezant treated himself with inhaled steroids. After the pharmaceutical company AstraZeneca supplied Budesonide inhalers, he offered the same treatment to every firefighter willing to take it. More than 2,700 signed up, but most dropped out right away. Some started but stopped after a day or two when they saw that results were not immediate. Others may have been scared off because they confused the medications with anabolic steroids. Only 158 stuck with the program for the full four weeks of treatment. A subsequent analysis, funded by the drug company and conducted by Prezant, showed that although corticosteroids should not be used in place of adequate respirators, those who tried the medication had better lung function and quality of life 18 months after 9/11 than those who hadn't used it.[1]

Prezant's own health issues were not dictating the course of treatment he prescribed for the department, but his health did make him much more aware of what the responders were going through. And that, combined with the medical evidence he was collecting as the burly firefighters, most of whom had been in peak physical condition before 9/11 (documented in the regular physicals they underwent), came to him weakened by a nagging, dry cough, led him to the early conclusion that this should be treated as an exposure incident instead of as a fire.

In the first weeks after the attacks, as Prezant continued to see firefighters with disturbingly similar symptoms, something bothered him. If EPA tests were showing only trace levels of hazardous material, why was the cough persisting for so long? He suspected that he was missing something, but what?

Something else weighed heavily on his mind. Both he and Kelly had for years dealt with the unfortunate legacy of an earlier tragedy that was deeply troubling to the city's firefighters—and to firefighters around the world. In 1975, a fire had broken out at a telephone company switching station at 13th Street and Second Avenue in downtown Manhattan. In the 11-story building, miles of cable wrapped in polyvinyl chloride had carried the immense volume of calls into and out of the financial district. The fire had been started by a short circuit or arc at an open splice in the PVC cable deep in a basement vault. It then had spread up to the main distribution frame on the first floor, spewing acrid smoke and dangerous gases. Firefighters had been exposed to the smoke throughout the 16 hours it had taken to bring the fire under control.

"Every firefighter is 100 percent certain that everyone who fought the telephone company fire died, and nothing anyone can say can convince them otherwise," Prezant commented. Self-contained air tanks had not been widely used in the 1970s, and the fire department's medical staff was not as attuned to the dangers of chemical exposures as it would become in later years. No coordinated screening and monitoring program had been established following the telephone company fire. Prezant and Kelly had tried to reach out to survivors in the mid-1990s, without much success. "Because there was no testing, and no monitoring, there are no answers," Prezant remarked. Without data, the belief that everyone exposed to the smoke had been poisoned by it and eventually died of cancer had become widespread. But the rumors were undoubtedly worse than the facts. Prezant concedes that some firefighters did die from cancer and emphysema— but how many, no one could tell. Proving that it was the chemicals unleashed by the telephone company fire instead of by other fires in an area of the country that already has elevated cancer rates turned out to be nearly impossible, given the absence of careful study.

That 1975 disaster and its aftermath had stoked mistrust between the rank-and-file and the department that Kelly and Prezant worked hard to overcome. In 2001, facing a new disaster, they had many questions and faced many uncertainties. But they knew they could not afford to repeat the mistakes of 1975. They had to have data. They had to give reliable answers. "Dr. Kelly and I heard about this a million times, and we did not want that to happen again," Prezant recalled. Within a week of the 2001 attacks, they began to consider options for dealing with the persistent cough and whatever else might come at them. Kelly was also extremely concerned that because of the horrors they had witnessed at ground zero, firefighters would be especially vulnerable to post-traumatic stress disorders (PTSD).

The doctors decided to see firefighters at department headquarters in Brooklyn and geared up to receive significant numbers of them. They stockpiled medicine and began to develop treatment protocols. With the help of the International Association of Firefighters, Kelly and the director of her department's counseling unit, Malachy Corrigan, recruited mental health counselors to supplement their small staff, anticipating an influx of firefighters needing help. But hardly anyone showed up. Firefighters still believed there were people to be rescued, and that left little time for taking care of themselves. Still, a few did straggle in, and their conditions showed that something definitely was wrong. Those initial impressions convinced the doctors that they needed a comprehensive medical monitoring and treatment program for everyone. But first they needed to get the fire department brass on board, including the nonuniformed fire commissioner, who deals directly with City Hall.

"Dr. Kelly and I went to see Tom Von Essen, who we had previously worked closely with on a variety of health and safety efforts," said Prezant. "We told him that we have to have this monitoring program." Von Essen, Mayor Giuliani's civilian Fire Commissioner, thought it was the right thing to do, but he anticipated what City Hall and others might ask: Why was monitoring necessary, and wouldn't it imply that the dust was dangerous, contradicting what the EPA and the mayor were saying? Those who were less interested in firefighter health and safety than those at headquarters might ask why the department should go out of its way to look for problems. Kelly and Prezant reminded the commissioner of the telephone company fire in 1975. "The fire department didn't look then, and the message that came out was that 100 percent of the people there got cancer," Prezant told him. He argued that even if, by actively looking for symptoms, they found that 10 or even 50 percent of the firefighters had come down with some illness (a highly unlikely possibility), it would still be far less than the perception created by the phone company fire, which was that the smoke had killed everyone. He firmly believed that the facts would turn out to be far less frightening than the rumors.

Von Essen found this argument persuasive and convinced Giuliani to back this ambitious effort. Kelly and Prezant then had free rein to advocate for a monitoring and treatment program, and they convinced everyone that they were acting directly on behalf of the mayor, which was a slight exaggeration. Kelly spoke before Congress, and Prezant before the International Association of Firefighters. Both met with the Federal Emergency Management Agency (FEMA) and the National Institute for Occupational Safety and Health (NIOSH). They convincingly argued that they had the credibility and experience to make such a program work. A strong point in their favor was that only the fire department had medical data, including pulmonary function tests, that predated the September 11 attacks. Comparing those records with current data would be the key to objectively determining the impact of the dust and using that information to create a medical program that could actually help firefighters. Before long, they applied for and received help from the Centers for Disease Control (CDC) that amounted to $4.8 million over two years. Although the funding didn't actually arrive until December, Von Essen had the monitoring begin in October 2001, giving the fire department a monitoring and treatment program with full management and union backing long before anyone else.

Two important decisions were made at this initial stage that would significantly improve the data coming out of the department down the road. Kelly and Prezant convinced the CDC that, in addition to covering active-duty firefighters, the monitoring needed to include retirees. This later became a crucial aspect of the program, as thousands retired or went out on disability after the ground zero cleanup ended. The only way to come to any conclusions about causality was to follow the firefighters for a long time, including the years after they retired and left the job. The second critical step came when the CDC agreed to provide advanced biomonitoring, something the FDNY wasn't equipped to do. Prezant was concerned that, in the first hours after the buildings were struck, there had been no active air monitoring. Conditions for firefighters on the pile at that time were believed to be the worst experienced by any recovery workers, and the physicians were worried they may have been exposed to a brew of deadly chemicals that no air sampling had captured. The federal government agreed to do the tests. Blood and urine samples were taken from 321 firefighters who came in for help during the first four weeks. The samples were shipped to the CDC daily and were analyzed for heavy metals, dioxins, and PCBs. When the results came back, none exceeded what are considered safe thresholds. That provided important insights into the hazards present at the site, which came into play later when the federal government assembled a larger screening and monitoring program at a consortium of hospitals, including the Mount Sinai Medical Center. Because those early samples did not detect any heavy metals, it was decided that the consortium didn't need to test for them, a step that helped keep costs in check and freed up dollars to screen a broader range of people.

The testing also underscored another aspect of the scientific response—the importance of administering the right test and of understanding how to interpret the results. Early in 2002, the *New York Daily News* reported that the Port Authority had found elevated mercury levels in the blood of four out of ten Port Authority police officers. The results led the city's Department of Environmental Protection to threaten to shut down the site completely until the source of mercury could be isolated. There was conjecture that it came from the thousands of fluorescent light bulbs in the buildings. The site never was shut down, and the mercury scare soon faded as calmer heads pointed out that the proper test for environmental mercury exposure was urinalysis. Blood tests pick up mercury that occurs within a few days of exposure, and the mercury usually comes from eating fish. The fire department had done the more reliable test, urinalysis, and did not find mercury to be an issue of concern.

When the blood and urine samples from the 321 firefighters were compared with samples from others who had not been at ground zero, analysts found troubling results. Although so little time had passed, the firefighters showed trace amounts of nine different chemicals of concern—mostly, the scientists believed, components of the raging fires called polycyclic aromatic hydrocarbons. In and of themselves, the chemicals would not have been a concern in such low concentrations. But doctors were worried that these were signs of far worse things to come. They also had stumbled on what would eventually become a central tenet of the investigation, the string they would use to hold it all together. In most studies of environmental exposure, a key factor is dosage, the amount of time each individual is exposed to harmful material. Simply put, the more exposure, the greater the risk. Prezant believed that work records would show the amount of time firefighters had spent at ground zero, which would then permit him to calculate exposure. But he was disappointed to find that, in the utter chaos of the days right after the attack, uniform work records were far from error-free and were not suitable for use in the studies he needed to do.

Forced to seek a substitute for dosage, Prezant used the only firm data he had: time of arrival at ground zero, based on the assumption that conditions were worst immediately following the collapses.[2] He divided the responders into four groups. The first consisted of the 1,858 individuals who were already on the scene on September 11 when the towers plummeted to the ground and, consequently, were engulfed by the dust clouds. The next group, made up of 9,435 individuals, had arrived on the afternoon of Day 1 and throughout Day 2, September 12. Those two groups represented the bulk of the department. Prezant created a third group for the 2,031 who had arrived for the first time on Day 3 or later. Finally, 187 members of the fire department who had not spent any time at ground zero became the fourth group.

Kelly and Prezant gave every member of the department a standardized questionnaire and then grouped the findings by time of arrival. The results were devastatingly clear for both physical health and mental well-being. The Day 1 group had the highest rates and greatest severity of every symptom: daily cough, shortness of breath, wheezing, chest pain, sinus congestion, lower-respiratory problems, acid reflux, and stress. The other groups had progressively less severe reactions the later they arrived at the scene. The bottom line: The race to get to ground zero first turned out to be a race to disaster and disease.

As he pursued this line of reasoning, Prezant oversaw the department's administration of standardized breathing tests to measure how being at ground zero had damaged the firefighters' lungs. These tests were particularly valuable because Prezant had already established baselines with similar tests that the fire department had administered every 12 to 15 months since 1997. This made it possible to compare with a degree of scientific certainty a firefighter's health before and after working at ground zero. Firefighting is dangerous under any circumstances, but it's especially hazardous in a city such as New York, where firefighters work in close quarters and are exposed to a vast range of pollutants. Under normal conditions, lung capacity decreases every year, from a combination of aging and the cumulative harmful effects of exposure to hazardous materials while fighting fires. On average, Prezant had calculated the loss to be about 31 milliliters a year from 1997 to 2001. But in the first year after the terrorist attacks, firefighters lost an average of 372 milliliters—that is, about the amount of air in a regular can of soda, and equal to about 6 percent of a firefighter's 6-liter lung capacity. Importantly, this is the equivalent of 12 years of normal lung function loss. As in Prezant's other studies, those who arrived first were hurt worst. The study also looked at steps the firefighters had taken to protect themselves, and it reported what was already clear to anyone who had watched the tumultuous activity at ground zero. Most of the people there had not worn respirator masks that could have shielded them from the worst hazards. Nearly 80 percent of the rescuers who were first to arrive on 9/11 said they rarely or never used a respirator. Many who had tried to protect themselves used flimsy dust masks that did little to keep out the smoke or loose asbestos fibers. And most of those who got hold of adequate masks were quick to whip them off when they became too uncomfortable. By the time respirators had become readily available, work habits had formed and intense exposures had already occurred.

By the end of September, most firefighters were being treated for what Prezant came to call World Trade Center cough, which he defined as a syndrome of persistent, almost continuous dry, nonproductive cough, accompanied by a range of upper- and lower-airway symptoms severe enough for the firefighters to be able to go on medical leave for at least a month. During the first three weeks, the men paid no attention to the symptoms as they raced to find survivors trapped in the debris. The fear of finding one of their brothers too late drove them into a frenzy, and they ignored their own health, ignored admonitions to wear protective gear, and ignored their own professional sense that the air at ground zero was too dangerous to breathe for even a short while. By the time some came to the fire department's clinic for evaluation, treatment, and answers, they had become the walking wounded, many fearing that their lives would be cut short and forever changed by this event.

Prezant's own medical condition improved after a few months. Over time, many firefighters who initially came in with trade center cough had stabilized or gotten better, and some were already back on the job. Yet others remained ill, with a few sliding deeper into their illness. Nearly 1,000 never regained the physical abilities to return to the life they loved; after they presented objective evidence of their impairment, they qualified for disability pensions from the fire department. Prezant developed an extensive body of knowledge about the dust that had covered his city. Working with Paul Lioy, he learned what it was made of and how it could hurt the firefighters. But what he didn't know yet, and this bothered him, was why the dust had had such a grievous impact on some firefighters while not at all affecting others. It really didn't matter to him what Christie Whitman or the *Daily News* said about the hazards of the dust. Clearly, something in the dust made it more harmful than ordinary demolition rubble. What he had learned about the physical characteristics of the dust, and the sheer volume of it in the air after the collapse, also made it clear that this health problem would continue far into the future. He was certain that some of the men would get better. He also figured that some would wind up not getting either better or worse, but would simply remain the same. And with the certainty he was forced to muster because of his scientific training, he knew that it was inevitable that some of them would, through no fault of their own, get worse, despite the assurances of the EPA and Giuliani that there was nothing to worry about.

But Kelly and Prezant worked for the city and would have to carefully measure their words, balancing their need to safeguard the welfare of the firefighters for whose health they were responsible against the requirements of the city that employed them as it tried to regain its footing. They worried that there probably would be pressure to keep some of the more distressing findings quiet, while broadcasting widely other findings that downplayed the dangers. They knew that advocacy medicine had its role but that it needed to be based on a strong foundation of credible evidence. They believed that the monitoring and treatment program needed long-term funding, not a short burst of emotional support. Prezant finally realized that God had saved him on September 11 for a reason. He had not rushed heroically into a burning building to rescue people trapped inside. But he was left in a position to help many who were desperate for answers. His goal now was to avoid the political blame game and remain true to the mission, which was to provide the best monitoring and treatment program, pursue the best science, and follow the results wherever they led.

Science would speak for itself.

Endnotes

[1]Prezant, David, "Inhaled Steroids Used as Preventative Treatment Post 9/11." Presented at the 73rd annual assembly of the American College of Chest Physicians, 24 October 2007, Chicago.

[2]Fire Department, City of New York, Bureau of Health Services, *World Trade Center Health Impacts on FDNY Rescue Workers: A Six-Year Assessment: September 2001–September 2007*. Available at http://home.nyc.gov/html/fdny/html/publications/wtc_assessments/2007/wtc_2007.shtml.

6

Building a science

The gasping firefighters who reluctantly dragged themselves away from the pile to see Drs. Kerry Kelly and David Prezant had responded immediately, and bravely, to the largest disaster they had ever experienced. On the enormous mound of twisted steel, shrouded in the choking smoke and ash of super-hot fires below ground—standing like sentries at the gates of hell—they became symbols of the city's resolve. But in truth, with their buckets and pick-axes, they were no match for the devastation left by the terrorists. If there was anybody left to rescue, the firefighters needed big help reaching them.

The help had started to arrive almost at once. Within days of the attack, an army of construction workers in hardhats and overalls was crawling over the debris pile alongside the firefighters who worked in their heavy bunker gear. And like the firefighters, many soon found that after working a 12-hour shift, their throats felt like they had been Roto-Rootered. They simply could not stop coughing. Unlike the firefighters, however, they did not have access to a central medical office. They had to see their own doctors, who, for the most part, were general practitioners who rarely, if ever, treated exposures to hazardous dust. They tended to misdiagnose the symptoms, fooled by the flulike runny nose and itchy throat, and prescribed antibiotics, which did no good at all. But most of the construction workers, driven by an overwhelming sense of patriotic duty at an extraordinary time, simply ignored the discomfort they were feeling, forgoing a visit to the doctor so they could keep on working.

By the beginning of October, a handful of non-uniformed ground zero workers had made their way to a busy uptown clinic just off Fifth

Avenue where they knew the doctors and the doctors knew them.
The clinic was the Irving J. Selikoff Center for Occupational and
Environmental Medicine at the Mount Sinai Medical Center. The
Selikoff Center had a long-established relationship with some of
New York's most powerful unions and, for decades, had been the
first place to go for workplace medical issues. That was never more
so than when asbestos exposure was involved. Most recently before
9/11, the clinic's work had shifted somewhat. Federally funded programs to remove asbestos in schools and other public buildings,
along with the end to the use of asbestos insulation in new buildings
in New York, had sharply reduced the number of asbestos-related
cases at the clinic. Its doctors now most commonly saw repetitive
strain injuries, torn muscles, and broken bones.

Then came 9/11. For a time, the 100-foot-high pile of steel and
concrete at ground zero represented the most dangerous workplace
in America. The construction workers suffered their share of broken
bones and eye injuries (but not a single fatality). They also thought
they heard Christie Whitman say the air was safe. But what they were
experiencing while they worked on the pile seemed to be anything
but safe. Adding to the confusion was what they saw there every day.
They knew that firefighters were, by nature, keenly aware of safety
issues because their lives depended on always knowing the dangers
they were rushing into. But there they were, digging through the pile
without wearing protective gear. The only logical conclusion the construction workers could reach was that wearing the uncomfortable
respirators and suffocating dust masks was unnecessary. They also
saw that visiting dignitaries did not even wear paper dust masks.
Nobody seemed to be taking seriously the advisories to wear protective gear. But one thing these guys did know: Working with the cranes
and grapplers that had been brought in to move the steel beams was
extremely dangerous. Those gigantic machines needed to be given a
wide berth, and when they were slinging a big load, nobody was supposed to be anywhere nearby. It made common sense to be in constant communication with the people around you, including the
operators of those behemoths. And to do that, you couldn't be wearing protective breathing gear that muffled your voice, or safety goggles that cut off your peripheral vision.

That's the gist of what workers told the doctors at the Selikoff clinic about the pile. For these doctors, the danger had been evident from the moment they watched the towers fall. Being located miles from ground zero, neither the clinic nor Mount Sinai had been directly involved in the immediate response to the disaster. Other hospitals, located closer to the trade center, had been put on standby to receive the wounded. On September 11, many of Mount Sinai's doctors who lived outside the city had been stuck on the George Washington Bridge and other crossings and had to turn around and go home. With much of New York City cordoned off and telephone service knocked out, several from the Selikoff clinic had decided to meet outside the city. They'd gathered at the Westchester County home of Dr. Jaime Szeinuk, an occupational medicine specialist at Mount Sinai. It was September 13, and reality had already sunk in. The doctors, like everyone else, had seen the twin towers turn to dust, and their stomachs had tightened as they'd repeatedly watched the towering plumes of debris steamroll through the city streets. But the dust meant more to them than to other New Yorkers because they had spent most of their professional lives trying to understand the devious ways that tiny dust particles and other microscopic bits and pieces can create havoc in the human body.

Few understood this more intensively than Dr. Stephen M. Levin, a driving force at the Selikoff Center for two decades. Levin was a nationally recognized leader in the field of occupational medicine. He had developed an abiding affection for working-class people and a penchant for making trouble for the corporations that exploited them. Levin had once been a protégé of Dr. Irving Selikoff himself. Selikoff had been a pioneer in the field, researching the links between asbestos and a range of diseases, including mesothelioma, which is almost exclusively connected to exposure to the fireproof mineral. Selikoff, too, had a long history of working with labor unions in the New York area, starting with a clinic he'd opened in the early 1950s in the blue-collar New Jersey city of Paterson.

After working in Paterson for several years, Selikoff had been approached by the local asbestos workers' union, which wanted him to take care of its members, mostly workers from the United Asbestos and Rubber Company plant that had produced asbestos insulation for boilers and turbines from the start of World War II until it shut its doors in 1954. As Selikoff screened the workers and treated them for various illnesses, he noticed an unusual pattern. The lungs of most of the men were badly scarred, which Selikoff suspected was the result of constant exposure to the asbestos fibers they had worked with. He also saw cases of mesothelioma every year when, statistically, the disease was so rare he should hardly have seen any among that comparatively small group of men.

His curiosity piqued, Selikoff collected the workers' medical records. Based on the evidence he found there, he eventually established a strong link between long-term exposure to asbestos in the workplace and such crippling diseases as asbestosis. He continued to study asbestos-related illnesses, sometimes running into resistance from the asbestos industry, which denied him access to employee work histories. But Selikoff worked around the companies by going directly to the unions, which understood the significance of his work. In a later study, he screened 17,800 asbestos insulation workers and firmly established the link between the mineral and the disease. Selikoff came to believe that even brief exposure to a small amount of asbestos could scar lungs and lead to cancer. He also explored the synergistic, or multiplying, effect of asbestos exposure and smoking tobacco. His studies showed that an asbestos worker who also smoked had a significantly greater chance of developing lung cancer than a worker who did not use tobacco.

As Selikoff continued his research, unions used his findings to seek compensation for workers at the United Asbestos and Rubber Company, Johns Manville, and other asbestos manufacturers. Besides the breakthrough research he was conducting, Selikoff's effectiveness came from being a master at taking his findings into the realm of public opinion. He often testified at public hearings, and he aggressively lobbied public officials, including President Lyndon Johnson, to restrict the use of asbestos. By the early 1970s, when Selikoff was a well-established occupational health researcher and an esteemed member of the Mount Sinai staff, legislative efforts to severely restrict the use of asbestos in new construction were enacted. Because of its ability to resist fire, asbestos had come to be widely used to fireproof the steel superstructures of new buildings. Before its use was officially limited (it has never been completely banned, even to this day), many builders decided to stop applying asbestos insulation altogether.

That included the Port Authority of New York and New Jersey, which, in the late 1960s, had embarked on one of the biggest construction projects ever, erecting the two tallest buildings in the world along with several smaller structures in a single complex in Lower Manhattan. The project moved from the drawing board to reality as the shipping industry left Brooklyn and Manhattan and moved to the new berths for containerized cargo ships that had been built on New Jersey's waterfront in the 1960s. As the old maritime port of New York faded, the tattered buildings of the Washington Market, an area near the waterfront in Lower Manhattan that housed produce stands and stalls selling radio equipment and other merchandise, were razed. On the cleared site, the Port Authority began construction of what it described as a new vertical port, grandly named the World Trade Center—twin 110-story cracker boxes that would realign the New York skyline. The steel of the North Tower was sheathed in fire-retardant material containing a relatively high concentration of asbestos from the ground level up to at least the 34th floor. But the spraying stopped there.[1] The Port Authority decided, under pressure from Selikoff and others, to switch to a different material, called slag wool, that did not contain any asbestos and that engineers showed was at least as effective as asbestos at holding back flames, without being toxic. That move represented a substantive victory for Selikoff that would have a profound impact on his legacy three decades later, when the towers disintegrated and the asbestos fireproofing was unleashed.

Levin felt a special kinship with Selikoff and saw in him an archetype for a rabble-rousing doctor who, through his clinic, stood up for working-class people. Similar to Selikoff, Levin had started out as a blue-collar doc in a blue-collar town—not his native Philadelphia, but Pottstown, Penn., where he had practiced for several years in the 1970s. He moved to Mount Sinai in 1979 to join Selikoff's occupational medicine team. He'd taken the position because it combined so many of his interests—public health, clinical medicine, research, teaching, and troublemaking. "It seemed like a satisfying thing to do, and Selikoff was a good model for that because he made lots of trouble for companies that did bad things," Levin said. They worked together until Selikoff's death in 1993.

As Levin and several other Mount Sinai doctors met in Szeinuk's home that September 13 morning, they had no doubt that tons of asbestos had been blown into the air above and around the pulverized trade center. They figured that the asbestos also had forced its way into offices and apartments in the area, spreading the hazards far and wide. Some of the doctors understood the enormity of the disaster because they had responded to an earlier crisis at the trade center. In 1993, terrorists had filled a rented truck with explosives and detonated it in the basement garage beneath the towers. The explosion blew a hole five stories deep, killing 6 people and injuring 1,000. A team from Mount Sinai, led by Levin, had been among the first medical personnel at the scene. He had rushed to the complex with respirator masks for responders, who were engulfed in the choking smoke from the explosion and fire. Levin had helped distribute the equipment, personally fitting the masks to the responders and making sure they understood how important it was to keep the protective gear on while they were working.

With that experience in mind, Levin was ready to help again after the twin towers fell. He'd called the New York City health department and offered to distribute respirators as he had in 1993. He had no idea how many would be needed, but he was willing to transport all that he had on hand, to help fit the workers with appropriately sized masks, and to show them how the masks were to be used. But the city was slow to respond. Levin thought it odd, but he persisted because he feared that the rescuers were being exposed to great danger every minute they worked without protective gear. Several hours later, he realized that the wait had been for nothing. When the city finally came back with its answer, it was, "No, thanks." It became clear that this incident was not going to be a repeat of 1993, although he didn't know why: "That was a disturbing indication to me that things were different now."[2]

At their first meeting in Westchester County, Levin and the other doctors hadn't worried only about asbestos. Watching television, they'd realized that underground infernos continued to release acrid smoke laced with toxic chemicals from the plastics and furnishings in the destroyed offices. They'd seen workers wiping dust from their eyes as they struggled to remain on the pile. Levin knew there was no way people could work in that environment without coming down with acute, and maybe chronic, respiratory problems. To him it seemed tragic that victims of the horrendous attack would be followed by more victims, this time victims of exposure to the dust. Victims upon victims. Casualties after casualties. And if Selikoff's experience with asbestos in Paterson was any guide, the problems would linger for three, four, or five decades.

The doctors vowed not to leave their meeting until they had come up with a plan. "We saw ourselves as part of the public health infrastructure," Levin recalled. "We were a repository of expertise. We thought that we ought to sit down and talk about what we were seeing, what we thought the exposure was going to be, what the potential health consequences were going to be, and put together an advisory for the medical community on treating patients."

They knew there were irritants in the air, not just from the smoke, but from other components of the dust, and that they were likely to trigger serious health problems. Levin, for one, had seen it before, in the 1975 telephone company fire that Prezant and Kelly also considered a watershed in the city. Years after the fire, he had examined retired firefighters who were exposed to the burning plastics in the phone company building. Some still had reactive airways dysfunction syndrome, often called irritant-induced asthma, 25 years later.

From experience, Levin and the other doctors knew that the dust released by the implosion of the huge towers was unique. Other violent events—volcanoes, earthquakes, and hurricanes—unleashed huge amounts of dust. But in an earthquake, buildings tend to topple over and the debris remains in large chunks. The towers had pancaked, each floor smashing into the one below, descending so quickly and with such compressive force that the concrete in the structures had been ground into particles so fine they could be drawn into the deepest airways of the lungs, causing lasting damage.

The doctors spent more than seven hours at the Westchester house that day, putting together a set of clinical guidelines that could walk a general practitioner through diagnosis and treatment of injured ground zero workers. They identified the likely skin rashes and outlined the high probability of post-traumatic stress, even among the uniformed responders who had been through disasters before, but never anything like this.

Levin then called the city health department again to say that the Mount Sinai physicians had prepared a clinical advisory, but that it would carry more weight and reach more doctors if the city put its name on the document and used its networks to distribute it widely. Once again, the department turned down Levin's offer. The city was more accustomed to putting out warnings of flu outbreaks or vaccination advisories. The health department suggested that Mount Sinai post the advisory on its own website. Levin argued that doing so would have limited impact because most doctors would not be looking for it there. Reluctantly, Mount Sinai did post the guidelines on its website by December, but it had little effect and the clinic saw widespread evidence that workers were continuing to be misdiagnosed. (The health department eventually did publish its own clinical guidelines, but not until 2006. Officials said they waited until they had sufficient evidence that the dust was linked to serious and persistent illnesses.)

Snubbed a second time by the city, Levin wondered what the department's actions really meant. "I had many friends at the department, and I could tell there was a policy being established above them that we are not going to acknowledge the health consequences and the risks of what was going on down there because we've got other compelling interests." To Levin, public health did not seem to be the Giuliani administration's overriding concern; getting the city back to business was.

Before their Westchester County meeting broke up, Levin and the other doctors decided to make the Selikoff clinic freely available to ground zero workers. The doctors agreed to take extra shifts to handle the anticipated onslaught of ill and injured. But when they returned to the city, they were in for a surprise. Levin was intent on spreading the word about the dangers. He went down to ground zero himself and attended safety meetings, urging contractors to have their workers wear respirators. The clinic's industrial hygienists met directly with union shop stewards at ground zero, pleading with them to get tough with workers who ignored warnings about personal protection. They told the union leaders that the uptown clinic was available for workers who needed medical care and urged everyone to come in. But for the first two weeks, no one did. The office space the clinic occupied on the ground floor of an apartment building at 5th Avenue and 101st Street on Manhattan's Upper East Side remained unnaturally quiet. Levin was baffled and began to think that perhaps he had misdiagnosed the problem and that the dust wasn't harmful. He asked the health department if patients were being seen elsewhere. He was stung again when the official reminded Levin that the department had said things were not so bad and that the irritations he thought he had noticed on TV were simply seasonal allergies. After all, it was autumn.

Just as Levin started to wonder where he had gone wrong, the first worker showed up at the clinic asking for help. Levin had worked with the man, a health and safety expert for one of the big unions, and knew he had been healthy and free of symptoms prior to 9/11. The man had spent two days at ground zero, and now he had a range of ailments, from sinusitis to new-onset asthma. Whatever doubts Levin had about sounding the alarm were dispelled by this first patient. After him, the floodgates opened. Workers and volunteers who had put off getting help for themselves so they could concentrate on the recovery at ground zero were by now too sick to continue working or no longer felt that it was unpatriotic to worry about their own health.

As more workers filed in, the clinic cobbled together a larger staff and additional equipment. But they were soon overwhelmed. There seemed no end to the people needing help. Union leaders realized that a big problem was developing. The Central Labor Council, representing the city's biggest unions, was already concerned about the loss of jobs and all the people who would need special assistance, and fast. The council reached out to the New York State AFL-CIO for help, and the state group got in touch with Sen. Hillary Clinton. She met with the union leaders and asked them what it would take to help their members. She encouraged them to think big and ask for everything they needed now, because in six months it would be a lot harder to get the government's attention. Ed Ott, a former health and safety officer for the Oil, Chemical, and Atomic Workers Union, knew that the trade center was about the last job in Manhattan that blew asbestos on the girders during construction. "That meant the guys were working on a toxic waste pile," he said.[3] He received a phone call from Joel Shufro, executive director of the New York Committee for Occupational Safety and Health, who was worried because so many of the workers he'd seen on television were not wearing masks. Ott knew that there was no way to get those guys off the pile while there was a chance of rescuing anyone still alive in the rubble. "They were in crisis mode," he said. Afterward, though, when it would become a recovery and cleanup operation, he expected there to be a need for clinical services and a way for workers to undergo baseline examinations to track any spike in ailments. It wasn't going to be enough for them to simply go to their own doctors if they felt ill. They'd need to come to a centralized location, whether or not they felt sick, so doctors trained in workplace hazards could check them out.

A long and mutually beneficial relationship had developed between the Selikoff Clinic and New York's unions. It initially arose because of Selikoff's asbestos research, and it expanded and matured under the guiding hand of Dr. Philip Landrigan, another Selikoff protégé and a pioneer in environmental and occupational medicine. Landrigan, a long-distance runner whose Jesuit education at Boston College left him with a quietly philosophical bent, became a prodigious researcher himself. After graduating from Harvard Medical School, he trained in pediatrics but also showed an interest in occupational medicine. He joined the Centers for Disease Control's Epidemic Intelligence Service and later went to Cincinnati to work with the National Institute for Occupational Safety and Health (NIOSH), a new arm of the CDC whose focus was the workplace.

Selikoff had helped clear the way for this new field and drew some of its earliest criticism. After his work with asbestos, he and others concerned about workplace safety did not want to be in the position of having to study linkages between toxins and diseases after they had already caused widespread suffering. Waiting until the diseases can be linked with medical certainty to exposure left the medical research community sitting on the sidelines while people died. The complex links between environmental contamination and disease are extremely difficult to prove with any degree of certainty, a situation not unique to occupational medicine, but one that brings the field a greater degree of scrutiny than other areas of medicine. The economic consequences for industries involved can be great. That sets up a high-stakes struggle that often gives the advantage to employers. Occupational disease specialists realize that, to get out in front of a problem, they need to urge limits on exposure before links can be proved definitively.

To put protective measures in place to avoid future health problems for employees, researchers have to gather enough scientific evidence to support a logical hypothesis about the connection between hazardous substances and certain illnesses. Making such links is not always an exact science, but it can prove invaluable if workers can be protected from disease.

Occupational medicine often pushed back the frontiers of medical knowledge, understanding that waiting for fail-safe proofs can be a death sentence for workers. Certainty is sometimes a luxury they cannot afford. Doctors in the field are constantly forced to walk the line between conclusive proof and informed guesses, between guarded warnings and alarmism, between science and advocacy. Epidemiological research can show the relevance of increased disease in a group of workers exposed to a certain contaminant. But it cannot so easily explain why an individual worker got sick. With his Jesuit training, Landrigan knew it was a fundamental epistemological problem, and one that big corporations—led by the tobacco companies—would always cite in their defense. In their work, the Selikoff clinic doctors staked their reputations on well-accepted criteria such as the consistency of their findings to substitute for absolute scientific certainty. The clinic's doctors also were willing to testify on behalf of injured workers who qualified for workers' compensation. These aggressive efforts to help workers forged bonds of trust with labor unions and made corporations—and sometimes government agencies—suspicious.

When Selikoff grew older and gave up administrative duties at the hospital, Landrigan was lured back from NIOSH to take over Mount Sinai's Division of Occupational and Community Medicine. He got to meet Selikoff there because the division oversaw the one-afternoon-a-week occupational health clinic where he saw patients. Dr. Ruth Lilis, a pulmonologist, had started the clinic in 1973 and spent the next three decades at Mount Sinai. After six years as head of the Occupational Epidemiology Program in Cincinnati, Landrigan arrived at Mount Sinai in 1985 with a firm commitment to occupational and environmental medicine, and a goal of expanding the work of Selikoff's clinic. But he needed to devise a way to pay for this greater role. Landrigan approached the state legislature, buttonholing Frank Barbaro, the powerful head of the assembly labor committee. Barbaro convened a public hearing about occupational health, and Landrigan testified that there was a great unmet need in New York. Barbaro proved to be sympathetic but unconvinced. He told Landrigan that he was uneasy about moving forward without proof of how big a problem the state had. They settled on a compromise, a $100,000 one-time grant that allowed Landrigan to document the extent of occupational disease in New York. Landrigan's final report produced startling conclusions. He estimated that there were 35,000 new cases of occupational disease a year in the state, some so serious that they led to as many as 7,000 deaths annually. Landrigan's task force calculated that the cost to the state of the top five occupational diseases was $600 million a year.

The approach worked, and when Landrigan returned to the assembly in spring 1987, he had already pulled together a large and powerful coalition of elected officials and labor leaders with the political weight to get the state to act. The legislature voted to create a statewide chain of occupational health centers, funded through yearly appropriations and coordinated through the New York State Department of Health. The head of the program who oversaw the new clinics was Dr. James Melius, an epidemiologist who had replaced Landrigan at NIOSH. (The two would work together again in the aftermath of 9/11.)

After so many years with government, Landrigan knew how dangerous it would be to rely solely on annual legislative appropriations. He rejoiced in having convinced the legislature to create the clinics, but he worried that legislative fiat could choke off any chance of success. Without long-term funding, it would be difficult for the new clinics to hire doctors, buy expensive medical equipment, or find reasonable space to rent. The legislature came up with a unique solution. It decided to tap the worker compensation premiums paid by employers and divert a small percentage of the money to the clinics. The one at Mount Sinai, named in honor of Selikoff, was, and remains, by far the biggest. The main clinic, and a series of satellite offices, receives about $2.5 million a year from the state, which is supplemented by funds received for providing clinical services.

The Mount Sinai clinic was able to jump in the way it did after the September 11 attack because of the bond that it had established with labor and because of the work it had done with the unions over the previous two decades. No other medical setting in the country may have been so well suited to respond to the unprecedented conditions at ground zero, and certainly none enjoyed greater confidence from the workers themselves. The Selikoff clinic was the biggest occupational health center between Boston and Washington. It was a leading research center in the field, and it had trained an entire generation of residents and fellows. Many of the ground zero workers who came to the clinic after 9/11 had been there before. They trusted Levin and the other doctors and agreed to be screened and tested by them. Many shared the same set of interlaced conditions—sinusitis, trade center cough, acid reflux, reactive airways problems—and worried about what was happening to them. This cascade of problems made them miserable and portended worse in the future.

By November, Landrigan's concerns about the potential health threat of working at ground zero had grown more urgent. In an article published in *Environmental Health Perspectives*, a scientific journal, he wrote that asbestos is "a major threat to the health of workers at the World Trade Center site," despite pronouncements from the EPA that the majority of dust samples the agency had collected did not contain dangerous levels of asbestos. In his article, Landrigan raised the specter of long-term health risks that included lung cancer and malignant mesothelioma. "Protection against these risks requires the provision of proper respirators to workers and the undertaking of health and safety training programs that emphasize the need for constant wearing of respirators, for proper fit testing, and for frequent changing and cleaning of filters." Landrigan also was one of the first to publicly call for a formal registry of workers at the site to keep track of who was there, when they arrived, and how long they stayed—all factors that would undergird later studies. He pointed out that baseline chest x-rays, establishing a worker's state of health at the time, would make it possible to accurately measure the effects of exposure to the dust, and he urged that blood samples be tested for PCBs, dioxins, and other toxins. Landrigan's long history in the field of occupational medicine guided him; he was both looking back on the way other exposure issues had been handled in the past, and flipping forward to anticipate what hard data he and others would need to make their case if the dust turned out to be as harmful as they feared.

By the end of 2001, Landrigan and the other Mount Sinai doctors were carrying almost the entire medical care burden for thousands of ground zero workers. The Church of Scientology offered rescue workers a detox and purification program that used saunas, high-dosage vitamins and oil, but it did not have the backing of the medical community, and most responders stayed away, even when they learned that actor Tom Cruise was paying most of the bills. The city government continued to focus on the recovery operation and offer limited help with health issues. The state health department had supported Dr. Joan Reibman, the director of an asthma clinic at Bellevue Hospital, when she canvassed downtown residents and compared their post-9/11 respiratory symptoms with those of city residents who lived farther from the disaster site. Reibman's study was one of the earliest to show that people who lived close to ground zero had a marked increase in immediate respiratory complaints. But neither the city nor the state offered medical screening or treatment for residents, students, or office workers.

Collaborating with Mount Sinai's doctors, the Central Labor Council had put together a funding proposal for a formal screening program. The demands of New York's congressional delegation, backed by the unions, had been heard in Washington, and $12 million had been appropriated for the workers. The funds took a circuitous route, from Congress to FEMA, to Landrigan's former employer, NIOSH. By the time the money was available to Mount Sinai in February 2002, severe restrictions governed how it could be spent. Because it was FEMA money, it could not be used for treatment. And NIOSH would not allow it to be used for research. From the very start, the unions insisted that no matter how much trust they had in Mount Sinai's doctors, they did not want the screening to turn into an academic research program. Ed Ott was firm: He refused to have workers treated like "lab rats." He wanted a health clinic that would check everyone on the pile and get them the help they needed. That position was markedly different from what had transpired at the New York Fire Department, where Kelly and Prezant, working with the full confidence of the members of the force and department brass, were able to launch detailed studies right from the start.

In July 2002, the World Trade Center Worker and Volunteer Medical Screening Program at Mount Sinai formally initiated operations with a total staff of about 25, including doctors, industrial hygienists, and clerks. They were still unclear on the range of diseases they would face because of the complex nature of the dust and smoke. Taking a cue from the fire department's screening program, they focused on three critical areas: respiratory problems, broken bones, and mental health issues related to extreme stress. Cancer screening was not included then because malignancies were understood to take decades to develop. The initial intake exam included a comprehensive questionnaire that established a worker's medical history, economic resources, and employment record. Each worker was given a chest x-ray, blood test, and standardized mental health evaluation. The doctors intended to create a baseline by conducting spirometry tests to measure breathing capacity, a relatively quick and easy way of looking for asthma or pre-asthma conditions.

It was to be a screening program only, but that raised an ethical issue for Landrigan and the others. If the doctors found something seriously wrong, they would have to refer workers to their own doctors for medical care because treatment costs weren't covered. But they knew that most doctors lacked the training to deal with exposure properly. And a good number of the construction workers might not be adequately covered by health insurance plans. They would have no place to go for the treatment, medications, or therapy the clinic prescribed. Landrigan turned to the Red Cross and several private philanthropies for help and was able to secure enough money to get the treatment program rolling, at least temporarily.

Despite the restriction against research, Landrigan realized that he would have to collect clinical information on the patients as they were being screened. As an advocate for the workers, he would eventually need hard data to overcome doubts about the dangers of the dust that the nation's top environmental official had said was not harmful. He also needed to make a strong case for workers to volunteer to be screened. Science—good science, based on quality data—would make the case for more funding, and that extra funding would provide for more monitoring. There wasn't money in the grant for sophisticated electronic data gathering, so the doctors put together a system on-the-fly. They used standardized printed forms and later transferred the information to electronic files. It was a time-consuming process that could be fraught with errors, but it was the best they could do under the circumstances.

In many ways, the Selikoff clinic was being forced to punch way above its weight. Although it had more expertise and experience than any other occupational medicine center in the Northeast, it clearly lacked the resources necessary to handle such a massive and open-ended job. It was a task more appropriate for government, but other factors prevented that from happening. The federal, state, and city governments were determined to show that the attack had only grazed the country, not wounded it mortally, and that things could return to normal quickly. Lingering health problems or, worse, a looming medical catastrophe could cripple the country's recovery. Besides, after what Giuliani and Whitman had said about safety, funding a big health screening program would be contradictory.

Landrigan worked with labor to establish a steering committee to oversee the screening program and to guide it as the doctors navigated between clinical care and research. As a model, they used the city's system of HIV clinics, which were run with the substantial input of the people they were serving. Mount Sinai received enough federal funding to screen about 9,000 people, but Landrigan did not really know how many workers were down at the pile and how many might come in to be examined. He assumed that intake would follow a bell curve, growing as more people found out about its existence and then tapering off as time elapsed. As the program expanded, space became an issue. The Mount Sinai Medical Center provided room, although administrators made clear they could not bear the cost forever.

As the clinical effort grew larger than anyone imagined, the unplanned way it was put together, improvising as everyone went along, inevitably caused trouble. The questionnaire given to incoming recovery workers ended up being 74 pages long, most of it self-administered, but with one part that had to be mailed in and another that was taken by an interviewer. With x-rays and a breathing test, the whole process could take more than four hours. Once word spread at ground zero, recovery workers thought twice before deciding to travel uptown to volunteer for a program that might find a medical problem but couldn't necessarily treat it.

Who did make the trip? The answer to that would have a profound impact on the studies Landrigan and his staff conducted over the coming years. Several fundamental flaws in the intake program could not be corrected. Despite his November 2001 call for a registry of ground zero workers, Landrigan never got an official count of who was down at ground zero and how much time they spent there. In time, however, Mount Sinai's programs, along with the fire department's outreach, would come to include a substantial number of responders. Together, they provided an acceptable approximation of the total and further backed up the reliability of their studies.

The federal government eventually recognized the need for a comprehensive study of the ground zero population. In July 2002, the same month in which the Mount Sinai program began, FEMA provided $20 million to establish a World Trade Center Health Registry. Everyone who worked on the pile, lived or worked or went to school downtown, or happened to be in Lower Manhattan on the day of the attack was eligible to sign up. The government expected more than 200,000 people to register, but the unions suspected that the city might manipulate the data to obscure the true health impact of the dust and discouraged members from cooperating. In the end, only 71,000 people signed up.

While the fire department could guarantee that everyone who was called in for a screening showed up, Mount Sinai's program was entirely voluntary. There was no telling who was coming in. One of the earliest attempts at evaluating the responders was done by the CDC, which looked at a sample of 1,138 workers and volunteers who had been screened by Mount Sinai between July and December 2002. They were predominately union members who worked on the pile from day one through Friday of that first week, when it rained. Three-quarters of them reported upper-respiratory symptoms such as sinusitis, runny nose, and cough.[4] Half had shortness of breath and other lower-respiratory problems. Among those who had never smoked, lung capacity tests showed more abnormalities than expected in the general population of nonsmokers. But who did this group represent? Were they the people who went to the clinic because they were coughing persistently, while others whose cough had improved stayed away? Did they include people who were sick from some cause other than the dust, while those who were healthy stayed away? Was the population skewed because the number of people who had symptoms was not a representative sample of everyone who had worked at ground zero during the recovery operations?

Those questions underscored a deeper, more mysterious question that the responders themselves had been forced to ask. As time went on, it became clearer that although some ground zero workers who had been exposed to the trade center dust had come down with a growing number of ailments, not all did, even though their exposures were similar. On top of all the other uncertainties that responders were living through, this one seemed to pinch the heart. The doubts that had arisen with the dispute over the EPA's early statements and that had colored so many negative reactions now started to hang over the responders as well. Despite some of the early indications coming out of the clinical research, questions were being raised about who was truly sick and who might be exaggerating. Without definitive answers, some in New York, Washington, and the rest of the country wondered, were they heroes, or victims, or whiners looking for pity?

Endnotes

[1]Gillespie, Angus Kress, *Twin Towers: The Life of New York City's World Trade Center* (New Brunswick: Rutgers University Press, 1999, reprinted 2001).

[2]Personal interview, 29 July 2009.

[3]Personal interview, 18 August 2009.

[4]Centers for Disease Control, *Physical Health Status of WTC Rescue and recovery Workers and Volunteers—NYC July 2002–August 2004* (10 September 2004).

7

It's not the dying

Few New Yorkers asked the fundamental questions of 9/11's aftermath—"Why me and not him?" or "Why him and not me?"—more often or with more apprehension than Marty and Dave Fullam. Both brothers were veterans of the FDNY on 9/11, and both had responded to the disaster; spent plenty of time on and around the pile; smelled the raw, penetrating, inescapable odor of burning flesh that they couldn't shake for weeks afterward; and went back to their homes doused in fine gray grit that clung to every exposed inch of their skin except the moons around their eyes. Both thought nothing in this world was nobler than being part of the fire brotherhood.

One brother came out of the fire scarred but whole. The other nearly died and will spend every day of the rest of his life taking a medicine cabinet of medications, keeping track of what he eats, keeping score of what he can no longer do, and hoping against hope that, with a new lung and a team of doctors who care, he can watch his three daughters grow into fine young women.

The youngest of those three girls, sweet little Emma, was born just five weeks before the September 11 attacks, but she knows the story by heart of how her daddy, firefighter Martin Fullam, Ladder Company #87, loaded nine fellow firemen into the cab and the bed of his red Chevrolet Silverado Z71 that morning and drove them as fast as he could to the muster point where they boarded buses that took them to the Staten Island Ferry. She has seen photographs of the truck, and she's heard her father retell the story of that day many times over. On the Saturday morning when Lieutenant Fullam recounted for me in painful detail what had happened to him, Emma stuck close by, frequently hanging on his wheelchair, at other times rubbing his short gray hair until it stuck straight up on his head. He never once shooshed her away or asked her to stop. They both seemed to realize how close they had once come to losing each other.

During the interview,[1] he sat at the same table where he had been sitting on that bright September morning. September 11 was his day off, and Marty was taking advantage of the extra time to brush up on a fire department manual. He had just completed 20 years as a firefighter for New York City and was preparing to take the test for lieutenant in a few months. With three young daughters, he couldn't even think about retiring. Besides, he loved being a fireman. His own father, Martin Thomas Fullam, had worked in a Manhattan corporate office and made the long commute from Staten Island before the Verrazano-Narrows Bridge had been built. But it was clear early on that life behind a desk wasn't for Marty. He loved helping people, and he loved everything about the fire department, most of all its sense of duty and its deep and heroic tradition. When he married, he chose the daughter of a battalion chief.

The morning of the attacks, his two older girls, Kelly and Caroline, had just gone off to school, and Patricia, his wife, was upstairs with the new baby. A neighbor knocked on the door shouting at Marty that a plane had crashed into the World Trade Center. A burly guy, slightly overweight, with pale eyes and an easy, glad-to-help smile, Marty rushed upstairs and turned on the TV in time to see the second plane crash into the towers. Without thinking, he prepared to do his job. He hopped into the red pickup, hightailed it over to the school to get Kelly and Caroline and bring them back home, kissed Tricia and the baby goodbye, and headed to Ladder 87, a few minutes away. Other guys piled into the truck there, and they rushed over to Rescue Five headquarters on Clove Road, where buses waited to bring firefighters from all over the southern half of Staten Island up to the ferry terminal on the north end for the tense trip to Manhattan.

It was an unusual response in many ways, but particularly because they left their rigs behind, along with nearly all their equipment. They boarded the buses with their bunker gear—the heavy pants and coats and their old-fashioned hardened leather helmets—and little else but their wits. At the ferry terminal, Marty walked aboard one of the huge double-ended, push-me/pull-me ferries along with maybe 200 other firefighters from New York City's most unlikely borough for the 20-minute voyage to Manhattan. It was a trip he'd made countless times, growing up on suburban Staten Island. None, however, had ever been filled with such tension and awe. On this extraordinary day, there were no private vehicles and no commuters as they headed toward a scene that no firefighter could imagine.

The firefighters landed at an empty terminal. But amassed outside were hundreds of commuters desperate to flee the chaos. As Marty and the other firefighters marched off toward the trade center site, the dusty people waiting there applauded, as though they knew something the men and women under the bulky gear did not.

Marty's first impression of the disaster scene was deceiving. He remembered that it was an unusually sunny day. "But then, looking up Broadway, it was like looking up at a night sky," he recalled. "As you walked up, you could tell it wasn't dark, but there was dust in the air. And the prevalent overwhelming smell in the air was—I know what it was, the smell of people, the people who died. Bodies burning. That's what we smelled overall. What you smelled for the whole time you were down there, for weeks you'd smell it. Then it got a little worse as the bodies started to rot."

As the corps of firefighters boldly marched up Broadway toward ground zero, Marty noticed the dust that seemed to be wrapped around everything. Pieces of the vertical aluminum tracks that made up the façade of the towers were everywhere, and then he saw something odd—a car parked a few blocks from the trade center site totally engulfed in flames, even though no building near it was burning. The fuel and fire expelled from the towers by the exploding jets had sent out incendiary bombs for blocks, torching parked cars.

Marty arrived at ground zero about 11:30 a.m. The towers had already come down, and the air was still thick with smoke and ash. He knew the conditions were hazardous, but all his equipment was still on his fire truck. Each firefighter normally is assigned a full face mask and a 30-minute tank of compressed air. Even if he had lugged his gear on the ferry, the air tank wouldn't have protected him for very long. And replacement tanks were hard to come by. Marty entered ground zero with nothing covering his face but a look of determination. As far as he and the other firefighters were concerned, the trade center—or the pile of rubble that remained of it—was still an occupied building, and the first thing a New York City firefighter is taught is to *never* give up an occupied building to a fire, mask or no.

Marty was assigned to work with a crew that was checking elevators, stairwells, and other areas of buildings 5 and 6 of the trade center complex. They searched for people who might have been injured or left behind. These two buildings were far smaller than the gigantic towers that had loomed over them, and they had been heavily damaged by the falling debris but were still standing. Marty knew there was a day care center in one of them, and thinking of his own girls, he searched thoroughly to make sure all the children had escaped. The firefighters did not find any civilians, but in the lobby of one of the buildings, they came across the still body of Father Mychal Judge, the department chaplain. His lifeless body had been found in the rubble earlier that morning and brought into the lobby. Now Marty, Lieut. Butch Pepe, firefighter Mark Heintz, and others carried him to St. Paul's Chapel, one of the oldest buildings in Manhattan, and carefully laid him on the altar.

Not for several hours later that day did Marty actually get to touch the debris pile, making his way in from West Street. "Where the sidewalk would have been, we found lots of debris there, and that's when we started to find people—firefighters, people, and stuff," he remembered, "but whoever was attached to what we found wasn't alive." They had to squirm through the tangled girders and piles of concrete dust, making their way down into a subway station where they recovered more bodies. Marty said there was heaviness in the air, caused not just by the intense emotion, but also by the contamination that had been aerosolized over the financial district. There was so much uncertainty at the time. No one knew for sure how many people had been in the towers when they came down. No one knew how many firefighters had been caught on the stairs when the world went dark around them. No one knew what was in the air they were breathing that day, but these were experienced New York City firefighters. "Oh, yeah, I went twice to a clinic to get my eyes cleaned out. My breathing, I could feel it. I mean, at that point, I was a fireman for 20 years. I knew it wasn't good. But that wasn't what I thought about that day."

Carefully worked-out firefighting protocols, refined over decades, went out the window. On this day, everyone did what it made sense to do, for as long as it seemed to make sense to do it.

About the only thing people could agree on was that if there were people to be rescued, there was no time to waste, even for something that might be as critical as making sure that the rescuers themselves did not become victims.

"The fire department has a lot of safety rules, but they weren't prepared for this large of an operation," Marty said. They knew they had lost so many men—an unthinkable number of the guys they had worked with, laughed with, exchanged family photos with, and played softball with—and they held out hope of finding them far longer than was reasonable. That, in the end, made worrying about protective gear seem selfish. "To stand around and wait for somebody to tell you to put on the right mask or the right cartridge, while maybe somebody's laying there still alive ... it just didn't make sense to us."

At about the same time Marty Fullam was marching into the dead zone at ground zero, his younger brother, David, was on duty at Ladder Company 46 in the Bronx. Dave, born on the Fourth of July 1963, was seven years younger than Marty and had come to the fire department indirectly. He had originally toyed with the idea of joining the police department, and he had done well on the test while he was still finishing his bachelor's degree in finance at the College of Staten Island. But Dave had turned down the idea of a civil service job to try Wall Street. A few years in the financial district convinced him to try something else, and by 1991, he had made up his mind to follow Marty into the fire department. Dave spent his first years on the job at a firehouse in midtown Manhattan. When he moved with his family to Orange County, New York, he transferred to the Bronx, shortening his commute considerably.

On the morning of 9/11, Dave's company had just come back from an easy run. He was on house duty and used the time to study for the lieutenant's test he planned to take in March 2002, the same time as his brother. He had turned on the television in the firehouse and saw what was happening in Lower Manhattan. Before any instructions had come in from headquarters, he used the loud speaker to tell the others to prepare to move fast. The firefighters scrambled to check their gear, grabbing coats and air tanks, and when the order came in, they were ready to roll.

They were sent not to the trade center, but to 2 Truck on Manhattan's east side, As the day wore on and the events downtown became more desperate, Dave's company itched to be sent down. But the fire dispatcher insisted they stay put, just in case something happened in that part of the city. From their position on 51st Street and Lexington Avenue, 2 Truck, now the relocated Ladder 46, could quickly respond to an emergency at some of the city's most notable landmarks—the Empire State Building, Penn Station, Grand Central Terminal, the United Nations. If the nation really was at war, any one of those buildings could be a target. The department was already stretched thin.

Dave had managed to get a call through to his mother, Helen, that first day. "Where's Marty?" he needed to know. His mother said he had called her from the World Trade Center. Marty was all right.

The first day after the attacks, a new crew relieved Ladder 46 so that it could return to its own house. Their tour ended, but instead of going home, Dave and four other guys in bunker gear crammed into their captain's Honda Civic and drove to ground zero to help. Almost no one was wearing a respirator mask that day or the next when Ladder 46 was officially sent down to work the pile. The dust made breathing difficult. Before Dave had reported for work that morning, he had picked up paper dust masks at a fire department depot. The masks wouldn't protect him from much, but he thought something was better than nothing.

By the beginning of October, when the department had established regular working shifts, Dave and the Ladder 46 crew started their tours by driving out to Shea Stadium in Queens. The department had established a staging area where firefighters could pick up gear, including proper respirators, before being bussed to ground zero. Dave was fit-tested there for a P-100 cartridge mask and told to wear it over his moustache and to change cartridges frequently. In the days to come, firefighters were able to pick up gloves and other supplies, too, including the hockey puck–sized asthma inhalers that Dr. David Prezant had recommended.

In all, Dave spent about 20 full days working at ground zero, starting the day after the towers went up in smoke and lasting through the end of 2001, after the fires were extinguished. "We were wearing masks on the pile," he said.[2] "There were some guys who wore them whenever they were down there ... others, as soon as they'd come off the pile, it was the first thing [they] took off. You did some of the worst things down there that you ever had to do. And as soon as you got off that hill, you wanted to start taking everything off, get relieved from that stuff. And the first thing you did was take off that face piece."

Marty and Dave never saw each other on the debris pile, but they knew what the other was going through. Their routines were slightly different. The established muster spot for Staten Island firefighters was the Homeport, an old Naval base on the island's northeastern shore. But Marty was too impatient to wait there for instructions. "You could kill hours there waiting," he said. Instead, he'd load up his Chevy pickup and drive into Manhattan, flashing his ID at the military guards so they'd let him through the barricades. He was able to park a block and a half from the site and report for work several hours earlier than he would have had he reported to the Homeport. That gave him even more time on the pile. But it meant he never was fit-tested for a respirator mask.

In all, Marty spent over 50 days at ground zero, winding down toward the end of the year just as his brother did. He worked there a few more days in 2002 before the cleanup ended. He'd never worn a P-100 respirator in 20 years on the job, and he didn't intend to change now, despite the possible consequences. "I knew better," Marty said. "I mean, I knew it wasn't good. I've done this long enough to know. But what are you gonna do? You're not gonna stay home."

That winter, Dave came down with pneumonia. He thought it was just a cold. Like most other firefighters, he had developed World Trade Center cough. In time, his symptoms grew less severe. But then as temperatures dropped, his breathing grew labored. At one point, he felt a stabbing pain in his chest every time he took a breath. Even simple motions, the kinds of things he'd done for 20 years, became so painful that he was forced to go out on medical leave. A doctor diagnosed pneumonia. Dave had never had pneumonia. He was still studying for the lieutenant's test, and the stress was affecting him in ways he hadn't expected. Two days before the test, he was driving somewhere, thinking about all the funerals for fellow firefighters he'd attended and worrying about how he'd do on the exam. Suddenly he felt a pain shooting down his left arm. He couldn't feel his hands. Certain he was suffering a heart attack, he thought he'd never see his wife or daughters again. He pulled over, closed his eyes, and tried to calm down. When he started feeling better, he went home.

Two days later, Dave and Marty took the lieutenant's test, and both passed (Dave got the higher score and rarely misses a chance to remind his older brother). Both were later promoted—Dave in January 2003, Marty in March. But that didn't end the anxiety. Dave was eventually diagnosed with post-traumatic stress disorder. He put on extra weight, and he thinks the added pounds may have contributed to him blowing out his knee so badly he couldn't work. Lieut. David Fullam retired from the fire department in May 2006 and tried to put everything behind him to start life anew in Syracuse, where his wife, Lynda, had grown up. The fire lieutenant who had once thought of becoming a cop took a position with the safety department at Syracuse University, analyzing risk. He tries not to dwell on ground zero and has not joined the responders, including his brother, who sued the city of New York for not providing them with the protective equipment that might have kept them safe. He just wants to forget 9/11.

Marty continued working at Ladder 87 until his promotion, when department regulations required him to move to another house. He chose 10 Engine on Liberty Street in Manhattan, a few yards away from ground zero. Marty and Tricia continued working on the renovation of their home in the suburban Annadale section of Staten Island and eventually completed a pool in the backyard. But by 2005, something was terribly wrong. Marty was nearing 50; he knew time would eventually take its toll, but not like this. Almost overnight, it seemed, he lost most of his upper-body strength, a significant setback for a firefighter who loved skiing, biking, and swimming. He was sleeping up to 14 hours a night and still waking up exhausted. Local doctors couldn't diagnose anything definitive, although they suspected a range of diseases, from carpal tunnel syndrome to lupus. Finally, Tricia convinced him to see a specialist in Manhattan. In November 2005, Marty went in for a blood test. The following morning, the doctor's office called back with an urgent message: Get to the hospital immediately.

The telltale sign that had set off the alarm was an abnormality in Marty's blood. Because he had complained about fatigue and a lack of strength, the physicians had ordered a complete blood test, including an intensive look at what was happening to his muscles. The test had calculated the levels of a particular enzyme—creatine phosphokinase, or CPK—that floods the bloodstream when muscles are damaged. Normal CPK levels are less than 200. When Marty came in, his were raging at about 15,000, a clear indication that he had done some serious damage to his muscles, although the doctors didn't know what had triggered such a severe reaction. He was admitted to New York University Hospital on November 12, 2005. In the ensuing days, he grew progressively weaker, until he couldn't even sit up in bed. He had to admit that he felt like a tired old man. At this time, he wasn't connecting his deteriorating condition to his work at ground zero. He just knew that he was sick, and he was scared. Tricia thought she was going to lose him.

Marty never returned to work at the firehouse. Eventually, the doctors at NYU Hospital diagnosed polymyositis, a disease in which the body's own immune system, designed to protect against infection and disease, attacks itself. In Marty's case, the target was his own muscles, which the immune system suddenly became intent on breaking down, causing widespread damage that released the flood of CPK enzymes. During a particularly long night at the hospital, when he was feeling depressed and angry, one of his doctors bent low over Marty, drew close to his ear, and said, "This is from 9/11, and we're going to prove it." That was the first time anyone had told him there might be a connection between the dust and what was happening to his body. Proof, however, would be hard to come by. As with many autoimmune diseases, including sarcoidosis, the cause of polymyositis is not at all clear. Some evidence suggests environmental links, although none that have been proven conclusively.

After a five-week stay in the hospital, Marty regained enough strength to return home. Although he had some good days, his condition steadily worsened. When he suffered a relapse in 2006, tests showed that his lungs were stiffening. Every breath of air became a struggle, even if he walked just a few feet. Tests showed he had only 34 percent of his breathing capacity, and he had to drag around an oxygen cylinder to keep from suffocating. He also developed an intense interstitial lung disease, called pulmonary fibrosis. By this time, Dr. Prezant had taken a direct interest in his care, lending a degree of consistency to what had become an increasingly chaotic and frightening situation for Marty and his family. Prezant was also aware that although Dave was fighting his own demons, he had gotten off much easier than his brother. Both had been exposed at some point to the same stuff, although Dave had sometimes worn a mask and Marty had not. Marty was told repeatedly that although he and Dave shared the same background, something in his makeup made him more vulnerable than his brother.

The situation was becoming dire for Marty. He started on physical therapy during his hospitalization, but his lungs were so weakened that sitting up in bed was an ordeal that took three days to master. He lost 60 pounds and much of his optimism. He stuck with the therapy, and eventually his lung capacity went back up to 60 percent, but that didn't last long. By 2006, he had dropped back to 40 percent, and doctors wanted him to start thinking about a very drastic step: a lung transplant. They were clear: A transplant was not a cure. It was simply a way to tame the disease he'd have to live with for the rest of his life. In November 2008, Marty's name was added to the lung transplant list at Columbia Presbyterian Hospital. By then he was pretty banged up. He hadn't been in the backyard pool for years. In fact, he couldn't do anything without his oxygen mask. His Staten Island home resembled the set of a science fiction movie. "I always knew when Marty was coming down the hall then because he sounded like Darth Vader," Tricia recalled.

Marty finally caught a lucky break. After a little more than four months on the transplant list, the call came in from Columbia Presbyterian. Doctors replaced his severely damaged left lung with a donor organ. Tests on the lung that was removed showed not only the fibrosis, but glass shards embedded in the tissue, probably from the pulverized glass, fiberglass, and asbestos at ground zero. A few weeks after the surgery, Marty was allowed to go home and begin his long recuperation. Tricia gave up her job as an insurance broker to take care of him. Marty doesn't expect to jump into the backyard pool for quite a while, but Dave gave him a mountain bike that he hopes to someday take for a ride. He's confronted daily with just how much his life has changed, from skipping fresh fruits or vegetables (for fear of infection), to never working at a firehouse again.

At first the fire department did not link polymyositis to ground zero and denied his application for a line-of-duty pension. But just before the transplant surgery, the department reversed itself. The updated diagnosis of polymyositis with interstitial lung disease was presumed to have been connected to his work at the trade center site.

What truly bothers Marty is not that he had to adjust his routine to include more than 40 prescription pills a day, along with regular checkups and physical therapy, but that when he is at the doctor's office, he runs into other firefighters who also worked ground zero and who, like him, are struggling with polymyositis. The typical age group for the disease is between 50 and 70, but the normal incidence in the general population is about 1 in 200,000. Marty counts five other firefighters with it, and Prezant believes there could be even more, which would push the incidence rate way beyond the expected. Because Marty also had interstitial lung disease, he has so far been the only firefighter with polymyositis to undergo a lung transplant. He joined the lawsuit against New York City, one of the thousands who believe the city did them wrong. If the suit is successful, he would win additional compensation beyond his fire department disability. But Marty doesn't expect the money, if it comes, to change his life. He once thought of moving away to someplace warmer, but now he's reluctant to leave his network of doctors, especially Prezant. He plans to stay in Staten Island and use the money to pay for the girls' college—and maybe draw attention to the other guys who were hurt. That's it. As for himself, his second chance at life is a sweet enough reward: "I just want to live in peace."

Two brothers with the same job—similar exposures, different outcomes. That leaves mysteries for science to ponder and emotions for the two men to come to grips with. Did the respirator Dave wore make the difference? Or was it something else? "Yeah, absolutely, I do consider why it happened to him and not me," Dave wrote in an e-mail. But Dave didn't come out of it unhurt. He must deal with survivor's guilt because he is still strong, whereas his brother nearly died. And he lives with uncertainty, always the worry about what might happen to him in the future. "Through it all, every little thing that feels different inside my body leads me to ask, 'Is this it?'" With the stress he's lived with since 2001 everything that goes wrong is multiplied. "There are small issues, but right away you think the worst." That's what happened on September 11, when he heard that Marty had gone down to the trade center. And that's what he's felt while watching his older brother struggle with the disease and then recover, only to get even sicker. Inevitably, Dave has thought about the possibility of his brother dying, about the funeral and the eulogy he'd be asked to deliver. He hates having those thoughts and not knowing why he was kept whole but his brother was not, and this has made his own emotional recovery even more difficult.

And although Marty certainly is glad to be alive, delighted with the prospect of watching Emma and her sisters grow, he has asked his doctors the same question about chance and science. "Ten thousand people could be exposed to the same thing in the environment, but for some reason, my genetic makeup allows that switch to be thrown and my body can't fight this condition," Marty said. "That's all there is to that. That kind of answered it for me, why I got it and not somebody else."

✻   ✻   ✻

In all, more than 60,000 people may have responded to the disaster at ground zero, among them many from outside New York City who came to help. They included alpine climbers who could venture far deeper into the debris looking for survivors than Marty or Dave Fullam ever could go, Red Cross disaster response specialists, and search-and-rescue teams such as Sarah Atlas and her specially trained German Shepherd, Anna.

Atlas is part of the 135 volunteers with New Jersey Task Force One, a search-and-rescue outfit that works in coordination with the state's Office of Emergency Management and the New Jersey State Police. They train at the Lakehurst Naval Air Station, the sprawling military base deep in the New Jersey Pine Barrens that was the scene of the famous accident that destroyed the German airship Hindenburg in 1937. Atlas was a career emergency medical technician who did ambulance runs for Virtua, a multihospital health care system in southern New Jersey. Her real passion, though, has always been her dogs. She was one of the rescue team's ten handlers who, with their 14 search-and-rescue dogs, were trained to respond to urban disasters. Like other members of the team, Atlas kept a travel bag packed and ready to go 24/7.

When her beeper went off on the morning of September 11, she was still in the middle of a 4 a.m.-to-11 a.m. shift with the ambulance corps. She rushed to her home outside Camden, rousted Anna—a three-year-old German Shepherd, mostly black, with reddish-tan darts on her husky legs—threw her emergency bag into the truck, and headed for Lakehurst, about 90 minutes away. She mustered there with the other members of the rescue squad. Soon they were on the road, barreling up the New Jersey Turnpike. They made it to Manhattan just after the towers fell, when there was still hope that people had somehow survived the cataclysm and were trapped beneath the rubble where only the dogs could find them. Fires were still raging, the air so thick they had trouble seeing, and breathing was tortuous. Atlas and Anna had been to many disaster sites before. Atlas had seen the damage left by floodwaters and the paltry remains of houses leveled by gas explosions. But this dwarfed her imagination. She struggled to reconcile the scene with previous disasters, and for a few minutes she was overwhelmed. Then her training kicked in. The responders on the scene, mostly firemen, had started to buzz with a nervous excitement because, Atlas could hear them murmuring, "The dogs are here." They knew that if anyone had survived the collapses, the dogs could find them.

Rescue dogs go through years of training and act as though they are part Daniel Boone, part metal detector. Anna was known as a "live find" dog. She had been taught that once she sniffed out someone in distress, she must stay on guard, staring intensively at the spot where the survivor was trapped and barking constantly until her human partner checked it out. This was what Atlas and Anna hoped to do as they crawled over the debris pile for ten days. "We were all hoping for miracles," she remembered.[3] But for ten days, Anna never barked the intense bark that would have indicated she had found someone alive.

The dogs scrambled over the busted concrete and the jagged steel, running up and down the valleys created by the debris. Anna crouched so low that her belly fur was scorched by pieces of melted PVC conduit. One rescue Border Collie had the fur on its paws singed by the heat.

Atlas and Anna worked with very little sleep for the ten days. Atlas was so overcome by the thick smoke that she developed World Trade Center cough, and it has stayed with her, on and off. She and the other rescuers were sore and mentally fatigued, never more so than when they realized that the chances of finding anyone alive were fading. In the meantime, Atlas remembered hearing that the air was fine, so she didn't panic when all she had for protection was a paper mask; Anna, of course, had nothing. When the rescue phase ended, Task Force One returned to a hero's welcome in Lakehurst. Townspeople organized a ceremony for them and celebrated their courage. But what should have been a joyous homecoming was another difficult step for Atlas. "There was a big party with speeches, but when my father met me at the base, I broke down crying." The days in New York had been packed with so much emotion, exertion, and exposure to the contaminated air that they had left her drained. When Atlas drove home after the ceremony, she was so agitated that she zipped right past her own house. A week later, she was hospitalized with intense sinusitis and pneumonia. She was out of work for two months.

Anna came back from ground zero equally exhausted, even though she was used to hardship. When she was just a year old, she had been hit by a car. Atlas and her veterinarian had agreed that if Anna ever developed arthritis because of injuries from the accident, she would not be worked anymore. Atlas was as committed to her rescue work as she was to the welfare of her dogs. "They put their own health on the line to help others. How can you put a price on that?" she asked. Two months before 9/11, she had taken Anna to the vet for spinal x-rays and extensive blood work. Everything seemed to be all right; Anna was allowed to continue to work.

But when Atlas was rushed to the hospital after returning from New York, her dog showed signs of weakness, too. By the time Atlas was discharged, Anna just wasn't right. She acted like she was sore and exhibited signs of pain if anyone touched her, which was not like her at all. Atlas took her to a vet, who found lesions on her spine. Later Atlas enrolled her in a study of rescue dogs that was being done by Dr. Cynthia Otto, a veterinary specialist and associate professor of critical care at the University of Pennsylvania. Atlas sent over Anna's x-rays and blood samples. Less than a year after 9/11, when Anna was just four, she became so sick that Atlas had to make an excruciating decision. Shepherds like Anna have an average life span of close to 13 years. But Anna was in such pain that Atlas reluctantly had her put down.

In her study, Otto eventually examined nearly 100 search-and-rescue dogs that had worked at ground zero.[4] She compared their medical records to those from a control group of rescue dogs that had not been exposed to the contaminants in the air of Lower Manhattan. After examining Anna, Otto determined that she had developed a fungal infection called aspergillosis that had quickly spread throughout her body, attacking every major organ. German Shepherds are predisposed to this infection, and Otto did not think it was linked to ground zero dust. Overall, Otto found no evidence of a correlation between the dust and the kinds of diseases that had troubled Anna and several other dogs.

Mindful of the concerns about asbestos in the ground zero air, Otto and her colleagues had closely examined chest x-rays of the dogs in the study. With the dogs' shorter life span, the two-to-three-decade latency periods for asbestosis and mesothelioma to develop in humans would have been expected to narrow to just a few years, making the dogs the canine equivalents of canaries in a coal mine. If dust caused cancer in the dogs at a higher than expected rate, there could be worrisome implications for humans. But the exams showed nothing unusual. Within four years of the attacks, 15 of the 97 dogs in the study (including Anna) had died. Eight of them had cancer. Otto found that the death rate and the number of dogs with cancer were not significantly different from what had occurred in the control group.

While she respects the work Otto has done, Atlas questions the validity of the study, saying that the results are skewed because they excluded many of the rescue dogs that were brought to New York from other parts of the country. In her mind, it was clear that the dogs had been exposed to toxic air and hazardous surroundings, and that raised questions about her own health. Anna had not spent one minute on the pile without her, and if, as she believed, the dust and gasses had fatally harmed the dog, what had it done to her handler? Atlas had come back from ground zero in one piece, but her life was not the same. She experienced bouts of dizziness when her blood pressure fell precipitously, at times going as low as 40/20. She'd drop into a dead faint, scaring everyone around her until they could get her to a hospital.

Within a year after 9/11, Atlas was suffering this kind of attack two or three times a month, and her doctors had no clue what was causing them. Then one day she used a commercial hand sanitizer and immediately afterward passed out and had to be rushed to the hospital emergency room. It appeared to be a severe allergic reaction. As the years passed, such attacks became more severe and occurred with greater frequency. She experienced one spell right after she took a Tylenol gel-cap. Another time she was driving with an open window and caught a whiff of something in the air. Finally, in 2007, after she had a severe attack while at work, she was forced to go for comprehensive testing. The doctors' conclusion surprised her. They diagnosed idiopathic anaphylaxis, a potentially fatal condition in which blood pressure drops sharply and the person suffers shortness of breath, coughing, wheezing, and fainting. Other ground zero responders say they have developed severe sensitivity to a wide range of chemicals. But in most cases, doctors have no idea what causes it. Atlas was given an EpiPen to inject herself with a powerful counteracting drug in case she suffered an especially bad attack. She was put on a regimen of antihistamines—and Prozac, because doctors realized that stress was also setting off the attacks.

Atlas was drawn into the cycle of separate but related symptoms that many ground zero responders have claimed. In the following months, she developed severe acid reflux. Later it was chronic obstructive pulmonary disease and irritant-induced asthma. She signed up for monitoring at the University of Medicine and Dentistry of New Jersey, which runs a satellite World Trade Center screening and monitoring program. She was given medications to lessen the physical symptoms, but nothing relieved her anxiety about what had happened to Anna and what the future might hold for her.

With the help of neighbors in southern New Jersey who raised the money for her, Atlas was able to replace Anna with Tango, a sable German Shepherd from the Netherlands that already had been trained as a live-find rescue dog. Atlas found that as she continued Tango's training, she had to give him commands in Dutch. She recently added another dog, a thinner but more energetic version of Tango named Kaylee who came from the Slovak Republic. Atlas now works Kaylee as a cadaver dog that can climb a ladder, leap over rebar, and sniff out decomposing flesh. When Kaylee finds what she has been trained to look for, she sits erect with her back to the remains until Atlas comes to investigate.

Atlas turned 54 in 2010 and continues to volunteer with New Jersey Task Force One. But in her regular job, she no longer goes on ambulance runs. Since the anaphylaxis was diagnosed, she has worked inside the Virtua hospital system, taking blood and administering EKG tests. She's still, as she says, "for the animals." Tango and Kaylee romp around her backyard, gnawing on big red balls they've torn open. Atlas also cares for a few birds, including a temperamental white cockatoo that isn't crazy about strangers. On the étagère in her living room are a dozen statuettes of German Shepherds, along with Anna's cremains, which she keeps in a handsome clay pot made by a local artist. "She was no different from any of the other dogs," Atlas says, "but they are all special because of what they do." She has started the Search and Rescue Dog Foundation to provide a little bit of help to the volunteers who pay for the entire cost of buying, raising, and training their rescue dogs.

It bothers Atlas that some people don't believe that Anna's premature death, and the death of other dogs that worked at ground zero, was caused by the dust. She realizes that the doubts also extend to her own medical problems. People see her working and think she must be all right. "But my health records speak for themselves," she said. She keeps them all in plastic binders, each a couple inches thick and growing. As more time passes, she realizes that attention has shifted from terrorism to the economy. Except for the 9/11 conspiracy theorists who call her on a regular basis to check out something they think she said about molten steel at ground zero (she didn't say it), she said she finds few people willing to listen anymore to the difficulties that she and other responders have faced, just as she and other responders find that they have trouble moving on with their lives.

At one time she had found people who believed her and were ready to help. She had gone to the September 11th Victim Compensation Fund in the last month before the fund stopped taking applications in December 2003. She won a comparatively small award, around $5,000, in 2004 that helped her recover from the months out of work because of her immediate respiratory problems. Now with the anaphylaxis and asthma and other chronic health issues permanently on her medical record, she, like Marty Fullam and thousands of others, decided to join the lawsuit against the city.

"I don't really expect anything to come of it, to be quite honest with you," she said. Even though her settlement with the compensation fund prohibts her from suing, she agreed to join the case against the city after plaintiffs' lawyers approached her. She said she did so because she was concerned about what might happen down the road, when who knows what else might suddenly pop up and prevent her from working with her dogs at disaster sites. She also had another reason to sue the city: She wanted to use the lengthy litigation to send a message. "I thought it was also important," she said, "that people realize that so many of us are sick."

※ ※ ※

A few months before September 11, Kevin Rogers and the 117 men and women who worked with him at Con Edison's Brooklyn-Queens Emergency Electric Operations Unit opened their hearts and their wallets to donate $10,000 to a local children's hospital. Each of them gave away a portion of the $400 bonus they had received for achieving the remarkable standard of working as a unit for more than a million hours without an accident. Considering the kind of work they did—on call all day, every day, responding to power outages and other emergencies during the worst weather conditions—escaping injury for so long was quite an achievement. Rogers, who managed the troubleshooting unit, had more than 25 years of experience with Con Ed and was known for being careful, a trait he passed along to those he worked with.

On the day of the biggest emergency he'd faced in that quarter-century of work, Rogers had made the trip up from his home in Toms River, N.J., to report to Con Ed's emergency operations unit in Brooklyn as he normally did. After the first plane struck the North Tower, he had been dispatched to Lower Manhattan, where the crowded streets of the financial district formed the heart of the city's electronic grid. Disruptions on or near Wall Street could be disastrous for all of New York City. Con Edison was worried about 7 World Trade Center and the giant substations beneath it. They represented a critical part of the city's electrical system, and now they were threatened.

Rogers led four crews into Lower Manhattan to assess the conditions at Number 7 World Trade Center. He arrived just as the first tower crumbled, and the wave of dust and debris swept over him. The heavy soot and airborne debris had just begun to settle, allowing in some sunlight, when the second tower gave way. Rogers again confronted the dark plume that had once been one of the world's tallest buildings.

As an on-site emergency manager for Con Edison, Rogers had to call on his decades of experience to figure how to stay ahead of the escalating calamity. As he assessed damage, he was constantly aware of the dangerous conditions all around him. He was one of the last people still inside 7 World later that day when authorities determined that it, too, was in danger of falling. He evacuated and then, for a third time that day, was covered by dust and ash when the building collapsed. He continued working through the afternoon and evening, and he stayed on the job without a break until September 14. Besides minding the electrical system, Rogers searched for a missing coworker who had been killed in the collapse of one of the towers. He took turns on the bucket brigade alongside firefighters and volunteers. As the immediate emergency was brought under control, he got some sleep and cut back his hours to 18 a day. In the following weeks, Con Ed installed 36 miles of cables above ground to take the place of the ruined subterranean infrastructure that the debris had made inaccessible. Rogers worked without a day off through October 13. He was 58 at the time, and the physical and mental effort he put into the ground zero operation left him exhausted.

Rogers continued to help coordinate Con Ed's response at ground zero, but he told his wife, Kathleen, a registered nurse, that something wasn't right. Although he said he had not had any pulmonary problems before 9/11, Rogers wasn't the same after being exposed to those three tidal waves of dust. He developed trouble breathing, and like so many others on the pile, he started coughing and couldn't stop, even when he was away from ground zero. He wasn't able to work around the pile after November, and he reported to Con Ed's medical office with breathing problems in February 2002. He kept going back month after month, and his condition grew worse. In August, doctors diagnosed chronic obstructive pulmonary disease. On November 4, 2002, he was forced to stop working altogether because of respiratory failure.

Rogers continued his rapid downhill slide. In January 2003, he was found to have new-onset asthma. He went in for a checkup at Con Ed's Occupational Health Department in February, and the report filed there stated "extensive WTC exposure" and said he had "also developed respiratory problems." In March, Rogers signed up for Mount Sinai's "Health for Heroes" medical monitoring program. There Drs. Laura Bienenfeld and Rafael de la Hoz put him through a series of tests and found that he—as with other workers who had come to Mount Sinai to be screened—had symptoms of all 10 of the most prevalent ailments then connected to exposure to ground zero dust, everything from persistent dry cough to acid reflux and post-traumatic stress disorder. Doctors put him on corticosteroids to ease some of his respiratory problems, but the drugs had a devastating side effect and he developed diabetes. In November, Rogers went to the Deborah Heart and Lung Hospital in southern New Jersey, not far from his home, for tests. There he underwent a CT scan that showed "glass opacities," defined as fine shards of glass and significant amounts of fiberglass material in his lungs. They also found signs of scarring from exposure to asbestos.

Unable to work, Rogers filed a claim with the New York State Workers Compensation Board. The doctor who had examined him at Mount Sinai told the board that Rogers was disabled and suffered from a range of respiratory illnesses, including chronic obstructive pulmonary disease. His own personal physician, Dr. Bertram Newman, whom Rogers had been seeing for 25 years, also reported to the compensation board that Rogers was unable to work. In January 2004, the board awarded him its highest payment, $400 a week, for the rest of his life. He also applied for compensation from the September 11th Victim Compensation Fund for the injuries to his lungs, and he won an award. On June 12, 2004, two years after the cleanup at ground zero ended, Rogers, who was then 60, died at Community Medical Center in Dover Township, N.J. No autopsy was done. The official cause was listed as sudden cardiac death due to coronary artery disease, which the doctors at Mount Sinai later attributed to his exposure to the dust. Dr. Newman, his personal physician for more than a quarter-century, concluded "with reasonable medical certainty" that Rogers's death was "directly attributed to his exposure to the toxic dust at Ground Zero." He outlined the basis for his medical opinion in a letter he wrote for Kathleen Rogers when she filed for survivor's benefits from the state workers' compensation board. "Kevin was in good health prior to the exposure at the WTC site. Subsequently, he suffered severe pulmonary and respiratory symptoms which were getting progressively worse until his death." In other words, Rogers had been healthy, had gone to ground zero, got sick, and died. What else could it have been but the dust?

✷　✷　✷

On the tough city streets and in the back alleys where middle-class people like him are not expected to go, Mike Valentin was known as the White Devil. He was one tough undercover detective, and his best stealth weapon was his fluency in Spanish, which he used to ferret out information from drug dealers, pimps, and other low-lifes who never suspected that the 40-something white guy at the end of the bar was actually a New York–born Puerto Rican cop.

Valentin knew how to pull information out of the air. He had been taught some of the tricks of the street by his partner, Ernie Vallebuona, who had started on the job as a New York City undercover detective a few years before Valentin joined the force. Vallebuona had the heart of a poet, an intellectual bent that led him to study the scoundrels he was after. It also gave him the courage to walk into a bar full of Russian gangsters and observe drug deals going down until a back-up team burst through the door and arrested them. He knew that if he blew his cover, he'd be dead, but he was confident that he was smarter than most of the thugs around him and would always be able to beat them at their own game.

Valentin and Vallebuona started working as a team in 1998. The more time they spent on all-night stakeouts and undercover investigations, the better they got to know each other and the street that was their office. They lived far apart, Valentin on Long Island and Vallebuona in suburban Staten Island. Before heading back to their precinct house after a stakeout, they'd sometimes try to squeeze in a few minutes for their real passion. They kept fishing poles in the trunk of their unmarked car, and they'd make their way to the nearest open water, whether up at Pelham Bay or over at the concrete banks of the East River if they had to, just to put a line in the water.

On the morning of September 11, they completed a late tour and went home. Valentin had just dozed off when his wife, Joan, woke him. "Mike, you've got to get up. A plane just hit the towers." On Staten Island, Vallebuona had made an early morning run to a local Home Depot with his son when he heard the news on the car radio. He turned right around and sped home. Amy, his wife, was waiting for him on the front steps, panic tugging at her face. "Work called. They want you to come in."[5] But she didn't want him to go. It didn't look safe, she said. But Vallebuona heard some other voice, an inner voice, telling him clearly, "You're a detective in the New York City Police Department. You know what you have to do, what you're trained to do." Vallebuona called in and was ordered to a mobilization point on the West Side Highway, just north of Vesey Street, the northernmost perimeter of the trade center.

Meanwhile, Valentin had put the flashing light on top of his car, picked up other detectives, and made his way in from Long Island, fighting against the frantic traffic scrambling to get away from Manhattan. They crossed the river into Manhattan's crowded grid and stared at the utter chaos unfolding around them. A woman wandered by in a daze, covered in dust and bleeding from cuts on her face. A firefighter dropped to his knees, crying out loud. "I asked him what happened, and he said he had just lost his best friend," Valentin remembered. He felt like he had walked into World War III. "What people write about wars and hell, that was it," he said. "All at once, it was all there, and I was numb to it. We all were numb to it."

Valentin and Vallebuona met up near the West Side Highway piers, just north of the trade center site. "You couldn't see for blocks because the cloud of dust was so dense," Vallebuona said. "It seemed like we were walking for a couple of blocks and just weren't getting any closer. It was such intense dust, we had to back out a few times. We were coughing—there was just too much dust to breathe in. We didn't have any breathing apparatus. We each just had bandanas over our face."

The bandanas—big handkerchiefs printed with American flags that Joan Valentin had bought for them—weren't nearly protection enough. After being on the scene for a few hours, the partners got word that 7 World was tottering. They watched it come down. "We were looking at this thing falling, and this plume of dust hits us, like a wave."

They spent the rest of that day and night transporting people out of the danger zone. Afterward, they were sent to search rooftops for body parts. They worked the bucket brigade for several days. They remained at ground zero, on and off, for nearly three months, retrieving body parts, helping people back into their apartments, and controlling onlookers at the edge of the pile. When the rescue turned into a recovery operation, and the recovery into a cleanup, their assignments changed. As the city got back on its feet, they got on with their work.

It was Valentin who first realized something was wrong. Like so many others, he had developed a dry cough that he couldn't get rid of. By 2003, he had lost a lot of his energy. He developed night sweats and put on weight. He told his regular doctor that he felt awful, but the doctor couldn't find anything wrong. Intent on not depriving his family of anything because he wasn't at the top of his game, Valentin took everyone on a vacation to the Midwest in 2004. The native New Yorkers got a kick out of the Indiana State Fair, enjoying the people as much as the amusements. But while he was walking the fairgrounds, Valentin's ankles turned purple, his chest tightened, and he had trouble breathing. They rushed home and got him to his doctor for a complete physical. That's when he was told they had found a tumor in his chest between his aorta and his trachea that was causing his breathing problem. Surgeons removed the tumor—specifically, a mediastinal mass—but in a short time, it returned. Valentin was back on the operating table. Doctors believed a haywire lymph node was causing the trouble, but they didn't know what to do about it. They ordered more tests. He continued to struggle with his breathing. Doctors said it was irritant-induced asthma. Valentin often sounded like he had run a marathon when, in fact, he had just climbed a few stairs.

At around the same time, Vallebuona was dealing with his own problems. In summer 2004, he took his family to a street fair on 116th Street in East Harlem, an old Italian-American neighborhood of Manhattan that is now mostly Latino. He caught a glimpse of a Hispanic street vendor slicing fresh fruit and gave in to desire. A local treat, slices of cantaloupe and melon on a stick sprinkled with chili powder, looked delicious on a hot summer day. Vallebuona devoured it, but afterward he felt like he was going to die. He herded his family back into the car and broke out in a sweat, convinced that the street vendor's knife must have been contaminated with bacteria that had infected his fruit stick. At that moment, it was the worst thing he could imagine happening.

Vallebuona made it back home and tried to recover. Nothing helped. He went to see a gastroenterologist the next day. As soon as the doctor examined his stomach, he felt a mass and ordered him to the hospital immediately. There doctors quickly did other tests and diagnosed B-cell lymphoma. The cancer was speckled throughout his body. He began treatment immediately. Vallebuona eventually had to undergo the rigorous challenge of a complete bone marrow transplant.

Both partners were facing serious health challenges, but they didn't know it. After 9/11, they had been reassigned to different precincts. Vallebuona had moved from Staten Island to Rockland County, just north of the New York–New Jersey state line. He heard from another detective that his old partner was sick. That's when he broke with deeply rooted police tradition concerning sicknesses in the ranks and called. Valentin was surprised to hear from him. "A lot of guys don't want to hear the bad news," Valentin explained. "They kind of put you off to the side like they were saying 'He's a sick dog—let him die in peace, don't bother him.'"

At that time, Vallebuona was just finding out the bad news about his own health. As he prepared for the bone marrow transplant, he was put in strict isolation. Valentin wasn't allowed to visit, so they talked on the telephone. Those conversations brought them even closer than they had been on the street. They became each other's medical consultant, life coach, and psychiatrist. "There were days we cried on the phone because we didn't know what to do," Valentin recalled. "We didn't know if we were going to live or die, and if we died, what would happen to our families."

If cops are a special breed, undercover detectives form an exclusive subspecies based on courage, smarts, and a taut sense of reserve. You need to have that kind of *sangfroid* if you are going to break up a drug deal or infiltrate a gang. You keep your cards close to the vest. You say what needs to be said and no more. And you never, never admit to anyone but your wife that you are scared. Even then, you never unveil the whole truth.

The code is universally followed on the job, and when it comes to being sick, it is doubled. Valentin says complaining about an ailment or illness is bad *mojo,* upsetting the natural order of undercover cops. But because both were sick, these partners could express their fears to each other without crossing the code.

Part of their emotional sensitivity grew out of the steroids they were taking at the time. The medication exaggerated their feelings, making them more expressive than undercover detectives liked to admit. "You have this machismo of being a cop, you know. We walk right over dead bodies," Valentin said. But at times he and Vallebuona spent hours on the phone talking about their feelings. They found they could talk to each other about anything, even the one thing they couldn't easily bring up with their spouses: what they feared most about dying. It wasn't the dying itself. All those years on the street had made them accept that possibility. They had lived a fair amount and had escaped death many times already. The physical act of being extinguished was comprehensible. What bugged them was the thought of leaving their families unprotected when they were no longer there to take care of them.

Both had applied for disability pensions from the police department, just as many firefighters who were sick had asked their department for help. But the police brass had much tougher standards of proof and were rejecting pension applications that lacked conclusive science linking a disease to the dust. Both men did receive partial disability payments, but it was based on a percentage of their regular salaries. As many other detectives did, they relied on overtime to pay their bills, and overtime did not play into the disability computations. Valentin eventually had to sell his house and move in with his father.

Cops were treated differently than firefighters after 9/11, and the partners thought they knew why. Every member of the fire department had been anointed a hero. Their turnout coats had become symbols of courage for the wounded city. The police, however, received far less sympathy, despite their own losses and a general feeling of patriotism. "Everybody loves the firemen," Valentin said. "But who loves the cops?"

Eventually, New York State passed legislation recognizing that firefighters and police who had worked at ground zero and later got sick should be presumed to have developed their respiratory disease and other illnesses because of their work. (The legislation is modeled after an older law that considers active-duty heart attacks to be related to work.) After the ground zero presumption bill passed, both Valentin and Vallebuona were granted full line-of-duty pensions. As the years passed, their health fluctuated. Some days were definitely better than others.

Although they lived far apart, the partners tried to retain their special bond as they rebuilt their lives. They'd meet on a quiet Long Island beach for a day of surf casting, standing on the edge of North America with 15-foot poles in their hands, facing the ocean and the uncertain future they knew awaited them. Both relatively young men who could no longer work, they also threw themselves into helping others facing similar problems. They realized that they had been lucky enough to have each other, but they knew that many of their colleagues had no one to turn to when things looked darkest. They volunteered at the detectives' union, joined the big lawsuit against the city, and later launched their own foundation to help others deal with the legacy of the dust. Valentin became the more active by far, often traveling to Washington to testify before congressional committees and urge members to not turn their backs on the responders. That had already happened once, in their eyes. "The city had to do what it had to do in the first two weeks to preserve life," Valentin said. "But after two weeks, it was a cleanup. There was no need to move so fast after that. There was no life at stake." He thinks somebody should have been there to say, "Stop." It's not right to put others in danger when there was no need. "We were a well-oiled machine," he said. "Somebody should have protected that machine. But that didn't happen."

As Valentin got more involved with the victims' group, Vallebuona turned inward. As time went on, he, like Dave Fullam, felt a need to put the dust and the ash behind him so that he could focus on the future. Just as mysteriously as he had gotten sick, he had been given a second chance to live and he was intent on taking full advantage of it. He wanted to spend more time with his family and his boys, Ernest and Ethan, fully tasting the life he had feared he would not have. When his lymphoma had proved hard to defeat, Vallebuona had been riddled with doubts about his own ability to survive and care for his family. He had been advised to keep a medical journal, recording medications and his reaction to them. But focusing so much on himself quickly got boring. He was far more concerned with his family, especially his boys, whom he was afraid would have to grow up without him. He pushed aside the medical journal and began collecting in a small notebook the words of wisdom he had once expected to pass along to them personally. He wanted to warn them to stay away from drugs and to respect women, of course. But he thought they'd need to know other things he had picked up on the streets at a different time, well before 9/11. "My guys are like little shrimps right now," he said, recalling what it was like when he was in school and there were bullies in the hallways. So he wrote this: "If you're the little guy and you're outnumbered, always punch the big guy first and then run away. This way, at least they'll respect you."

Vallebuona knew what it was like to come up against guys bigger and tougher than he was. And now his work on the pile had forced him to face a different kind of bully: a disease that ravaged his body despite his best efforts to fight back, and a system that dug in its heels and continued to doubt that he and his partner had surrendered their health, and the stability of their families, by going to work. That enraged him. "I realized that politicians would love for these problems to just go away," he said. He was not afraid of dying, but for the sake of his family, and the families of other men and women who had gotten sick, he was determined not to simply go away. He vowed to get in the face of anyone who denied that something bad had happened at ground zero.

Valentin and Vallebuona were just two of the thousands of people whose futures had been altered by their work at or near the pile. By 2010, more than 28,000 people who had worked the pile—cops, steel workers, volunteers—had been screened by Dr. Stephen Levin and the crew at Mount Sinai. But an entirely different group of people, a group just as large as the responders and volunteers, had been exposed to the dust and smoke of ground zero for months on end. And this group was being routinely ignored by the federal, state, and city governments. Even Mount Sinai's screening program, comprehensive as it was, had been closed to them from the beginning. For these people, ground zero was not a rescue operation or a crime scene.

It was home.

Endnotes

[1]Personal interview, 6 June 2009.

[2]*Ibid.*

[3]Personal interview, 6 November 2009.

[4]Fitzgerald, S.D., Rumbeiha, W.K., Braselton, W.E., Downend, A.B., Otto, C. M.. "Pathology and Toxicology Findings for Search-and-Rescue Dogs Deployed to the September 11, 2001, Terrorist Attack Sites: Initial Five-Year Surveillance," *Journal of Veterinary Diagnostic Investigation* 20 Issue 4(2008): 474–484.

[5]Various personal interviews, 2007–2009.

8

Life and dust

The vast concrete plaza at the base of the twin towers, a windswept butte that architectural critics and office workers alike recognized as sterile and uninviting, was the perfect place for Catherine McVay Hughes's two sons, Philip and Matthew, to learn to ride their bicycles. On weekends, when the suits and briefcases were nowhere in sight, the big space was all theirs. Children of the city, they also ice skated there in the winters, when the Port Authority installed a rink to break up the plaza's bleakness. For the Hughes family, the plaza became a substitute backyard. Their own home was a roomy apartment on the 14th floor of an old loft building on Broadway, just one block away. The huge copper windows of their apartment looked out over the roofs of lower buildings across Broadway and down Cortlandt Street for a block directly west onto the South Tower of the World Trade Center. Their apartment actually is located on the 13th floor, but by New York tradition, it is designated floor 14. Despite the old superstition, McVay Hughes likes to think of it as being the 13th floor, her lucky 13. And never did good fortune grace her and her family more than the time following September 11 when they escaped unharmed and the disparate chapters of her life came together to help her represent tens of thousands of New Yorkers who felt that they had been abandoned by their government and left to fight for their homes on their own.

McVay Hughes has a tall woman's lanky grace, accented by bright eyes, a mellow voice, and a highly structured practical mind. At a time when few women made their careers in technical fields, she had studied hydro-geologic engineering at Princeton, where she had met her future husband, Thomas, an English major. Her relationship with the trade center complex went back to her first job after graduation in

1982 with ICOS, an Italian company that had designed and built the famous slurry wall that lined the cavernous basement of the trade center and kept the murky waters of the Hudson River at bay. After working in engineering for several years, she returned to school, this time for an M.A. from the Wharton School of Economics at the University of Pennsylvania. That was followed by a stint in New York finance, which convinced her that the world of Wall Street was not for her, either. Something important was missing. At Princeton, she had been schooled in the idea of "service to the nation," and her own family history made service an integral part of a complete life. Her father, Scott McVay, was the influential president of the Geraldine Rockefeller Dodge Foundation in New Jersey and was known for his dedication to community and the arts.

When Catherine McVay married Tom Hughes in 1987, she moved into the funky 14th-story loft he had purchased on Broadway a few years earlier. One day, returning from the investment house where she worked, McVay Hughes, dressed in a business suit, decided to stop in at the downtown offices of the New York Public Interest Research Group (NYPIRG), an advocacy organization founded by Ralph Nader, who had been a classmate of her father's at Princeton in the 1950s. She didn't realize how out of place her business attire would look among the jeans and sneakers that were the dress code at the nonprofit group's office. Regardless, she was interested in what they were doing and wondered if there was some way she could help. With her background in business and engineering, she was well suited to take over the group's fuel oil purchase program, a cooperative effort to buy discounted home heating oil and pass along the savings to needy families. When the job was formally offered, she took it. Later she helped run NYPIRG's lead abatement program, eventually coauthoring a residents' guide called "Get the Lead Out." When she found out that asthma among city kids was a growing health concern, she started Asthmamoms.com, a web site that provided information and guidance to families dealing with asthma.

After her son Philip was born in 1991, and then Matthew in 1995, the downtown Manhattan community where the Hughes family lived became even more important to her. In 1997, McVay Hughes joined Community Board 1, the local liaison between downtown residents and city government. In New York City, community boards make decisions about liquor licenses, street fairs, and other local issues that, in the hothouse environment of Manhattan, can quickly become quite heated. McVay Hughes's dedication to her children was well known when it came to the community amenities that the financial district lacked. She believed that Wall Street could be the kind of 24/7 neighborhood where it was possible to put down deep roots and raise a family. Her one exception was education. She and Tom sent the boys to the Packer Collegiate Institute, a private school in Brooklyn with a 1-acre garden where they could get dirt under their fingernails.

On the morning the towers were attacked, McVay Hughes was in Brooklyn. She had taken the subway with her boys, then 9 and 5, and dropped them off at Packer Collegiate. But she had stayed to attend a session with the school's music teacher, to find out which instruments were available for students to study. To take advantage of a beautiful September morning at the beginning of the school year, she'd planned to walk back home, crossing the Brooklyn Bridge on foot. She had on her sneakers, and in her fanny pack she carried her driver's license and an American Express credit card. She did not have a cellphone then.

McVay Hughes had just started on her way when she heard that a plane had hit the trade center. She thought it surely was a small private plane that had gone off course. She couldn't see the towers and couldn't call anyone to find out what had happened, so she and a few friends continued their stroll. When they got to the bridge, a swarm of people came toward them from Manhattan. As the true scope of the disaster became clear, McVay Hughes immediately turned back toward the school to pick up the boys. She gathered them up and used a school phone to make sure that Tom, who worked at 99 Church Street, just a few blocks from the trade center, was safe. Then her practical side kicked in. She withdrew money from the bank and went to the hardware store to buy N95 dust masks. She made the boys wear the masks as she took them to the Brooklyn promenade overlooking New York Harbor and Lower Manhattan. They stood there in the blizzard of paper and ash that was raining down from the towers and gazed out toward their home. "I want you to see what's going on," she told them.[1] Even if they didn't quite understand what had happened, she wanted them to have some idea why they wouldn't be going home for a while.

The boys wouldn't sleep in their own beds for more than four months.

Although it wasn't damaged when the trade center fell, their building had been invaded by dust. The National Guard had evacuated all residents, but by breaking through the glass front doors, they opened a way for the dust to infiltrate the lobby and be tracked upstairs. As president of the building, Tom Hughes later had to negotiate for the common areas of the building to be professionally cleaned. Cleaning inside each apartment was left to the individual owners. Although McVay Hughes had shut the old copper-framed windows in her apartment when she had left that morning, they were far from air tight. A thick layer of grayish dust had seeped in and settled over everything. Luckily, the building's superintendent had acted quickly to shut down the central ventilation system, preventing even more dust from being blown into every apartment and all the common areas. Still, whatever dust had seeped in made the apartments unlivable.

Her training and professional experience, her work with lead paint and diesel fumes and asthma, and all that she had learned and put into practice until then led McVay Hughes to believe that the collapse had contaminated her home and her neighborhood. She was puzzled when Christie Whitman and Mayor Giuliani encouraged residents to return home and get on with their lives. The dust she saw everywhere, the acrid smells and throat-burning smoke, the news she read in the tabloids, just didn't correspond to what she heard the officials saying. She was urged to register with FEMA, and about a month after the attack, she did. An inspector from the agency came to check the conditions in the apartment. It already had been professionally cleaned, but when the inspector saw the cloth-covered white sofa in the living room, he smacked it hard. Dust billowed up. There's only way to be safe, he told her. Get rid of the sofa. It was fairly new, and she thought that dumping it would be wasteful. But when she saw that dust, she decided it had to go. She threw out other upholstered furniture, fabric curtains, and mattresses. All of the boys' stuffed animals went out, too, except for three special ones, which she put through the washing machine several times. She recalled what the FEMA inspector had told her when he saw the apartment. He had urged her to think twice before moving back. "He said, 'Ma'am, I used to be a firefighter down South. This is what you call a toxic fire,'" she said. He told her that being there would be unhealthy for everyone, but especially the boys. "If you have kids you should not return until the fires are out."

She had filed a disaster claim with FEMA for one air purifier. She ran it constantly and was surprised to find that the filter that was supposed to last six months became so clogged in two weeks that it needed to be replaced. That's when she decided to buy several more units, along with the filters to go with them.

It took a long while for McVay Hughes to be satisfied that the area was safe enough for her children to return. She had read Juan Gonzalez's columns, and she knew that Joel Kupferman's tests for asbestos had come back positive. As a member of the Lower Manhattan community board, she pressured City Hall to acknowledge that the contaminated air around ground zero endangered local residents and that many of them needed professional help cleaning up their apartments. One month after the collapse, she attended the first public meeting on health concerns. Others on the community board tried to discourage her from speaking out about the hazardous conditions. It would be unpatriotic to even bring up such things while the city was hurting, they said, and so many people had so much more to worry about. But she insisted.

Her building had a good insurance policy that paid for a top-to-bottom professional cleaning. Her own insurance replaced furniture and clothing that had to be discarded. But many other downtown residents didn't have such good coverage and couldn't afford to pay for the work themselves. Some lived in buildings whose landlords refused to cooperate, fearing that authorizing a cleanup would leave them legally liable if something went wrong. Those residents had turned to the EPA for help, but the agency told them it had no legal responsibility for indoor spaces. Nonetheless, in the days just after the attacks, the agency had come to understand the severity of the indoor contamination. After federal agents tracked dust into the lobby of its own building, just a few blocks up Broadway from McVay Hughes, the EPA undertook an extensive decontamination of its space.

A discussion of what needed to be done in Lower Manhattan had just gotten underway when New York City notified the EPA that it intended to handle the job itself. But how it was going to do so wasn't clear. New York City's Department of Environmental Protection claimed it had jurisdiction only over building exteriors. After complaints from residents about dust on building facades, the department started a large-scale effort to wash them. Finally, the city's Department of Health (under Mayor Michael R. Bloomberg, it was renamed the Department of Health and Mental Hygiene) acknowledged that the potential presence of contaminants inside residences constituted a public health hazard that needed to be addressed. But the way it responded only added to the confusion and increased the fear.

The city health department issued step-by-step guidelines for decontaminating apartments. It distributed pamphlets and posted notices on its website advising residents to use vacuum cleaners, mops, and wet rags for the job. The instructions were not very sophisticated, and they may well have violated city laws that require licensed asbestos removers to handle asbestos abatement. For years afterward, critics—led by Rep. Jerrold Nadler, a New York Democrat whose district covers most of Lower Manhattan, including ground zero—ridiculed the city for suggesting that residents facing hazardous contamination arm themselves with mops and wet rags.

The critics also raised alarms about the way the city reopened offices, businesses, and schools after the attacks. For some, the city's handling of the schools was a microcosm of the government response to the whole disaster and was marked just as strongly by lack of information, mistrust, and angry confrontation.

All New York City schools were closed on September 11. Seven in Lower Manhattan, which served more than 6,000 children, remained closed for weeks or months afterward. The classrooms stayed empty despite Giuliani's immediate response to the catastrophe, which was to ask the schools' chancellor, Harold O. Levy, to reopen them the following day to prove that the city was unbowed. But just as President Bush's advisers had warned him that reopening Wall Street too soon would be a disaster, Levy told Giuliani that the schools should not be reopened until they were thoroughly cleaned and proven safe. Students of the seven schools closest to ground zero were encouraged to attend classes in other schools until their own buildings were decontaminated. Some schools did not reopen until February 2002.

The biggest of those schools, with more than 3,000 students, was Stuyvesant High School, one of the city's most selective. Almost as soon as the students had fled on the morning of September 11, Stuyvesant had been taken over by the city's Office of Emergency Management, which held meetings there. The city used a nearby dock to load trade center debris onto barges bound for the reopened Fresh Kills landfill on Staten Island. Dump trucks loaded with twisted steel and pulverized concrete rumbled past the school 24 hours a day.

By October 9, under intense pressure to restore normalcy to New York, the emergency management office was ready to hand back control of Stuyvesant to the board of education. Levy went out of his way to prove that the building had been cleaned adequately and was safe. He told parents that air monitors had not found any significant amount of asbestos or other hazardous material, and he vowed that testing would continue for the rest of the year or longer. But soon after they returned to their desks, students complained of headaches, persistent coughing, and other symptoms of respiratory distress. After more testing, officials determined that the students actually weren't getting enough air. By keeping the school's windows closed and shutting air intakes to prevent the ground zero dust from recontaminating the school, they had inadvertently choked off the building's supply of fresh air. Carbon dioxide built up, causing headaches and other problems. The school principal, Stanley Teitel, reported that when the Board of Education sent a nurse to check on conditions, 57 students and 31 teachers went to see her. The Stuyvesant parents' association, however, said far more students than that felt ill, but the line to see the nurse grew so long that many got tired of waiting and left before being examined.[2]

The mistrust that had overshadowed the city's relationship with the responders had spread to the schools. Many Stuyvesant parents were themselves power players in New York City—finance executives, media managers, people who understood how to rally support for their cause. They demanded more rigorous testing and cleanup before they would allow their children to return, and they pressed the Board of Education for more resources. The city insisted that the schools were safe but nonetheless complied with requests for additional cleaning. Parents in some schools hired their own consultants and, later, their own lawyers. One group of parents tried to get a court injunction against the board. They resented being forced to choose between keeping their kids out of the reopened school (and, therefore, isolating them) or sending them into buildings that they felt could cause cancer in some of them decades into the future. Stuyvesant parents hired Richard Ben-Veniste, the Watergate lawyer, to represent them before the board. By challenging the board, the parents in some schools were able to delay their children's return by at least a month. Stuyvesant parents had to settle for closing the school in mid-July 2002 for a comprehensive six-week cleanup.

Despite the precautions and several surveys indicating that the majority of parents felt the city had done all it could, some students came down with serious illnesses, including Hodgkin's disease, that were blamed on the dust although there was no scientific proof of any link. Still, worried parents continued to demand more information about what was happening to their children. Few satisfactory answers came.

Nor were residents satisfied that their condos and co-ops had been made safe. Those with the means to have their own buildings cleaned and tested were horrified to find that even after the visible dust was gone, their apartments still were contaminated because the dust had gone under beds, behind bookcases, and in the louvers of air vents. "Suddenly, the idea of dust bunnies under the bed had a whole new meaning," McVay Hughes recalled. Residents took their findings to Sen. Hillary Clinton and other officials, who demanded the EPA do something.

Clinton understood that she was facing an uncooperative Republican administration that seemed to consider lingering problems at ground zero a rebuke of its claim that the terrorists would not win. Recognition of disease, or persistent danger, would tarnish the administration's success in showing the terrorists how resilient the city, and the country, could be. By ignoring anything that was contrary, the administration was holding up its own "Mission Accomplished" sign at ground zero.

As frightened residents grew increasingly concerned about the extent of the contamination they were left to clean, they found Senator Clinton to be a willing listener. Since taking office early in 2001, following a campaign in which she was called a carpetbagger, she hadn't strongly connected with any New York issue. This was different. She had made her way to ground zero soon after the attacks and quickly immersed herself in the fight to win billions for New York's reconstruction. She listened to the health concerns of the unions and others who represented responders working on the pile, and she worked hard to get them adequate medical attention. In a political sense, ground zero also meant that she could go toe to toe with the Bush White House and the Republican establishment she had been fighting for so long. She had walked the tattered streets of ground zero with her one-time and potential future rival, Mayor Giuliani. Clinton sometimes wore a dust mask and later said she had been certain from the beginning that the smoke and dust wasn't good for anyone. As fears about the effects of the dust mounted, she became more involved and seemed to realize that she had found an effective way to defy the Bush administration; to stand apart from the Republicans who were running the city, state, and federal governments; and to begin to build a base for an eventual run for the Democratic nomination for president. In ground zero health, she would have a perfect foil to Giuliani's claim to be America's mayor. Contaminated schools, poisoned offices, and apartments where babies crawled along carpets that could be laced with asbestos fibers all would counter Giuliani's claims about securing the city's future the way no one else could.

For five months following the attack on the towers, the EPA did not test indoor air anywhere in Lower Manhattan, insisting that it was the city's responsibility, a position that elected officials and local residents disputed. They cited various federal directives that seemed to make clear that in the response to such an attack, the EPA, with its expertise, was empowered to take the lead in handling contamination, whether outdoors or inside. Soon after the attacks, local elected officials—including Rep. Nadler, Rep. Carolyn Maloney, Sen. Clinton, and Sen. Charles Schumer—formed a task force and demanded answers about the hazards facing residents, students, and downtown workers. Within days of their first meeting, the officials ordered an independent assessment of contamination in downtown residences.

When the results came back in mid-October, they showed cause for alarm. Concentrations of asbestos found in dust samples and in the air within apartments were significantly elevated. Any movement—even someone plopping onto a sofa—would propel the thin fibers back into the air. Analysts issued a bleak warning, urging that, unless proven otherwise by testing, "all dust should be assumed to be asbestos-containing,"[3] and that removal should be done only by trained professionals. At a city council hearing a few weeks later, Dr. Philip Landrigan of Mount Sinai testified that children's exposure to trade center dust should be minimized. He urged that a registry of children potentially exposed to the dust be created, to monitor their health and pick up potentially harmful trends as quickly as science permitted.

As revelations about the apparent disparity between the EPA's assurances and the actual results of tests became known, residents took their complaints to the EPA's national ombudsman, Robert Martin (a member of the Makah Indian Nation, he wore a business suit but kept his long hair in a ponytail). Early in 2002, Martin held public hearings into the EPA's conduct. At the hearings, the agency was sharply criticized for turning its back on residents and passing the buck to the city, which clearly wasn't capable of testing and cleaning the interiors of hundreds of buildings. The city's environmental protection commissioner at the time, Joel A. Miele, admitted as much, saying his department was basically a "water and sewer agency," without either the expertise or the equipment to handle a massive cleanup. Despite the EPA's assurances that the air was safe, warnings had been issued the day after the attacks in a memo to the EPA by Dr. Edwin M. Kilbourne, associate administrator of the federal Agency for Toxic Substances and Disease Registry. When the White House asked for a fact sheet on asbestos for the public, Kilbourne wrote to the director of biopreparedness and response at the Centers for Disease Control, saying it was far too early to even think about letting people back into Lower Manhattan. "[We] are concerned about even being asked to write a document for the public about re-entry at this point. Does this mean that unrestricted access to the WTC vicinity is imminent?" Kilbourne, a world-renowned epidemiologist, felt that the 4 percent asbestos that had been found in some early samples constituted a "substantial concentration," but he feared there was more than just asbestos to worry about. "Contaminant groups of concern include acid gases, volatile organic compounds, and heavy metals," he wrote. He was worried because the White House hadn't even asked about them.[4]

At around the same time Kilbourne sent that warning, Whitman was assuring New Yorkers that her agency was prepared to do everything in its power to ensure their safety. She told *Newsweek* magazine, "Everything will be vacuumed that needs to be, and filters will be cleaned. We're not going to let anybody into a building that isn't safe. And these buildings will be safe. The President has made it clear that we are to spare no expense on this one, and get this job done." Reassuring words, but hardly the way the agency proceeded when, in the following months, it repeatedly tried to duck responsibility for the indoor cleanup.

At the two-day ombudsman hearings early in 2002, the EPA had refused to show up or testify, convinced that it would not get a fair hearing. Martin sent a letter to the Region II administrator, Jane M. Kenny, stating that Stuyvesant and other schools were being recontaminated, a problem that "must be addressed immediately." Martin followed up with a long memo outlining the conclusions of his investigation into the agency's ground zero response and made several recommendations, among them that the EPA use its authority under the National Contingency Plan and President Clinton's Directive #62, to clean all the buildings—inside and out—that had been contaminated by trade center dust.

By this time, Martin and Whitman were engaged in an all-out struggle for control of the ombudsman's office, a spat that predated September 11. Since he had been hired for the position in 1992, Martin had intervened in many individual cases on behalf of local communities involved in EPA hazardous waste and Superfund programs. He had gotten toxic wastes removed, residents relocated, and pesticides investigated. As an independent representative of the communities, he had often pressured the EPA to be more transparent and to respond more quickly to the community concerns. But during the Bush administration, Martin's activism rubbed some the wrong way. The EPA under Whitman had started to push back, seeking a way to rein him in. She decided to move the duties of the ombudsman's office to the office of the Inspector General for the

EPA, essentially bringing it into the EPA's own house and truncat-
ing its independence. Martin fought back, lining up congressional
support to remain independent. It wasn't enough, and in April
2002, Whitman succeeded in her plans to take control of the
ombudsman's office. In protest, Martin resigned.

That same month, under growing community pressure, Whitman
formed a special task force to look into the issue of contaminated
indoor air. In late April, Bloomberg asked the EPA to take the lead on
indoor air, and in May, the city, along with the EPA, announced the
start of a voluntary cleanup program paid for with federal funds.
When she outlined the program, Jane Kenny, the regional administrator, said that testing and scientific analysis made it clear that residents weren't facing any immediate risks from dust in their homes.
The agency was moving ahead with a program because "people
should not have to live with uncertainty about their futures." She
stated, flat out, "There is no emergency here."

The World Trade Center disaster was not the first calamity in
which the EPA was expected to take charge of indoor space as well as
the air, soil, and water outdoors. In Libby, Mont., a town contaminated by tailings from an asbestos mining operation, Whitman had
just a few days before 9/11 told residents and local businesses that the
EPA would protect them from ever having to assume the cost of
cleaning up their own homes.

In New York, the federal agency became a reluctant participant
in the widening ground zero cleanup. Pressure from the ombudsman,
local officials, and the increasingly well-organized residents themselves left little choice but to step in. The EPA contracted with the
New York City Department of Environmental Protection and the
city's health department to undertake the cleaning of thousands of
apartments and residential common areas. The EPA itself would handle the analysis of air and dust samples from the buildings.

Many New Yorkers saw the EPA's method of selecting those residences as a symbol of the agency's mishandling of the whole disaster.
Up to this time, the EPA had not done any kind of systematic testing
to determine the physical extent of the contamination. Although logic
and experience dictate that such testing should precede any serious
cleanup, neither the EPA nor any other agency had undertaken the

work. Instead of starting at ground zero and moving out in concentric circles while sampling for contaminants in apartments and offices (where the contaminants would be sheltered from the rain and wind that had washed away some of the hazards on the streets) until none were found, the agency relied on visual evidence from aerial photographs along with anecdotal information to set the boundaries of the cleanup program at Canal Street, the broad commercial strip that cuts across Lower Manhattan about a mile north of ground zero. Any resident or landlord below Canal Street could ask to participate. Even though a number of independent surveys found significant contamination in buildings several blocks north of Canal Street and in parts of Brooklyn, those residents were out of luck. If they wanted their residences cleaned, they'd have to foot the bill—which Martin estimated could run as high as $10,000, not including the cost of testing to make sure it had been done right.

When the federally funded cleanups began, crews hired by the city showed up with vacuum cleaners, mops, and rags to wipe up visible dust and then test to make sure the contaminants were gone. Many of the workers were immigrants without legal documents who had little or no training in handling asbestos-containing dust. They worked in jeans and T-shirts, often without respirator masks. They wiped down surfaces and vacuumed where they could—hardly the kind of cleanup the EPA recommends for loose asbestos fibers. It was a half-hearted approach that gave the agency the right to say it had responded. But it was doomed to failure. Multifamily residential buildings were treated as an aggregate of individual units rather than a single, interconnected system. Because the program was voluntary, it could not guarantee that contaminated material had been removed from an entire building, no matter how vigorously an individual apartment had been scrubbed. This led to the real possibility that even apartments that had been cleaned could be contaminated again by dust from the apartment next door or down the hall that had not been cleaned. Common spaces such as lobbies and hallways also could spread dust through the rest of the building if not cleaned properly. And just as a person's lungs and circulatory system can carry dangers throughout the body, heating systems and ventilation ducts could spread contamination through every apartment in a building. Some residents refused to participate, and many landlords, worried about potential liability, did not let the cleaning crews in.

Some of the earliest health studies undertaken at this time gave residents ample reason for concern. Dr. Anthony M. Szema, a professor of medicine at Stony Brook School of Medicine on Long Island who had been following children with asthma in New York's Chinatown for several years, looked at how exposure to the dust had affected those children.[5] He found a significant increase in the number of times kids with asthma who lived within 5 miles of ground zero went to the doctor in the year after the attacks. They also received more asthma prescriptions, indicating that the dust had significantly worsened their conditions. Independently, researchers from Mount Sinai found that, among 187 women who were pregnant on September 11 (including 12 who were inside the towers that day but escaped before the collapse), there was a twofold greater risk of low birth-weight babies at delivery, which raised concern about their future growth.[6]

And Joan Reibman, the NYU pulmonologist, worked with the New York State Department of Health and the New York Academy of Medicine to canvass 2,166 residents of Lower Manhattan in the months immediately following the attacks.[7] Because mail delivery had been interrupted, the researchers went door to door to question some residents in their apartments. Their medical conditions were compared with those of a control group living more than a mile away from ground zero. Reibman found that the residents of Lower Manhattan who said that before 9/11 they were healthy were significantly more likely to report coughing, wheezing, and shortness of breath after the attacks than were those who lived uptown. People who had asthma and breathing problems before 9/11 reported that their symptoms had gotten worse and that they were forced to use asthma medications more often. Based on what she found in the limited polling she did, Reibman expanded her asthma clinic at Bellevue Hospital to treat residents who had developed respiratory symptoms after being exposed to the dust. She also agreed to see the undocumented (and uninsured) immigrant workers who had cleaned the apartments.

By the time the voluntary cleanup ended in summer 2003, only a small portion of more than 20,000 downtown residences had been tested. The EPA analyzed samples from 4167 apartments in 453 buildings in Lower Manhattan.[8] The agency also tested samples from 793 common areas in 144 buildings. But it did not attempt to clean any of the 330 office buildings, stores, warehouses, and schools below Canal Street. Nonetheless, the EPA touted the results as proof that there was little or no danger in the air. Only about 40 apartments, or 1 percent of the total tested, had asbestos contamination above the agency's own standard for long-term risk. The program had lasted two years and cost $37.9 million. Of that amount, $7.5 million went to the EPA itself to cover oversight and sample analysis. The rest, $30.4 million, went to pay the cleaning contractors.

But what Catherine McVay Hughes and other residents found most worrisome was that the cleaning crews had never gotten around to the hard-to-reach places, such as behind bookshelves or under beds, where asbestos dust could have settled into carpets or seeped under floorboards or wood trim. Parents knew instinctively that the space beneath a bed was anything but inaccessible for little children, who could use it as a hiding place, a fort, or a shelter during a thunderstorm. Moreover, the testing methods used to determine whether there was asbestos in the apartments were inadequate. Fibers that settled into carpets and drapes had to be aggressively moved around with a high-powered fan to be detected. That didn't happen.

A report by the EPA's Office of Inspector General sharply criticized the cleanup, taking issue with its voluntary nature, the way it used inadequate testing equipment, the way it ignored commercial buildings where people worked, and generally, its inability to achieve the minimum standards needed to ensure pubic health.[9] The inspector general's office made several recommendations. It urged the agency to verify that apartments that had been cleaned and or tested had not been recontaminated. It also called for the EPA to get ready for the next emergency by developing clear guidelines for handling indoor contamination.

With so much criticism heaped on the initial cleanup effort, an effort that the majority of downtown residents had ignored, the residents again turned to Senator Clinton. At the time, President Bush nominated Michael Leavitt, who had replaced Whitman at the EPA, for secretary of the U.S. Department of Health and Human Services. During the confirmation process, Clinton made it clear that she would block Leavitt's nomination unless the EPA responded to the mounting fears of downtown residents. James. L. Connaughton, chairman of the President's Council on Environmental Quality, signaled that the administration was willing to meet Clinton's demands, even if there was little scientific need for more testing. In a letter to Clinton, Connaughton wrote that the agency was willing to take certain steps "to provide greater collaboration in ongoing efforts to monitor the situation for New York residents and assure them of their current safety," as if their safety were assured.[10]

The EPA agreed to set up a panel of technical experts to "recommend any steps to further minimize the risks associated with the aftermath of the World Trade Center attacks." The panel included individuals who had been studying the 9/11 dust since 2001, including Dr. David Prezant of the fire department and Dr. Paul Lioy of the environmental institute at Rutgers. After protests, the agency also agreed to include on the panel a single liaison to the Lower Manhattan residential community: Catherine McVay Hughes.

McVay Hughes was surprised to be asked to participate in a panel filled with geologists, medical doctors, and technical experts. Her own scientific training was limited to hydraulic geology and what she had picked up at NYPIRG's lead abatement programs, although the difficult months since the trade center had been destroyed had given her a crash course in chemistry, physics, and toxicology. She was committed to representing the families of Lower Manhattan, along with the workers, the students, and the visitors who were living with the remnants of the dust clouds.

The panel itself would not have the power to decide what should be done next. Its role was to simply advise the EPA. Given the high profile of its work, the pressure from Clinton, and the EPA's urgent need to shore up its own damaged reputation, it was widely thought that the panel's recommendations could be rejected only at the agency's peril.

However, it became clear from the outset that action wouldn't be the panel's trademark. Unwieldy at 15 members tapped from positions all over the country, and meeting in public gatherings in Lower

Manhattan not far from ground zero with an uncertain mandate from an agency that had an indelicate connection to the problem, the panel was put together like a bureaucratic camel, and everyone knew it. Its first meeting in spring 2004 had to be halted soon after it began because the auditorium in the old Customs Building in Lower Manhattan where it was being held sprang a leak. Water flooded down the stairs, and though there was no panic, it was generally taken as a sign of just how unpredictable and difficult to control the entire process would be.

For residents and downtown workers who rarely had a chance to face Bush administration officials, the panel's meetings became a prickly forum for venting years of anger and frustration. Responding to the outpouring of emotion, the panel agreed to go beyond the EPA's central promise of retesting already-cleaned apartments. Members listened to residents and office workers testify that they had been misled, misinformed, ignored, and abused. "It's all very well to talk about the recontamination issue, but you haven't begun the work of finding out what was contaminated in the first place,"[11] testified Robert Gulack, an attorney who said he had developed asthma from working in a downtown building that had not been cleaned properly. Downtown resident Barbara Caporale told the panel, "We're tired of being considered collateral damage,"[12] as she pleaded for federal help to extend far beyond the arbitrary Canal Street boundary. Listening to the passion and fear in their voices, the board agreed to broaden its mandate into other areas of the city and to determine more stringent levels of abatement than the original program. But first it had to settle a basic question of science.

From the first moments of the catastrophe, asbestos had been fingered as the worst villain, but as Paul Lioy well knew, the trade center dust that he kept in his cold room consisted of many different substances besides asbestos. To expand the cleaning program, there would have to be a way to determine whether any hazardous material that was encountered had indeed come from the trade center site. Looking for traces of asbestos in a crowded old city such as New York would be an insurmountable task because so many different sources of asbestos fibers exist—pipe and boiler insulation, car and truck brake pads, roofing material, and more. Merely finding asbestos in the settled dust of an apartment would not be proof it had come from the trade center. Similarly, lead could not easily be singled out as having come from computer monitors and TV screens at ground zero. Dangerous amounts of lead dust could be found in any apartment with lead-based paints. The EPA knew it would find those contaminants if it looked for them, and it understood that following that trail would lead down an endless rabbit hole costing billions and lasting years. The agency also had to be aware that unless it discovered a way to distinguish trade center material from common urban dust, the cleanup program would leave the impression that the tower's destruction had, indeed, created a public health hazard of immense proportions, which was the opposite of the agency's position.

Scientists on the technical panel agreed that some other kind of distinguishing marker or unique signature was needed. After studying different materials for more than a year, they settled on slag wool, the fire-retardant coating sprayed on steel beams in the towers after asbestos insulation was no longer used. The panel believed that if slag wool showed up in dust samples from the residential, institutional, and commercial buildings within that test zone, the EPA could conclude that they had been contaminated by the trade center disaster and would perform a cleanup free of charge.

Moreover, the panel recommended a way to eliminate the uncertainty left by the earlier cleanup. Using statistical analysis, it proposed sampling 150 buildings in a measured grid twice the size of the original, extending above Canal Street and over to parts of Brooklyn. If slag wool were found in the test buildings, they would be cleaned, along with all other buildings in the zone. This time, commercial buildings would be included and entire floors of buildings would be decontaminated. When the boundaries of the cleanup area were established, the panel wanted to offer a far more thorough cleaning than before, extending to the areas under beds and behind heavy furniture. Crews would be instructed to look for four different contaminants of concern: asbestos, lead, vitreous (fiberglass) fibers, and polycyclic aromatic hydrocarbons (soot from uncontrolled fires). The air testing also would be more aggressive, with powerful fans used to stir up remaining fibers so that delicate testing instruments could detect them.

It was an ambitious extension of the first cleanup, and as the panel broadened its scope, residents continued to demand more, as if the panel could undo all the mistakes of the past. The EPA was not comfortable with the mission creep. But before any decision could be made, independent outside experts had to review the data used to justify a slag wool marker. The peer reviewers criticized the panel's conclusions. They believed that because slag wool was heavier than other elements in dust, it might not have traveled far, and its absence could give a false reading about whether World Trade Center dust was present.

By this time, Lioy and other panel members were becoming increasingly frustrated. The EPA was giving clear signs that no matter what the panel suggested, it was going to do things its own way. And certain groups of residents kept demanding more from the cleanup program, while attacking the panel members for being unresponsive. Lioy felt shell-shocked at the end of some of the meetings, where he was portrayed as representing a recalcitrant government agency that was digging in its heels no matter what New Yorkers said.

As residents continued to snipe at the panel, Prezant and another panel member, Jeanne Mager Stellman, from the Mailman School of Public Health at Columbia University, drew up an alternative plan that would dispense with testing and simply clean indoor spaces within a designated perimeter, assuming that any contaminants that were found should be removed, regardless of where they had originated. But the EPA wasn't interested. It was still on record as saying there wasn't anything to be worried about.

When the peer reviewers formally rejected the slag wool marker, chaos ensued. Some panel members accused the EPA of having deliberately sabotaged the effort by sending incomplete data for review. Others, including Lioy, argued that the reviewers had been tripped up by the way the material had been presented and that, with slight modifications, the slag wool studies could be accepted. But the EPA was impatient. The chairman of the panel, E. Timothy Oppelt, acting head of the EPA's Office of Research and Development, was scheduled to retire at the end of the year. He showed little enthusiasm for the panel's work continuing indefinitely. McVay Hughes was dumbstruck. She had believed that the EPA had initially planned on "doing the right thing" for downtown residents and workers. But after the slag wool setback, signs of goodwill vanished.

What came next stunned even the members of the expert panel and outraged the Lower Manhattan community. Oppelt announced that the EPA had rejected all the panel's recommendations. Instead, it would repeat the original voluntary cleanup program, with one catch. It would exclude apartments that had been cleaned before, obviating the possibility of doing what the agency had originally promised to do about determining the extent of recontamination. A few commercial buildings were included, but Brooklyn was left out again. The abridged program was given a budget of $7 million, the amount of money left over from the federal appropriation for the 2002–2003 program. It was a quick and easy accounting step intended to put a lasting end to the cleanup. After announcing the changes, Oppelt abruptly shut down the panel, thanked the members, and left for his retirement. Lioy, disappointed, told Oppelt it seemed clear that the EPA "felt this panel was the child of a lesser god" and strongly urged the agency to reconsider its decision. Prezant proposed a special one-day meeting to review modifications that would make the plan acceptable to the public and to the agency. Stellman called the new plan pointless. Downtown residents were the angriest, saying they felt betrayed by a process that only reaffirmed their belief that Washington didn't care.

McVay Hughes and all but two of the remaining members of the technical panel refused to endorse the plan. One member said publicly that he would not, under those circumstances, recommend that anyone participate in the second cleanup because doing so would accomplish nothing. Micki Siegel de Hernández, who represented the labor community, saw the EPA's decisions as a cynical move that reflected the worst aspects of Washington's mishandling of the September 11 response. "This plan is the Bush administration's plan," she said at the panel's last meeting. "This is not the panel's plan and this is not the community's plan."

By the time the technical panel was disbanded, the downtown community's anger toward Washington was palpable. Several fed-up residents had already banded together and, with help from Joel Kupferman, filed a class action lawsuit that accused Leavitt, Whitman, and the EPA of having endangered the public with false and misleading statements about safety around ground zero. The suit collected all the community's grievances against Whitman and her agency, contending that they amounted to "a shockingly deliberate indifference to human health." Although George W. Bush wasn't named in the suit, it was clear that they believed every decision had been directed by or cleared through the White House. A district court judge sided with the residents, calling Whitman's actions following the attacks "conscience shocking." But in 2008, a federal appeals court overturned the ruling and dismissed the suit against Whitman and her agency.[13]

The EPA had organized a semiformal reception for panel members following the disastrous last meeting. McVay Hughes skipped the event. She was greatly disappointed in the agency's actions and in the way the panel's advice had been dismissed. After cooling off with some friends, she walked back to her apartment on Broadway, eager to make sure her air purifiers were working properly.

When registration for the second EPA cleanup was opened to the public in 2007, turnout was just as poor as the panel members had predicted. The residents of just 183 downtown apartments out of the thousands eligible signed up for it, along with the owners of 21 residential and commercial buildings who wanted the EPA to test lobbies, corridors, and other common areas. By the time the samples were taken, seven years had passed since the towers had come down. Most of the samples were negative for asbestos and other hazards. With its budget of leftover dollars, the EPA eventually cleaned only 16 apartments and the common areas of 14 of the 21 buildings. Rep. Nadler called the program an absolute failure. He was so outraged that he demanded an investigation by the Government Accountability Office. After reviewing the unfortunate history of the program, the office found that the EPA had obscured the results of its first cleanup, depriving residents of valuable information about the hazards in their apartments. The report criticized the agency for not calculating a realistic budget for the second cleanup and simply using up the $7 million left over from the first program. Finally, the report found that the EPA had not done anything in the second program to correct the errors of the first—or to better prepare the agency to handle future disasters.

A short time after the technical panel's disbanding had caused such anguish in Lower Manhattan, McVay Hughes received a lumpy package in the mail from the EPA. Inside was a framed certificate honoring her for her work on the technical panel over the previous two years. The agency had used a padded shipping envelope, but not enough cushioning had been used to protect the glass on the picture frame. When McVay Hughes opened the package, glass shards fell out. She felt it was an appropriate metaphor for her experience with the EPA. The formation of the technical panel in 2004 had seemed like an important achievement, but the process had broken down and ended in a trust-breaking fiasco. "Any expectation that the right thing would be done was shattered," she said. "None of the goals that [the] EPA set out for the panel were realized. It was a public relations fiasco for the EPA and federal government. I think that the federal government was trying to wear the community down so that the will to find out the truth would diminish. However, in this case, it did not work."

In the years since, she has often stood before the big copper-clad windows of her apartment, watching the reconstruction of ground zero grind ahead slowly. At times she has wondered about whether the EPA ever really did intend to do the right thing for the people downtown or was merely placating all those who were angry and frustrated. She is thankful that her boys are healthy, that her husband has not suffered any ill health effects, and that, despite being diagnosed with reactive airways disorder, she can still breathe normally if she just avoids construction sites and other dirty environments. The family's lucky 13th-floor loft still feels like home to them. And although McVay Hughes never received any compensation from FEMA except to cover the cost of one of the six air purifiers she keeps running all the time, she is grateful for the FEMA inspector who cautioned her not to bring back her family until the fires were completely extinguished. But she worries constantly about her downtown neighbors who haven't been so lucky, such as one woman who came down with pancreatic cancer and another who can't walk more than a few feet without stopping to catch her breath, and all the others who felt abandoned by Washington at the time of their greatest need.

Endnotes

[1]Personal interview, 1 June 2009.

[2]Bartlett, Sarah, and John Petrarca, *Schools of Ground Zero*, American Public Health Association and Healthy Schools Network, Inc., 2002.

[3]Chatfield, Eric J. and John R. Kominsky, Ground Zero Task Force, "Characterization of Particulate Found in Apartments after Destruction of the World Trade Center," October 12, 2001.

[4]Gonzalez, Juan, "Doc's WTC Note: Don't Hurry Back," *New York Daily News*, 28 October 2003, p. 19.

[5]Szema, A.M., Khedkar, M., Maloney, P.F., et al., "Clinical Deterioration in Pediatric Asthmatic Patients After September 11, 2001," *The Journal of Allergy and Clinical Immunology* 113, no. 3 (March 2004): 420–426.

[6]Berkowitz, Gertrud S., Wolf, M.S., Jancvic, T.M., et al., "The World Trade Center and Intrauterine Growth Restriction," *The Journal of the American Medical Association* 290, no. 5 (August 2003): 596–598.

[7]Lin, Shao, Reibman, Joan, Bowers, James, et al., "Upper Respiratory Symptoms and Other Health Effects Among the Residents Living Near the Former World Trade Center After the September 11 Disaster," *Epidemiology* 15, no. 4 (July 2004).

[8]U.S. Environmental Protection Agency, Region 2, *World Trade Center Residential Dust Cleanup Program: Final Report, December 2005*. Available at www.epa.gov/wtc/finalreport/pdfs/full_final_report.pdf.

[9]U.S. Environmental Protection Agency, Office of Inspector General, *EPA's Response to the World Trade Center Collapse: Challenges, Successes, and Areas for Improvement*, (21 August 2003), 47.

[10]Read into the Congressional Record, 27 October 2003, 13, 250.

[11]EPA Technical Panel hearing, 31 March 2004.

[12]*Ibid.*

[13]*Benzman, et al v. Whitman, et al.* United States Court of Appeals for the Second Circuit, April 22, 2008, Docket Number 06-1166.

Part III

Doubt

9

Such money grubbers as these

On September 11, 2001, a Republican triumvirate controlled the White House, the State House in Albany, and City Hall in New York City. But with the exception of Republican Vito Fossella of Staten Island (the city's most conservative borough), New York City's congressional delegation was chock full of Democrats. This political and ideological gap made it all but inevitable that there would be a deep chasm between the parties, even over something as tragic and non-partisan as ground zero.

Besides Sen. Hillary Clinton, those who had most aggressively demanded that Washington pay attention to the dust were the unlikely pair of Rep. Carolyn Maloney and Rep. Jerrold Nadler. Both were outspoken critics of the Bush administration, and both—by their attitudes and their accents—were children of New York, even though Maloney had been born in North Carolina and had managed to modulate her moderate Southern drawl with brash New York overtones. Maloney, whose district included the silk stocking Upper East Side as well as parts of Queens, is tall, blonde, and loud. Nadler, a born New Yorker who graduated from Stuyvesant High School and Columbia University, and who spent 16 years in the State Assembly before going to Congress in 1993(the same year as Maloney), is short, round, and aggressively insistent on getting attention for his district, which includes ground zero. The two of them, and their staffs, doggedly challenged an uninterested Washington to assume responsibility for what they argued time and again had been not just an attack on New York, but a deadly strike at the heart of the nation, requiring a response not just from the city and its allies, but from the whole country by way of Washington. Their most powerful weapons were outrage, anger, and, at times, invective and exaggeration.

Clinton, Maloney, and Nadler were practiced in the art of political denunciation. All three were Capitol Hill veterans who understood the power of sound bites, punchy quotes, and a measure of scorn. They freely tossed around the term *hero*, using it to refer to the tens of thousands who had flocked to the pile, as well as to those who died in the attack. For them, there often was little difference between the firefighters who scrambled over the debris looking for survivors, individuals who came months later when it was strictly a demolition site offering unlimited overtime, and those who, driven by their own desires, came to ground zero and did little more than hand out water bottles. All were heroes, all deserving of the government's attention, all liable to have become sick because of the administration's mishandling of the unprecedented rescue and recovery operation. There was little sense of reckoning that if everyone was a hero, then none could truly be heroes. Equally, no distinction was drawn among their symptoms. One responder's runny nose became the moral equivalent of another's scarred lungs; one's skin rash equal to another's burned thorax.

In front of the cameras, the elected officials denounced the Bush administration's distracted attitude toward what they believed was New York's health emergency. Nadler and Maloney both regularly appeared at rallies with responders, condemning the White House for its failure to act. Some of the hard work of forcing a reluctant administration to acknowledge that the cleanup had come at a tragic price fell to their staffs, who spent long hours digging through documents, reaching out to angry responders all over the nation, and focusing attention on a problem that, despite the rhetoric shaping it as an attack on America, most people in Washington considered a local issue.

Although the entire New York delegation played a role in this effort, Maloney and her staff often led the charge in getting the government to provide some measure of healthcare for those who needed it. Hundreds of her constituents died in the attacks, and on that first morning, she had worried about several close friends who worked inside the twin towers. She had driven back to New York in a panic that day and was at ground zero almost immediately, breathing in the dust and seeing through teary eyes the impact it was having on those who worked there. She tirelessly crusaded on behalf of the responders, appearing with them so often over the years that she came to know many by their first names. Maloney was supported by a strong staff, led by Benjamin Chevat, her chief of staff, and legislative aide Edward Mills, who demonstrated the two-tiered way Washington works. On one level, the cameras focus on the elected officials. But behind the scenes, the grunt work that goes into the passage of controversial legislation gets done by those whose names never appear on a ballot.

Chevat, an attorney and former Chief of Staff to the Speaker of the New York State Assembly, has worked the trading floor of persuasion his whole adult life. Mills started as a junior staffer in Maloney's office. Each had a personal stake in the events of September 11. Chevat's mother, Edith, 77 at the time of the attacks, was a resident of Battery Park City, a housing development built on the edge of the Hudson River just to the west of the World Trade Center. A former New York City school teacher, she lived on the 19th floor of a building little more than a block from the twin towers. On the morning of 9/11, Ben Chevat was in Maloney's Capitol Hill office when he first heard the news. He called his mother to tell her she needed to get out of that building. She had made her way to the street when the first tower turned to dust. She and other Battery Park City residents were evacuated by ferry to New Jersey. When Chevat finally was able to visit her in New York a few weeks later, he saw that debris from the towers had ripped a gash in her building.

Mills found out that a friend from his hometown of Hull, Mass., had driven to New York that night to help in whichever way he could. He'd spent days on the pile and later developed respiratory problems. And just as it was for so many other ground zero volunteers, he wasn't covered by state workers' compensation programs.

Schumer and Clinton helped secure an initial commitment of $20 billion from President Bush to get New York back on its feet. The money covered cleanup, reconstruction, and compensation for the families of the dead, but not, at first, health monitoring or medical care for those who survived. Schumer later left most of the health issues to Clinton, who negotiated the release of the first $10 million for monitoring after meeting with Ed Ott and other labor leaders. But New Yorkers quickly found out that what the Bush administration promised about ground zero, it didn't always deliver. Many suspected that the reason for that recalcitrance went back to the first days after the attacks when the message seemed to be that there was no danger. Authorizing money for sick workers directly contradicted that stance. That made getting anything—money, programs, attention—a matter of putting pressure on Washington and keeping it there until promises were kept.

Sniping about the federal response began almost immediately. And because New York's senators and Manhattan's representatives were Democrats and the House, Senate, and White House were controlled by Republicans during most of the Bush years, the sniping inevitably turned partisan. Nadler could see the way things in his own district were being handled, and he did not like what he saw. After Joel Kupferman's early investigation of the contaminants in the dust, Nadler took on the issue with evangelical passion, working with the EPA ombudsman until that office was dismantled, and then taking charge himself. While Nadler largely focused on the cleanup, Maloney's office took greater control of the health issues. Even at this early date, the trade center cough was a widely recognized medical phenomenon, at least outside Washington, and increasing numbers of responders were showing up at Mount Sinai with worsening respiratory symptoms.

Washington reacted with a yawn. By the first anniversary of the attacks, the Bush administration was threatening to rescind $90 million that had been set aside for responder health programs. Many Republicans couldn't understand why local workers' compensation laws couldn't take care of those who were legitimately injured. With Clinton trying to gain ground on the Senate side to keep the money in the budget, it became clear that the support that might have been expected for such a request—from New York City and the state of New York—was strangely absent. Gov. George E. Pataki supported the idea of a trade center health registry and didn't think anything more was needed, even though the registry was not designed to provide treatment and never would. What the registry could do was track a large group of responders and monitor whether they improved or got sicker. At City Hall, Mayor Michael Bloomberg, at one time a registered Republican, early in his administration had taken a hard stance on the health issue. Mindful of the city's potential liability, he repeatedly insisted that it was imprudent to link any illness to contact with the dust unless there was hard scientific proof. If the city were seen lobbying Washington for treatment money, it could be interpreted as an admission that, in fact, people who had worked on the pile had been sickened by the dust, inviting lawsuits.

Washington already was aware of the tremendous liability connected with any admission of culpability. In November, 2001, Rudy Giuliani had bypassed the congressional delegation and gone directly to the administration with a specific request for liability protection for the city that was similar to what had been given the airlines after 9/11 to avoid bankruptcy. That blanket protection allowed the families of victims to surrender their right to sue the airlines in exchange for monetary compensation from a September 11th Victim Compensation Fund. Although Giuliani had repeatedly insisted that there was no lasting danger from the dust, he had been told that the contractors who worked for the city were worried about liability. The city's own advisors determined that the city needed more than $1 billion of coverage beyond its own self-insurance reserves, and the contractors represented additional liability, depending on the extent of their own insurance coverage. But the city was unable to buy much more in the commercial market. The lack of an agreement on liability had kept the city from signing a formal contract with the four major construction companies or the more than 100 subcontractors who worked at the site for the entire nine months of the $225 million cleanup.

Giuliani returned from Washington with a verbal commitment for $1 billion from the Federal Emergency Management Agency (FEMA) to establish a unique insurance company with just one client—the city of New York—that would be protected against lawsuits arising from the cleanup for a period of 25 years. That was based on a general understanding that, as it had been for soldiers exposed to Agent Orange during the Vietnam War, some illnesses might take decades to develop. The agreement was formally announced in March 2002, with FEMA recognizing the expense as a part of the cost of the city's recovery. The insurance company, called a captive because it dealt with only one client, had to be chartered to operate in New York State, and that required special legislation in Albany that took 18 months.

Maloney realized that unless the House stood up for them, the workers would have no one with power in Washington on their side.

The labor unions had already pleaded for the monitoring program at Mount Sinai, but the administration found it was possible to ignore them and to take away with one hand the money it had given with the other. Within five months of the attacks and the President's pledge of unconditional support, the administration showed another side of its attitudes about responder health. By then, a little more than half of the promised $20 billion in federal aid had been appropriated. When the new federal budget was delivered in February, it included no additional aid for New York. The White House budget director, Mitch Daniels, said he was going to count $5.5 billion for victims' compensation as part of the rescue package, an accounting maneuver that went against the basic understanding of everyone involved about what the administration had promised. When Maloney, Nadler, and others in the delegation complained, Daniels dropped all pretense and laid out his true feelings about New York's problem. "It's strange to me to treat this as a little money-grubbing game," he scoffed.[1]

New Yorkers didn't like being called money grubbers. Maloney and her staff responded by doing what they had done before when faced with blatant hostility: build a case based on documents and data. They put together a chart showing where the money from the promised $20 billion had gone and where it had never appeared, despite promises.[2] It was a way to put pressure on an administration that, at least when it came to ground zero, felt it could ignore its promises. Clearly, the White House was trying to avoid being drawn into a messy and open-ended environmental and health problem that would only slow down the nation's recovery from the 9/11 attacks. Maloney made the chart available to reporters, who wrote about the missing dollars, embarrassing the administration and, importantly, keeping the issue alive.

That process—maintaining vigilance, holding the administration accountable, leaking information to the press, and keeping the controversy alive—became standard operating procedure for the Maloney team. They fell back on it time and again over ensuing years, relying on the strategy to take the place of the allies who normally would have stood up for the city but were now silent. Other House staffers had warned the Maloney office against taking on the Bush administration without adequate support from home. "Informally, they were like 'Come on, do you really want to do this?'" recalled a staffer. "They said, 'It's going to be really expensive and Pataki isn't even pushing for it. He's got the Registry and can't understand why you need anything else.'"

Maloney felt there was no alternative but to push on. The first obstacle was the administration's plan to renege on the $90 million pledge for responder health issues. About $25 million of that money was supposed to go to Dr. David Prezant's monitoring and treatment program at the fire department, with a similar amount for Mount Sinai's World Trade Center efforts, along with other programs, including outreach for police. Maloney sent signed letters from the delegation to President Bush in August 2002 urging that the money be restored. Additional letters went out in October and January asking for the budget to be restored. They weren't getting much traction on the issue until her staff came up with the idea of inviting sick responders to attend the President's State of the Union address. In January 2003, members of Congress from New York and New Jersey gave gallery passes to nine ground zero workers so they could plead their case in person. It took another year of lobbying and relentless pressure, but by March 2004, $81 million was available for Mount Sinai and other medical institutions in the New York area to fund a rigorous screening program. Still no money was available for treating workers with persistent symptoms.

The Democrats continued to press the issue, pointing out that not one cent of federal money had gone to provide the medical care the "heroes" needed. By August 2004, New Yorkers were again being called "money grubbers" for demanding aid. Once more, sick ground zero workers were invited to the State of the Union address, after which Maloney and Nadler introduced two critical pieces of legislation: one bill to provide treatment and another to extend the September 11th Victim Compensation Fund to cover workers on the pile whose illnesses had developed after the fund expired.

Those legislative efforts were doomed, but in 2005, an opportunity arose for the Democrats to get some of what they were looking for. The Bush 2006 budget proposal rescinded $125 million in federal funds that were to have been used to reimburse the state workers' compensation fund for awards to injured ground zero workers. It also would have provided some money for worker training. The congressional staffs mobilized—organizing rallies, transporting ground zero workers to Washington to testify, and trying their best to embarrass the administration into not cutting the funds. Maloney then added a new tactic: shaming the federal government for letting down its own workers. She went after a special program that had been set up to provide medical assistance to the thousands of federal workers who had been sent to New York during the recovery, or who had helped out simply because their offices had been located in lower Manhattan in 2001. Repeatedly requesting information about the program from the Department of Health and Human Services, Maloney's staff found out that fewer than 400 federal workers had been screened before the program, meant to provide ongoing monitoring for thousands, had simply disappeared. At Maloney's request, the Government Accountability Office (GAO) investigated. Its conclusion: The program had accomplished almost nothing. The Bush administration's agonizing response to Hurricane Katrina provided Maloney with an effective put-down. "If this administration can't even get a list of federal workers who worked at ground zero, let alone manage a program that treats their injuries, what have they been doing for the last four years?" she said in a statement released with the GAO report. "There is no way we can be confident of a sound response to Hurricane Katrina's health effects—or any future disaster, for that matter."

By the end of 2005, Maloney's strategy seemed to be working. The House not only restored the $125 million, but it provided the first federal dollars for treatment. Of the $125 million, $50 million would reimburse the state workers' compensation board for ground zero claims. In addition, $75 million was set aside for screening, monitoring, and treatment at Mount Sinai and other institutions, representing the first steady source of federal funds. Mount Sinai finally had the ability to offer the procedures, medications, and therapies that ailing ground zero workers expected.

As 2006 began, the contours of the health crisis grew increasingly complex. More than four years had passed since the attacks, and ever more workers and volunteers were registering with Mount Sinai for screening. Some also needed comprehensive medical treatment. This underscored a fundamental problem that the advocates would constantly have to contend with. It is fairly easy to connect physical

injuries such as a broken leg or the loss of a finger to a worksite accident. The worker compensation system files are full of such cases.
But it is substantially more difficult—and, in many instances, impossible—to prove that a respiratory illness or a disease such as pulmonary fibrosis or cancer, which could have many origins and take
many years to develop, was caused by a specific chemical exposure.
This left many workers out in the cold, even after a special
compensation program had been set up to help them.

The federal government has a long history of offering compensation to the victims of disasters, tragedies, and calamities. Among the
earliest federal compensation programs were payments made to
people who were victimized by the Whiskey Rebellion on the Pennsylvania frontier during George Washington's first term in 1794.
People who lost property in storms, floods, and fires, as well as
those caught in the path of the warring armies in the war of 1812,
received federal payment without much political dissension. Troubles followed, however, as victims became claimants, and expectations rose—along with the resentment of those who had suffered
some tragedy but were not covered by a government program.[3]

The September 11th Victim Compensation Fund was given an
unlimited budget to provide monetary compensation to the families of
those who had been killed or injured in Washington and New York that
day. A Washington lawyer who had experience in settling the Agent
Orange lawsuits, Kenneth R. Feinberg, was put in charge and given
the broadest prerogative to decide, in essence, how much each life was
worth.

Even amid the emotional tempest that followed the terror
attacks, there had been some mild disagreement about the September 11 fund. The victims of other recent disasters—primarily the
1995 bombing of the federal building in Oklahoma City, and the 1993
bombing at the trade center itself—had not received federal compensation. But patriotism and cooperation were the backdrop of the post-
9/11 moment. The criticisms were noted but then gently dismissed.
Nearly all the families of the 3,000 victims of the trade center, the
Pentagon, and the jet that came down in Shanksville, Penn., agreed to
accept the money Feinberg offered in exchange for surrendering
their right to sue the airlines.

But a lesser-known part of the fund's work saw Feinberg compensating people who were injured as a direct result of the attack. Those who had suffered burns, cuts, and broken bones during the first four days, and who reported the injury within a short time after it occurred, were considered victims. Feinberg's work, then, was to devise a way of calculating what each injury was worth.

That criteria didn't fit so neatly with respiratory injuries, which had quickly become the most prominent result of exposure to the dust. For these cases, Feinberg was not legally obliged to prove the injury was related to the disaster "beyond a reasonable doubt," as would have been the case in a courtroom. Instead, he looked for a preponderance of evidence that would lead to the conclusion, all else being the same, that the injured person probably had been hurt as a direct result of the disaster.

Some 1,300 people received awards from the fund for physical injuries such as burns or broken bones. Another 1,377, mostly recovery workers, had come to Feinberg with respiratory problems that had begun soon after their work on the pile.[4] Feinberg used broad discretion, asking for evidence of the first visit to a doctor as proof of the date the illness was noticed. But the fund stopped accepting applications at the end of 2003 and made all its payouts to the injured (totaling more than $1 billion) by the following June. By then, many recovery workers were only starting to develop symptoms. They were shut out of the fund.

For those people, the alternatives were to apply for state workers' compensation and enter the monitoring program at Mount Sinai or hospitals in the surrounding area, including the University of Medicine and Dentistry of New Jersey, where Sarah Atlas had been treated, and Stony Brook Hospital on Long Island, which took care of Mike Valentin. But until federal assistance became available in 2006, the hospitals could not offer treatment or cover the cost of prescriptions.

Despite facing stiff odds and the lingering suspicion in Washington and New York that there were frauds in the growing number of people who claimed to have been sickened by the dust, New York's congressional representatives kept fighting. Then, a few days into 2006, the fears of many New Yorkers seemed to be realized when it was widely reported that New York Police detective James Zadroga, who was just 34 years old, the highly decorated son of a veteran Polish-American police chief from New Jersey, had died of respiratory and cardiac failure. Zadroga had worked at ground zero.

In his own written account,[5] Zadroga recalled how he had been on his way back from an arraignment in New York City that morning and was making the long drive from Queens, where he was assigned to the Street Crimes Unit, to his home in a rural part of upstate New York, about 90 miles north of the city. He was about halfway there when he turned off his Kenny Chesney country music CD, turned on the radio, and heard the news about the World Trade Center. At home, his wife, Ronda, who was seven months pregnant, was just waking up. They turned on the television, uncertain how the events that were unfolding on the screen would affect them and the life they were trying to put together. She begged him not to go back to the city, but he knew it was his duty. He arrived at ground zero after the towers collapsed and was assigned to perimeter traffic. But he felt he could do more. He helped out where he could, securing buildings, working on the bucket brigade, or recovering human remains. He was caught in the dust cloud after Building 7 came down. In all, he spent 20 hours there that first day and into the next morning. In the following three weeks he accumulated 120 hours of overtime, along with his regular 12-hour shifts. He was exposed to the heaviest and most dangerous dust for many hours, and it appeared to affect him severely. Within a year, he was seeing a pulmonologist, who recorded a rapid decline in his health. By October 2002, tests showed that his lung capacity had been cut in half. That doctor was the third to attribute Zadroga's deteriorating condition to trade center dust. But Zadroga was having trouble convincing the police department, which had classified him a habitual sick leave offender and threatened to fire him.

In 2003, Zadroga went to the Deborah Heart and Lung Center in Browns Mills, N.J., where biopsies were taken of his lungs. Three strips of lung tissue, each about an inch long, were sent to independent specialists. A doctor at the Mayo Clinic hospital in Scottsdale, Ariz., found the tissue scarred and tainted by prominent black streaks, typically found in smokers and people who work in dusty conditions, and usually not considered life-threatening. The slides of

Zadroga's lung tissue also were sent to the Armed Forces Institute of Pathology, a national forensic center with expertise in analyzing autopsy results. A doctor there found signs of mild fibrosis in the lung but said its cause was undetermined, and he suggested further testing. Zadroga appeared at a hearing before the medical board with a portable oxygen tank and a nasal cannula. Gasping for breath, he told the board that he was often so weak that he spent whole days in bed. He had seen a psychiatrist and was on 80 mg of Prozac and 10 mg of Valium daily. He was also taking medication for asthma and acid reflux, and when his breathing became excessively labored, he took prednisone. He looked gaunt and told the board that he had lost more than 70 pounds. He was sent to the Police Department medical offices for breathing tests, and his lung function was measured at about 66 percent of normal capacity. The board withheld action on Zadroga's application and sent him back to Deborah for more testing. By July 2004, when the results of the additional tests came back, the Medical Board of the Police Pension Fund formally determined that Zadroga was disabled. And although the board was unable to determine the exact cause of the lung disease that had disabled Zadroga, his documented exposure to the trade center dust during the weeks he had worked there led to the board's determination that Zadroga's disability was work related.

Zadroga was given a line-of-duty disability pension, equivalent to three-quarters of his salary. He had already won a large award from Feinberg's compensation fund. His health continued to deteriorate, and when his wife died suddenly at the age of 29, Zadroga blamed her death on the stress caused by taking care of him and their baby daughter. He moved in with his father on the New Jersey shore and grew steadily worse.

By January 2006, Zadroga was spending most of the day in his room. One night his daughter woke up, calling for a bottle. He got up to take care of her but never made it to her bed. When he didn't come down for his medication the next morning, his father, Joe Zadroga, checked in on him. He found his son on the floor, the baby's bottle still in his hand.

Joe Zadroga demanded an autopsy. The Ocean County New Jersey Medical Examiner's office officially linked his son's death to exposure to the dust. During the autopsy, Dr. Gerard Breton, then a

73-year-old retired pathologist who had been trained in Haiti, found "innumerable foreign body granulomas" containing material he described as "consistent with dust." Breton concluded with standard medical phrasing that, in this case, carried great weight because it was the first formal scientific link between trade center dust and death. "It is felt with a reasonable degree of medical certainty that the cause of death in this case was directly related to the 9/11 incident," Breton wrote. He had not tested the material, nor had he consulted with doctors who had seen other responders. In his New Jersey shore community, Breton normally saw very little but the diseases of the elderly. Yet he said that what he found in Zadroga's lungs left no doubt about the cause: "I cannot personally understand that anyone could see what I saw in the lungs, and know that the person was exposed to ground zero, and not make the same link I made." Zadroga's death became a sentinel case that focused attention anew on the aftermath of September 11, playing on the fears of so many people that the dust represented a gathering storm of disease and death. For others, it was a reason for caution. "We'll see what other doctors say," Bloomberg remarked, unwilling to accept Breton's conclusion as the last word. "Generally, there are lots of other contributing factors."

Within a few weeks of Zadroga's death, the federal government responded to increased pressure from New York to take a greater role in the ground zero health issues. Michael Leavitt named Dr. John Howard coordinator of 9/11 federal health programs. Howard headed the National Institute for Occupational Safety and Health (NIOSH), a part of the Centers for Disease Control that had provided the earliest grants for the medical monitoring program at Mount Sinai. A distinguished pulmonologist, as well as a lawyer, Howard was a natural choice for the position. But his appointment reflected the Bush administration's general lack of interest in moving beyond public relations when it came to ground zero. Howard was given responsibility for coordinating all federal 9/11 health responses but was not allotted additional staff or budget to get the job done. He was notified of his appointment by an assistant secretary of the Department of Health and Human Services, who told him rather apologetically, "You seem like a nice guy—I hate to do this to you."

Howard was put into a delicate and, ultimately, uncomfortable position. Because of his training in medicine and law, he understood the nexus between politics and medicine better than most. As head of NIOSH, he also knew the difficulties of the workplace and was dedicated to protecting workers. But he was part of an administration that didn't share those views and that would be anything but cooperative as he tried to resolve specific problems. Howard soon found that the administration wasn't willing to pour resources into taking care of an issue that it didn't recognize in the first place. He became the government's point man in New York, taking the heat when responders condemned Washington's inaction, but playing it straight about the scale of the problems. When Maloney once asked him at a congressional hearing how long ground zero workers would need to be monitored, he answered, "For the rest of their lives," which made the administration's budget people shudder.

Before he completed his first year as 9/11 health czar, Howard was picked to appear on *60 Minutes* to defend the administration's attitudes, which he clearly did not share. Katie Couric had decided to do her first *60 Minutes* segment on the health effects of the attacks. Her producers wanted to talk to Leavitt, but the secretary decided that Howard should stand in for him. The department hired a media consultant to give Howard two days of preparation for being interviewed in front of television cameras. During the session, a nervous Howard asked what he was supposed to say if Couric wanted to know whether he talked to Leavitt regularly about the health issues. He had been the national 9/11 health coordinator for eight months and had not spoken to Leavitt once. Aides quickly set up a meeting with Leavitt and other top-ranking officials of the department, who again asked why the New York state workers' compensation system wasn't fit to take care of the problem.

The discussion reflected one of the Bush administration's principal problems with ground zero health claims. The administration believed the federal government should be the payer of last resort and that workers' compensation and private health insurance should pay first. Howard argued that New York's workers' compensation system was not set up to respond to this kind of crisis. It is a confrontational system, more suited to handling broken arms and other physical injuries than environmental ailments that might not develop for years. Even if, following extended adversarial proceedings, claimants are successful, the maximum compensation provided by the New York system was the $400 a week that Kevin Rogers of Con Ed received until he died. For most disabled workers, it was not nearly enough to cover living expenses or medications.

Howard argued that there was a moral issue involved, because many union workers have health insurance plans that peg coverage to the number of days they work in a year. In the economic slowdown that followed 9/11, many went long periods without work and, therefore, had little or no insurance to cover their mounting health expenses. Illegal immigrants who had taken jobs cleaning apartments and offices had no insurance at all, while many workers who held legitimate jobs had inadequate coverage. In Howard's view, Washington was obliged to help.

When he testified before Congress, Howard could tell that the doubt and skepticism that had arisen in the early days after the attacks had pervaded the views of congressmen outside the New York region. Ground zero workers were mostly faceless, which made them easier to ignore. That's why the death of Zadroga became so important. Zadroga's name became synonymous with the worst fears of all those who had been exposed to the dust. His father, a rugged former cop who habitually wore black suits and got teary eyed when he narrated the sad saga of his son, became a regular witness at public hearings about mounting health concerns. The Zadroga name also was wrapped around a legislative attempt by Democrats to fund an ambitious program to monitor and treat ground zero workers. The James Zadroga Act, sponsored by Maloney, Nadler, and others, sought to reopen the September 11th Victim Compensation Fund so that all those who had developed breathing problems, stomach issues, posttraumatic stress, and a long list of other ailments would get the care they needed and the compensation they felt they were owed.

During the remainder of the Bush administration, the bill would go nowhere.

Another opportunity to personalize the tragedy for Washington's sake arose later in the same year Zadroga died. This time, attention was focused on the plight of a single American family and the police officer father who had become so sick after working at ground zero that he was dying. That officer, Cesar A. Borja, had been hospitalized with pulmonary fibrosis, the same serious lung disease that had struck Marty Fullam. Officer Borja deteriorated quickly after entering the medical monitoring program at Mount Sinai in 2006. He was 52 and needed a lung transplant to survive. His son, Ceasar, a 21-year-old journalism major at Hunter College in New York City, had sent e-mails to every New York City reporter he could reach over the Christmas holidays pleading for help finding a new set of lungs for his father. He found a sympathetic ear at the *New York Daily News*.

Ever since Juan Gonzalez had published his first damning columns on the dust in fall 2001, the *Daily News* had a special hold on the ground zero story. In July 2006, the tabloid had begun an unusual series of articles on 9/11 responders. It clearly was a campaign to force the government to take care of those who had become sick, regardless of the lack of scientific certainty linking their illnesses to the dust they had inhaled. It was a classic newspaper crusade that made every responder who came forward to tell his or her tearful story a tragic hero. Most of the accounts were based on the worker's own diagnosis that the injuries had been caused by the dust. The *Daily News* ran the pieces at the front of the paper, as though they were news articles. But they were called editorials, and that gave them the journalistic dispensation from the usual requirements of objectivity. The newspaper expressed outrage at the way the ground zero workers were being treated, without worrying about first obtaining proof that their sicknesses, in fact, had been caused by the dust. The editorials accused the city, state, and federal governments of not only failing to protect the workers during the recovery, but of letting them down again now that they were sick and needed help. The editorials repeatedly referred to Christie Whitman's early statement about the air as "the big lie," and they supported Gonzalez's earliest columns about the 9/11 fallout, including the ones his editors had initially questioned.

The *Daily News* wasn't the only news outlet to pick up the Borja story, but no one else ran with it the way the tabloid did. In an article on January 16, the paper used emotional tones to describe the way Officer Borja had rushed to the trade center on 9/11. According to the *News*, Borja volunteered to "work months of 16-hour shifts" in the rubble of the fallen towers. After toiling there for hundreds of hours, the articles said, Borja had become progressively sicker. He retired in 2004, and in 2006 doctors at Mount Sinai told him that spending so much time at the trade center site without respiratory gear had permanently damaged his lungs. Only a transplant could keep him alive.

As Officer Borja sank into a coma, his son redoubled his efforts to keep his father alive. He contacted Clinton's office, begging for help. The State of the Union speech was coming up, and in the past, that event had provided a highly visible stage for the responders' pleas for help. Sensing an opportunity to bring special attention to the dire situation facing Borja and other responders, Clinton invited the officer's son and several others involved in the fight—including Joe Zadroga and Marty Fullam—to attend the 2007 State of the Union Address. Clinton provided a gallery pass for Borja, and the *News* paid for his flight to Washington and back.

Clinton, who had been pushing for treatment and long-term health monitoring for ground zero workers, wrote directly to President Bush about Officer Borja, portraying him as a symbol of the ills of so many others: "Cesar Borja was a hero who served his country in her hour of need and sacrificed dearly for that service. Since the attacks of September 11, 2001, as Cesar's health deteriorated, he and his family endured a great deal of hardship but never lost sight of the needs of the other workers, volunteers, first responders, and victims who survived the attacks but did not survive unharmed."

Two hours before President Bush began his address, Ceasar Borja Jr. was having dinner with congressional staffers at a D.C. restaurant called Bullfeathers when he received a call from New York. He abruptly left the table, and when he came back, he announced that his father had died before receiving his new lung. The congressional staffers offered to help him get back to New York. Ceasar said no. He felt duty-bound to remain in Washington to plead for help, if not for his father, then for all the other responders who were battling ground zero illnesses.

After the State of the Union speech, the younger Borja returned to New York vowing to continue to call attention to the needs of responders who, like his father, had sacrificed so much to help the city recover. "Nine eleven did not end that day," he told reporters. The Borja episode, with its irresistible combination of pathos, heroism, and outrage, had lured in reporters and editors hungry for a way to bring an immense story into some kind of human perspective. The intersection of politics and science had, in this instance, combined to make Borja a tragic symbol. His son's presence in Washington on the night of his death seemed to highlight Washington's impotence and proved to be an embarrassment for the administration.

And for the congressional staffers who had cooked up the idea of the trip and watched it all come together, Borja seemed for a time to have pried open a soft spot in the nation's conscience.

A degree of compassion fatigue had settled over ground zero once the cleanup was completed in 2002. But years later, with treatment money allocated and Howard proving to be a receptive and understanding coordinator of 9/11 programs, with Zadroga and Borja as sympathetic figures the public could identify with to put a face on the issues, Maloney felt confident about completing her mission. She thought she had beaten back the skepticism of those who had called New Yorkers money grubbers. And she had reason to believe that national opinion was shifting to her side and the side of the responders. Proof of that seemed to come when Jon Stewart skewered the administration's handling of ground zero on the *Daily Show.* Stewart grabbed a videotaped segment of Whitman's testimony at a hearing before Rep. Nadler. In it, she defended her statements about safety in September 2001 as truthful. She insisted that her goal then had been to protect the residents, but also to get the city back to work. If Wall Street had not reopened quickly, she testified, the terrorists would have won. That gave Stewart a caustic opening: What Whitman seemed to have stated so emphatically, he mocked, was that "If we didn't breathe asbestos, the terrorists win."[6]

Endnotes

[1]Krugman, Paul, "Money Grubbing Games," *The New York Times*, 8 February 2002, p. 23.

[2]http://maloney.house.gov/documents/olddocs/Sept11/TheChart/TheChart.pdf.

[3]Landis Dauber, Michele, *The War of 1812, September 11 and The Politics of Compensation*, Stanford Public Law and Legal Theory Working Paper Series, December 2003.

[4]Feinberg, Kenneth R., "Final Report of the Special Master for the September 11 Victim Compensation Fund of 2001," 17 Novermber 2004. Available at www.justice.gov/final_report.pdf.

[5]Statement submitted by James Zadroga to the 9/11 Commission June 2003, published by *The Daily News* 23 October 2009. Available at www.nydailynews.com/opinions/2009/10/23/2009-10-23_the_pain_of_911__the_days_after.html.

[6]27 June 2007.

10

Degrees of certitude

Doubts about the safety of the air in lower Manhattan that arose immediately after the attacks occured generated a lingering skepticism that quickly spread from New York to Washington and then to large swathes of the country. As time went on, it became increasingly difficult to know whether the air was safe, as officials insisted, or whether it was life-threatening, as Joel Kupferman and Juan Gonzalez had charged. No one knew with certainty whether an epidemic was brewing in Lower Manhattan or whether New Yorkers really were money-grubbing opportunists, trying to exploit a nation's goodwill. Science had yet to prove that a series of deaths among ground zero workers was just the beginning of an epoch of misery and pain, not merely the actuarial consequence of an aging population subject to the same diseases and environmental insults as the rest of the country. Because almost everything ended up being questioned, almost nothing was certain—not even the number of people who had died as a result of the attacks.

Even after Dr. Charles Hirsch and a team of medical examiner's office staff, backed by voluntary pathologists, had meticulously examined thousands of remains to come up with a list of 2,749 people who had died when the planes smashed into the towers, doubts remained about whether that number was complete. Detective James Zadroga's name may have been on the massive compensation bill before Congress, but it was not on the official list of victims, although many people thought it should be. Neither were the names of Kevin Rogers, Cesar Borja, or dozens of responders who had already died at comparatively young ages. Although they all had toiled at ground zero and then died of causes that seemed plausibly linked to their exposure to the trade center dust, Hirsch's office did not recognize any scientific proof to back up such a link. Hirsch was the gatekeeper to the official list, and the list was the guide to the controversial 9/11 memorial. The mayor had decided that only names on the official list would be so honored, and only those deaths that Hirsch categorized as murder would be put on the list.

This situation raised complex issues of science and law, never a clear ground and now even more confused and entangled. The standards of certainty that applied to the courtroom differed, by necessity, from those that were applied in the morgue. "Beyond a reasonable doubt" was not achievable in pathology or epidemiology. Instead, doctors and scientists strived for a different standard that could be summed up in the phrase "with a reasonable degree of medical certainty," as Dr. Gerard Breton had written in Zadroga's autopsy report. But *reasonableness* and *certainty* were abstract terms that could be adjusted according to the views, beliefs, and goals of those who used them. Few, if any, absolute proofs could link the dust to a particular disease, especially at this relatively early point in the unfolding mystery. Thirty or 40 years into the future, epidemiologists might be able to provide strong evidence showing that a spike in a certain type of lung disease or cancer among the group of responders could be linked "with a reasonable degree of medical certainty" to the trade center disaster. But there would always be exceptions and a degree of doubt. This was a basic fact of life for epidemiologists and a constant source of puzzlement for people who had to confront the mysteries of illness. Countless people said of a loved one, "He was healthy before 9/11—played basketball with the kids and ran 3 miles every day—and now he has trouble climbing a flight of stairs. What else could it be?" Similar questions are asked all over the country whenever a cluster of illnesses is detected. Whether it was breast cancer on Long Island, or childhood leukemia in parts of New Jersey, attempts to link the outbreaks to the water supply or nearby industries were tantalizingly easy to make but frustratingly difficult to prove.

For some experts, looking for a plausible link between an event such as the trade center collapse and the occurrence of diseases in a certain group of people is similar to developing photographic film. When negatives are first placed in a chemical mix, the images appear blurry and indistinct. Only after several minutes in the developing solution do they become clear.[1] The same is true of science and certainty. Initial conclusions are indistinct and suggestive. It takes time, and effort, for the shadows to fade and the outlines to become distinct.

By 2006, five years after 9/11, Zadroga's death was the only fatality that had been linked by autopsy results to the dust. But because the findings had been reached outside of Hirsch's office, they did not meet the standard of proof needed to have Zadroga's name added to the official victims' list. However, little known to Hirsch and most other New York officials, one other death had been legally ascribed to the dust. But when the case was revealed, it opened another complicated and frustrating avenue of investigation.

Felicia Gail Dunn-Jones was an idealistic young black lawyer, a striver married to a pharmacy supervisor named Joe and the mother of two teenagers. Daughter Rebecca was enrolled in one of New York's most competitive schools, and Joe junior was a big kid with a big temper that his parents were disturbed to eventually find out was severe autism and a mild cognitive deficiency. To keep Joe junior's emotions in check, the family had adopted schedules for everything, and they had learned to live by those routines religiously. Changing even the sequence of the smallest steps could send Joe junior into a rage.

The morning of September 11, 2001, began no differently than any other. Dunn-Jones had gotten permission to be on a flex-time schedule at the U.S. Department of Education civil rights office in downtown Manhattan, where she worked investigating rights abuse claims. She normally was the first one to show up in the morning and one of the first to leave in the early afternoon so she could get back home on the North Shore of Staten Island before Joe junior came back from his special-needs school. That morning she left their house, an up-and-down duplex where the Joneses lived on the second floor, just as the day was beginning. She did not have any interviews scheduled that day, so she was dressed casually—jeans, sandals and a V-neck aqua blue blouse. It was not yet 6 a.m. when she walked the block and a half to the corner of Crescent and Westervelt avenues to catch the number 42 bus that would take her the short distance to the water's edge, where she would board the Staten Island Ferry for the quick trip across the harbor to Manhattan. It was her ordinary routine, even though this was not an ordinary day because of the scheduled municipal primary election. She always voted, and she planned to do so, along with all her other domestic duties, when she got back from work. When she disembarked at the southern tip of Manhattan, she walked a few blocks north to her office at 75 Park Place, one block above the trade center. It wasn't unusual for her to stop in the towers on her way to work. Her credit union was housed there, and the gym she went to regularly was located inside the Marriott Hotel in World Five. She had worked out at the gym on September 10.

But on the morning of the 11th, she didn't have time to stop at the gym or the credit union. When the first plane struck a short time later, Dunn-Jones and the other lawyers rushed to the window to see where the noise had come from. From the fourteenth floor, they could see the skyscraper on fire, smell the burning jet fuel, and hear debris pelting their building. No one was sure what had happened, but Dunn-Jones decided it was too dangerous to stick around. When she got to the lobby, a security guard stopped everyone, saying it was too dangerous to go outside just then. She and the others who had tried to flee were advised to go back to their offices. Dunn-Jones did as she was told. She had always believed that laws and rules were meant to be followed, which was one reason she became a lawyer. After she got back to her office, she joined the others at the windows as they watched the fires spread. Then the second plane hit. This time no one waited to be told to evacuate. Dunn-Jones headed down to the lobby and out into the street. To get back to the ferry, she would have had to walk past the towers, which she knew was impossible. Her exit route blocked, she wasn't sure where to go, but she didn't want to stay where she was. She made her way north, moving with the crowd away from the burning towers. Once she got to what she figured was a safe distance, she stopped to watch the disaster unfold and try to figure out what to do next. It seemed unreal, both frightening and fascinating enough to keep her from running away. At that moment, she was not far from where Mayor Giuliani was trying to establish his command center, or where Kevin Rogers was checking the grid, or where David Prezant was setting up his triage center. Then she heard the sky roar and watched the South Tower buckle and fall. Within seconds, the cloud of dust barreled toward her, moving faster than she could run.

Frightened, and thinking about her family spread out all over the city, Dunn-Jones ran for her life. The dust got heavier, and then the menacing plume of smoke and ash overtook her. She tried to cover her face, grabbing her blouse and pulling it over her mouth. She choked on the dust and was close to panicking when she ducked into a delicatessen, taking refuge there until the most blinding part of the dust cloud had passed. A few minutes later, though dust still blanketed the air, enough sunlight seeped through for Dunn-Jones to find her way. As she ran, she saw someone fall. When she stopped to help him up, she looked into his face and saw absolute shock in his eyes. She had just bought a bottle of water when the second tower gave out. Again she was smothered by dust. It clung to her skin and worked its way into her eyes, nose, and mouth.

The buses weren't running, the streets were filled with people, and no one knew whether there would be more attacks. Dunn-Jones was too scared to stay in Manhattan. The only option left was to get to the Brooklyn Bridge and then to her sister-in-law Joyce's house in Fort Greene, Brooklyn. She crossed City Hall Park, but by the time she got to the foot of the bridge, the police had put up barricades and were stopping everyone except emergency responders. Not knowing how long the bridge would be shut, she headed north, toward the Williamsburg Bridge, which would get her to Brooklyn. But it, too, was closed. Exhausted from the walking and the sheer terror, she decided to just wait until the police reopened the Williamsburg. Hours later, she joined the long lines of dust people staggering across the century-old bridge to Brooklyn, all of them looking as though they had marched, fully clothed in business suits, through a desert.

That morning had begun with a similar rush and routine for Dunn-Jones's husband, Joseph. Tuesdays and Thursdays were his favorite days of the week because he didn't have to be at work at the Reiter and Patio Pharmacy on Flatbush Avenue near Prospect Park until 11 a.m. That gave him time to have a relaxed breakfast or to stop for a few minutes at a morning concert as he made the long trip from Staten Island to Brooklyn. The one option he didn't have was to sleep late. Joe junior's need for routine kept the entire family on a strict rise-and-shine schedule. So as with every other day, Jones put his son on his bus to school at the regular time, took Rebecca to the day care to wait for her bus, and then walked to the ferry terminal.

The walk is a vigorous uphill climb and then a comfortable stroll down to the water's edge. Jones had just crossed a local park when he saw the water of New York harbor and a huge streak of black smoke cutting across the horizon. He adjusted his Walkman and heard the news. From the ferry slip, he had no sense of the extent of damage and figured it was just an unfortunate but small-scale accident, one he hoped wouldn't interfere with the ferry's scheduled 9 a.m. departure. Accommodating Joe junior's obsession with routine had left an imprint on the whole family, and anything out of the ordinary presented ominous possibilities. Jones boarded the big orange and blue ferry and moved to the far end, facing Manhattan, where other passengers had clustered. His eye caught another plane coming down over the water. He was used to seeing jets over the harbor. But this was very different—low and moving fast, he recalled, like a fighter jet coming in for an attack. Against the brilliant morning sky, the silhouette of the jet was black, and Jones watched it swoop over the harbor, bank sharply, and then get sucked into the South Tower, just blocks from Felicia's office. He thought of her gym and credit union, and hoped against hope that she had not gone to either that morning.

The 9 a.m. ferry never pulled away from the slip. The stunned passengers didn't need to be told to go back home. Jones rushed off, hoping to get to a pay phone to call his wife. She carried a cellphone, but he didn't. Plenty of other people had had the same idea about calling and were lined up in front of the few available public phones. Frantic to make sure Felicia was okay, he practically ran back home.

He turned on the television, watched the towers crumble, and saw the dust swallow the city. He tried calling his wife's office and then her cellphone, without any luck. Her mother, Carmen, who was staying with them, kept trying; finally, by early afternoon, she got through. Dunn-Jones said she was scared and caked with dust, but otherwise okay. Rebecca got home safely, and Joe junior's school in Brooklyn agreed to bring him back. It seemed the worst was over.

After Dunn-Jones finally crossed the Williamsburg Bridge, she was able to flag down a cab that took her to her sister-in-law's house. She washed up there as best she could, rested a while, and then prepared to start out all over again. She caught a subway and then switched over to the no. 53 bus across the Verrazano Narrows Bridge, where Jones was going to pick her up. It was 8 o'clock and the sun was just setting when Jones found her at a gas station near the bridge. Even though she had washed, she still wore a stubborn residue of dust. Her clothes were stained with it, and it was all through her hair. Her feet were sore, and she said she felt like the walking dead. When they arrived home, she wearily climbed the flight of stairs and hugged her mother, glad to be alive.

What happened next is still a blur for the Jones family. Dunn-Jones worked from home until a temporary office opened in downtown Brooklyn in early October. Although that meant she didn't need to go anywhere near ground zero and relive that horrible day, she was scarred, as were so many New Yorkers. She had a dry cough that wouldn't go away, and she felt tired all the time. She thought it was from the stress of living through a nightmare.

As 2002 began, her cough grew worse. She didn't see a doctor, despite her condition, in part because her doctors were located in Lower Manhattan and she wasn't ready to go back yet. She worried about how the events of 9/11 had set off Joe junior. He was stressed out, and his behavior upset the rest of the family. At times, Dunn-Jones was the only one who could calm him. She couldn't afford to leave him alone, even to see a doctor for herself. And she shared something at that time with many other New Yorkers. The scale of the disaster dwarfed individual concerns. She felt that seeking medical attention would be exceedingly selfish and unpatriotic. If other New Yorkers went to their doctors for such simple things, they would clog the system and monopolize services for people who were really sick.

Dunn-Jones continued to commute to the temporary office in Brooklyn, and she kept up her schedule of field visits all over New York State, monitoring compliance with civil rights regulations and investigating suspected violations. When her cough grew worse, Jones suggested strong nonprescription cough medicine. He was used to offering such advice in the drugstore. An outbreak of flu in her office made them even more wary. By early February, Dunn-Jones was not herself at all. One Saturday late in the month, she loaded the kids into the car and drove them to nearby Clove Lakes Park. While Rebecca and Joe junior played, she sat on a park bench reading. On the way home, she stopped at a Pizza Hut and sent the kids inside for a pie while she waited in the car. They came back a short time later to find her sound asleep. They thought it was odd but were afraid to ask what was wrong.

The next day Dunn-Jones grew weaker. By afternoon, she had fallen sound asleep in Rebecca's room. When Rebecca looked in on her, she was snoring loudly. Jones took the kids grocery shopping, and Dunn-Jones was still dozing when they returned. Worried, they woke her and asked if she needed to go to the hospital. All she wanted, she said, was a cup of hot tea. Joe prepared the tea, but when he brought it to her, she had stopped breathing. They called 911. Jones and Rebecca jumped into the ambulance with her. Joe junior was too upset to come out of his room. He never saw his mother again.

The ambulance rushed her to St. Vincent's Hospital on Staten Island. By the time it arrived, she was dead.

Jones was stricken with grief and totally mystified. "It all just came out of left field," he remembered, still troubled by his inability to notice that anything life-threatening was wrong. He had not considered any link to ground zero. He had been too worried about what he was going to do with Joe junior, afraid he would become even harder to handle without his mother. The boy had listened to her. But now she was gone.

Luckily for the family, Dunn-Jones had a good life insurance policy, though they needed a lawyer to help handle estate questions. Dunn-Jones's supervisor referred them to an estate lawyer in Manhattan who was willing to take on the case. Rick Bennett, who had helped Kevin Rogers, had earned a reputation for being scrupulously fair about his work. He asked Jones for copies of the insurance policy and all important documents, including Dunn-Jones's death certificate.

Because she had died so suddenly and at such a young age, Jones had asked for an autopsy to be done. Crazy things went through his head. There was that anthrax scare, and a few people had died, hadn't they? The only symptoms that Dunn-Jones had to suggest anything was wrong were the rashes on her chest and the inhaler she used when she thought no one was watching. When the death certificate was issued in May, Jones was puzzled by what he read. The immediate cause of death was listed as sarcoidosis with cardiac involvement.

Jones had become familiar with many medical terms while working in the pharmacy, but this one he had never heard of. Neither had Bennett, who asked his wife, Kiki, who works with him, to look it up on the Internet.

What she found stopped them cold. Among the references to sarcoidosis was a 1999 scientific paper that Prezant had written about the higher than normal incidence of the disease in New York City firefighters.[2] Sarcoidosis is a mysterious autoimmune disease in which small clumps of cells attach themselves to major organs, particularly the heart and lungs. Most people can live with it without any outward symptoms. But it can turn deadly. No one knows exactly what triggers it, but it has been linked to environmental exposures such as smoke, ash, and dust. The image of Dunn-Jones covered in dust on the evening of 9/11 came vividly to Bennett's mind.

"I called Joe and said dust may be the reason Felicia died," Bennett recalled. As he did more research, Bennett found additional information linking sarcoidosis to dust, which strengthened his conviction that her death was connected to ground zero. He read articles in the *New York Daily News* about firefighters and other ground zero workers coming down with sarcoidosis, further confirming his belief. At that point, they decided to file an application with the September 11th Victim Compensation Fund.

Bennett felt he had enough evidence to make the case that Dunn-Jones's death by sarcoidosis could be traced back to her exposure on 9/11. His first application to the compensation board was rejected in August 2003 without explanation. But he appealed the decision, gathered more documents, and brought in medical witnesses to testify on her behalf.

One of the experts was Dr. Alan Fein, chief of the Center for Pulmonary and Critical Care Medicine at North Shore University Hospital. Fein testified that Dunn-Jones had had regular checkups, including x-rays and echocardiograms, that were within normal limits

as recently as 2000. She had no history of illness and had not complained of any shortness of breath, fever, arthritis, or skin rash—all
signs of sarcoidosis. Fein cited Prezant's sarcoidosis study on New
York firefighters and their higher incidence due to constant exposure
to smoke and dust. His conclusion was clear-cut: "Because of the
rapid progression of Mrs. Dunn-Jones's sarcoidosis leading to her
death approximately four months after the World Trade Center
episode, it is my considered opinion that her death was due to the
development of this sarcoidal 'granulomatous reaction' involving vital
organs and was the result of an acute exposure to components in the
dust cloud released at the World Trade Center."

At the hearing, Fein told Kenneth Feinberg, the fund's special
master, "This was a healthy woman who should not have died at age
42."

The other expert was Prezant, who, because of his continuing
work on sarcoidosis within the department, was interested in finding
out more about Dunn-Jones's case. He had agreed to testify as a physician, not as a fire official. His findings supported Fein's conclusion.
Clear evidence from Dunn-Jones's medical records indicated that she
had not had the disease when she was examined in 2000. There was no
question that, as she had fled from her office in Lower Manhattan on
September 11, she had been exposed to contaminants in the dust
plume. And she belonged to a group, African-American women,
known to have higher than normal susceptibility to sarcoidosis.

Prezant told Feinberg, "[T]here is no dust exposure I am aware of
that had the acuteness and the chronicity of the World Trade Center."

But the fund had some very specific eligibility requirements that
posed a legal obstacle to making the link between the dust and Felicia
Dunn-Jones's death, regardless of science. According to the fund's criteria, claimants needed to have been present at the world trade center
and its immediate environs in the first four days after the attacks. Bennett argued that Dunn-Jones met that requirement because her office
building, just north of the North Tower, had been hit by debris from
the impact of the jet and, therefore, was in the "zone of danger" on the
morning of September 11. That rationale satisfied Feinberg. But it
was much more difficult for Bennett to show that Dunn-Jones met the
fund's requirement that claimants must have seen a doctor or checked

into a hospital within 72 hours of being injured. When this issue was raised, the hearing turned tense. "Feinberg was very thorough," Jones recalled. "As we were getting to the end of the proceedings, you could see that he would walk back and forth; he was really giving it consideration." Bennett argued that sarcoidosis generally has no outward signs that would have prompted Dunn-Jones to see a doctor until it was too late. In fact, he argued, from a medical point of view, she didn't really know she was sick until the day she died.

At that, Bennett saw Feinberg's eyes light up. He leaned back in his chair, looked at the doctors who were there to support his argument, and then looked at Bennett and Jones. "That's it," he said. It happened so quickly that Jones wasn't sure whether they had won or lost. Feinberg asked them to come back with more information about Joe junior's medical and educational needs so he could calculate the economic loss of Dunn-Jones's death.

Feinberg decided that her death was linked to the dust and awarded her family $2.6 million, a settlement that reflected the extra care Joe junior would require during his lifetime. But it would be the only instance in which Feinberg determined that a death had been linked to an illness caused by 9/11 contamination. Feinberg's ruling provided Jones with a way to put his life back together, and for that he was grateful. But that didn't satisfy his need to make sense of his wife's death. She had simply gone to work one bright Tuesday morning and come home, hours later, with a death sentence hanging over her. Jones felt she was a casualty of a war, the war against terrorists, and that, as any casualty of war, her memory ought to be honored in some public way. "We respectfully acknowledge the people who died on 9/11," he said, "but what about those who died after a couple of days, week, months, or even years later. Aren't they victims?" He wanted Dunn-Jones's name added to the official list of victims that is solemnly read each year on September 11.

"She was a victim as surely as if she had been in the building with the others," he stated several times as he made his case public. Bennett once again compiled his documents. He sent the testimony of the medical experts who appeared before the fund, along with a letter that Feinberg wrote, to Hirsch. In the letter, Feinberg explained that the extensive medical documentation that had been presented, along with the expert opinion, led him to determine that "Ms. Dunn-Jones's death, although five months after the September 11 attacks, was nevertheless the direct result of her exposure to the World Trade Center dust."

Hirsch was the dean of medical examiners around the country, a staid and respected figure who had spent nearly two decades as New York City's chief medical examiner. He looked over Bennett's papers but rejected the claim and refused to put Dunn-Jones's name on the official list of victims. He said that although he respected Feinberg's work, the burden of proof for the fund was fundamentally different than was his. Feinberg had operated as though the cases before him were civil court proceedings, which meant that he required "a preponderance of proof." At the medical examiner's office, where decisions can determine whether someone is charged with murder, the burden is far greater. What Jones and Bennett were asking for, by petitioning that Dunn-Jones's name be added to the official list of victims, was a judgment by Hirsch that her death was indeed a homicide. And the burden of proof there was similar to what was required in a criminal trial. Hirsch wanted "certainty beyond a reasonable doubt."

In October 2006, Hirsch wrote to Rep. Carolyn Maloney and Rep. Vito Fossella, who had intervened on Jones's behalf. "After careful deliberation and discussions with the medical examiner who performed Mrs. Dunn-Jones's autopsy and other senior medical examiners at our agency," Hirsch said, "we concluded unanimously that we could not link her death to inhalation of World Trade Center dust with certainty beyond a reasonable doubt."

Jones was disappointed and afraid he would eventually have to be satisfied with the local memorial that had been established to honor the memory of the nearly 270 Staten Island residents who had perished at the trade center. The process for compiling the victims list there was less discretionary than for the principal memorial in Lower Manhattan. The Staten Island commission's members were inclined to be more flexible about whose name could be included, and they had the benefit of a design that could easily accommodate additional names. In 2005, Dunn-Jones's name had been carved into a tablet placed on the memorial of stark white South American marble that now stands on the north shore of Staten Island, not far from the ferry slip where she left for Manhattan that day. Jones visited the memorial often and brought flowers to put next to his wife's name—roses or carnations, red ones, her favorite color. Joe junior refused to go to the cemetery with him, but he sometimes visited the water's edge, where they can see the empty space where the towers once stood.

The discrepancy between Feinberg's finding that dust caused Dunn-Jones's death and Hirsch's conclusion that her death could not be linked to the dust ate at Jones and kept him pressing for some kind of answer. After reading an article about his quest in *The New York Times*,[3] Rep. Maloney rounded up the delegation and had letters sent to Hirsch, urging him to reconsider. Bennett also redoubled his own efforts, compiling hundreds of pages of studies and reports, and appealing to Hirsch to take another look, arguing that Feinberg's decision in a quasi-judicial proceeding had already proved that the dust was deadly.

In May 2007, Hirsch reversed his earlier decision, concluding this time that Dunn-Jones's death was indeed connected to the dust. In his typically careful manner, he held on to some reservations. In a letter to Bennett, Hirsch said he found some aspects of the written opinions of her personal doctor "troublesome," without mentioning what they were. And he held on to what he said were reasonable doubts that the dust had *caused* her sarcoidosis. The autopsy had disclosed scars in the heart muscle that appeared to have been older than just the four months that had transpired between September 11 and her death, suggesting that she had a pre-existing condition.

Nonetheless, Hirsch cited "accumulating evidence" that trade center dust had caused sarcoidosis or an inflammatory reaction much like sarcoidosis. He was referring to Prezant's work on New York firefighters. Prezant had followed up on his 1999 sarcoidosis study with a revealing look at what had happened after 9/11.[4] Using firefighters' detailed pre-9/11 medical records and thorough examinations that had been conducted after the clean-up ended—including biopsies that confirmed the presence of sarcoidosis—Prezant found a startling increase. There had been 26 new sarcoidosis cases in the first five years after the attacks, more than for the previous 15 years combined. The steepest spike came in the first year, when 13 new cases were diagnosed. That produced an incidence rate of 86 per 100,000, five times higher than the rate of 15 per 100,000 for the department in the 15 years before 9/11. What bothered Prezant was not just the increase, but the clinical presentations of the new cases. Sarcoidosis often can be hard to diagnose because a person with the disease can live symptom free for years. The affected firefighters in the earlier study had not had many obvious symptoms, but the new group came in with a whole host of them, including liver problems, muscle or bone issues, and such severe sarcoidosis around the heart that one firefighter needed a pacemaker. This led Prezant to conclude that although firefighters were normally exposed to hazards that led to a greater occurrence of sarcoidosis than in the general public, something in the ground zero dust had a more potent effect, leading not just to more cases, but to cases that were far more severe.

Hirsch found the fire department data convincing, and even though it conflicted with his previous position, he changed his mind about Dunn-Jones. He concluded, "If WTC dust can produce such a reaction *de novo,* it is highly likely that the dust would have aggravated pre-existing sarcoidosis. Therefore, whether or not she had sarcoidosis prior to 9/11/01, it is likely, with certainty beyond a reasonable doubt, that exposure to WTC dust was harmful to her."

Dunn-Jones's death certificate was modified. The underlying cause of death remained sarcoidosis. Exposure to trade center dust was listed as a contributing factor. Importantly, Hirsch amended the manner of death from natural causes to homicide. He then recommended that Mayor Bloomberg add her name to the official list of World Trade Center victims that is read on the anniversary. And when a permanent memorial is built on the site, he believed that her name ought to be engraved there.

Jones's fight for his wife's memory represented a critical turning point for 9/11 health conflicts. It was just one case, but it was clear in the medical, scientific, and political communities that others would follow. As soon as Hirsch's reversal was reported, other families asked for the same kind of review. Hirsch agreed to take a second look for any family willing to provide documentation. Several came forward.

Among them were the families of Detective Zadroga and police officer James Godbee, Jr. Hirsch reached his conclusion about Godbee quickly. To some, the decision revealed a lot about his character and his adherence to a rigid rule of science and logic. Others saw it as proof he could be arbitrary and capricious. Godbee, a 19-year veteran of the police force, had been assigned to duty in the vicinity of the trade center on September 13 and had worked there 14 hours a day through the end of the month. He had continued there almost daily until the end of the year, and then sporadically through June 2002, when the cleanup was complete. In all, Godbee had put in about 850 hours but had never worn a respirator because he said none had been made available to him. He had never worked on the pile itself.

Godbee, a former Marine and 19-year veteran of the force, had been in good health before 9/11, but after working near the pile, he had developed breathing problems that grew progressively worse. By the end of 2003, he could barely get out of his chair. A chest x-ray the following February indicated that he had pulmonary sarcoidosis. His lung collapsed in March, and a biopsy confirmed sarcoidosis. By August, his persistent cough had grown far worse, and he had complained of tightness in his chest. Another x-ray showed that the sarcoidosis had progressed. By the end of 2004, Godbee, only a shell of his former husky self, suffered a heart attack at home and died at age 44. An autopsy conducted by Hirsch's office found nodules on his heart and lungs, and concluded that the cause of death was sarcoidosis.

Deciding whether to add Godbee's name to the list might have seemed relatively simple for Hirsch, since he knew that sarcoidosis had also killed Dunn-Jones and she had been declared a 9/11 victim. And Prezant's study made a strong case for linking the disease to ground zero dust. Yet there were no easy answers for Godbee's wife, Michelle Haskett Godbee, and her two children. The Police Pension Fund had denied her appeal for line-of-duty death benefits in 2005, based on its finding that sarcoidosis was not related to Godbee's police work at ground zero.

That left extreme contradictions between the positions of the fire department, which clearly linked sarcoidosis to ground zero exposure, and the police department, which did not. It also raised the issue of whether Hirsch would follow the precedent set by his decision on Dunn-Jones or uphold his conclusion that Godbee's death was from natural causes.

Hirsch notified Michelle of his decision in June 2007, a few weeks after his decision on Dunn-Jones. His ruling took Michelle and many others by surprise. Hirsch reasoned that every one of the 2,750 people on the official list (including Dunn-Jones) had been killed on 9/11 or were exposed to the dust caused by the collapse of the twin towers that day. Godbee had not arrived at ground zero until September 13, two days after the collapses. Even though the dust he breathed, and that may have caused or exacerbated his sarcoidosis, had surely come from the twin towers, Hirsch determined that his death could not be classified as a homicide because he had not been at the crime scene on September 11. Hirsch said his office had to adhere to the principle that "fatalities caused by work-related inhalation of dust are classified as natural deaths" and would not be considered homicide. He left unanswered the question of whether exposure to the dust had caused Godbee's sarcoidosis.

That decision infuriated many New Yorkers. Maloney, Fossella, and Rep. Jerrold Nadler fired off a statement criticizing the idea of an "arbitrary cutoff" and calling for the establishment of a panel that would take such emotional decisions away from the medical examiner's office. Bloomberg wasted no time rejecting the idea because he believed that any panel would insert politics into a realm that, by right, should be governed by science. He also defended Hirsch and his actions. "The medical examiner was asked to rule on whether or not the legal definition of death is homicide," Bloomberg told reporters. "This is strictly the legal definition based on what the law is, and the medical examiner made a finding. They did not look at what the actual cause of death was."[5]

But Hirsch did just that when he re-examined the circumstances around what had been called the sentinel case, the unfortunate death of Detective James Zadroga.

Endnotes

[1]Personal interview with Joseph Graziano, associate dean for research at the Mailman School of Public Health at Columbia University, October 2006.

[2]Prezant, David, Atheya Dhala, Andrew Goldstein, et al., "The Incidence, Prevalence, and Severity of Sarcoidosis in New York City Firefighters," *Chest* 116, no. 5 (Date): 1183–1193. Available at http://chestjournal.chestpubs.org/content/116/5/1183.abstract.

[3]DePalma, Anthony, "Medical Views of 9/11's Dust Show Big Gaps," *The New York Times*, 24 October 2006.

[4]Izbicki, Gabriel, Robert Chavko, G.I Banauch, et al., "World Trade Center 'Sarcoid-Like' Granulomatous Pulmonary Disease in New York City Fire Department Rescue Workers," *Chest* 131, no. 5 (May 2007): 1414–1423.

[5]"Bloomy Snubs WTC Hero's Kin, Backs Top City Doc on 'Natural' Death" *New York Daily News*, 27 November 2007: p. 2.

11

Beyond doubt

It would have taken a heart of steel to not be moved by the story of Ceasar Borja's valiant but ultimately fruitless quest to find help for his father. That tragic tale, and the heart-breaking coincidence of his big appearance in Washington on the very day his father died, drew national sympathy, one of the few times outside the anniversaries of the September 11 attacks that media from all over the country paid attention to the continuing saga in New York.

A week after he returned from D.C., Borja, along with his mother and his younger brother and sister, had a chance to speak directly with President Bush. Bush came to New York to give a major economic speech at historic Federal Hall, not far from ground zero, and made time to meet with the Borja family. What was scheduled to be a 15-minute private meeting following the speech turned into a counseling session punctuated by surprisingly direct lobbying. Bush was moved by what he had read about the Borja family and promised to do his best to help. Since delivering his State of the Union address, he had cleared $25 million for medical treatment for responders—the first treatment money ever written into a federal budget (earlier amounts had been emergency appropriations)—and ordered a review of possible ways to fill gaps left by workers' own insurance. Bush expressed sympathy for the Borjas' loss, and pledged even more support for sick responders. "If they were on that pile and if they were first responders, they need to get help," he said. Congress already had before it Sen. Clinton's bill to provide $1.9 billion in medical assistance to injured workers. While the President was at Federal Hall, a group of responders held a demonstration at the edge of ground zero to demand that he keep his word.

At about that same time Bush was meeting the Borjas, Joe Sexton, editor of the Metropolitan Section of *The New York Times*, was following a hunch. Sexton, a former sports reporter who had risen through the ranks of the newspaper on the strength of a sharp intellect and plenty of street smarts, was skeptical of Borja's tale. The blend of strong pathos and weak science struck him as another example of a sloppy tabloid approach to the question of whether exposure to the trade center dust had caused any illnesses. Sexton's skepticism had its roots in the newspaper's early coverage of the disaster, when it had generally accepted statements about safety made by Christie Whitman and Rudy Giuliani, and downplayed the possibility that the dust had posed a widespread danger. The *Times* had gone out of its way to make the case that Whitman and Giuliani had differentiated between the air on the debris pile, which they had said was dangerous, and the air in the rest of Lower Manhattan, which EPA tests had indicated was not contaminated. Repeatedly, the *Times* pointed out that firefighters, police officers, construction workers and everyone else on the pile had been urged to wear respirators, but many had ignored the warnings. Thus, whatever happened—and the *Times* reported that adverse health effects ought to be relatively mild and only temporary—could be blamed in large measure on the workers for not taking steps to protect themselves after they were warned about the risks.

Sexton assigned police reporter Al Baker and City Hall reporter Sewell Chan to look into Borja's claims about his father's work at ground zero. Chan had written an article about Caesar Borja's Washington trip, the only mention of Borja's quest that the *Times* had published. The article was a sympathetic look at Borja's campaign to help his father, and it did not raise doubts about the severity of Borja's illness or its link to ground zero dust. In fact, the article attributed to an unnamed congressional official a statement indicating that Borja's acceptance into Mount Sinai's treatment program, which was paying for virtually all of his medical care, was a tacit recognition that his condition was connected to his exposure to the dust.

Baker and Chan were able to obtain pension records and other documents detailing Borja's work schedule in the months after the attacks. Chan says the key break in the story came from Borja's family, which openly shared with him Borja's own log books. The books were revealing. The information contained there did not correspond to the accounts of Borja's heroism that had been published in the *Daily News* and other newspapers. The records suggested that Borja had not rushed to ground zero on September 11. In fact, records showed that on September 11 he had reported to the police car pound in Queens, his usual duty. His memo book, in which he detailed his daily assignments, did not mention volunteering at ground zero at any time. He had been assigned to the outer perimeter around the debris pile, but there was no record of it until December 24. By then, however, the underground fires had been extinguished, and some degree of normalcy had returned to New York. Over the three months that had transpired since the attacks, repeated rain and brisk winds had substantially cleared the air, although dust could still be kicked up whenever a girder was hauled away.

Sexton gave the reporters an exceptional canvas on which to tell their story. They produced a 2,849-word article that began on the front page and ran for a good portion of an entire page inside, a notable bit of newsprint.[1] Professional sniping at a cross-town rival also may have been involved: The reporters raised doubts about the version of the story published by the *New York Daily News*, which was aggressively campaigning for a Pulitzer Prize for its 9/11 coverage. Baker and Chan quoted the officer's wife saying that the account in the *Daily News* had not been accurate, but intimated that she had been reluctant or unable to correct it. The tale of Borja's heroism had taken on a life of its own that not even his family could control.

The *Times* article did not state categorically that Borja's illness could not have been caused by exposure to the dust, but it minimized that possibility. The paper pointed out that Borja was close to retiring in 2001, and extra work over the Christmas holidays had bolstered his earnings for the year. That inflated his pension, which would be based in part on his income during his last years on the job. The placement of the story on page 1 and its length left the clear impression that the *Times* was comfortable claiming that the Borjas had not told the entire truth and that the exaggerated account had duped the *Daily News*, Senator Clinton, and even the president. Some of the *Times* staff also delighted in the notion of puncturing the Pulitzer hopes of the *Daily News*.

The *Times* article created two separate sets of controversy, a regular pattern in ground zero issues. On one side were critics who lambasted the *Daily News*, Clinton, and the rest of the congressional delegation for being naive. They felt that the Borja saga was proof that responders were capable of attempting to bamboozle the government as they grabbed for assistance they didn't truly deserve. Even though the Borja family had not sued the city, their story became another cautionary tale about a system that painted every responder as a hero and every government action as a deception. On the other side, the *Times* was criticized for dragging the honor of Officer Borja through the mud by intimating that he had engaged in deception. These critics insisted that Borja had put in two decades as a police officer and had spent time near ground zero while the cleanup was still ongoing. To them, his illness—which Mount Sinai's doctors attributed to exposure to the dust despite the fact that he had once been a heavy smoker—underscored just how dangerous ground zero had become. In their eyes, Officer Borja had died from pulmonary fibrosis that he had gotten by working near the pile. Their underlying message was simple: If this could happen to someone who was there in December, imagine how dangerous the pile had been earlier.

In truth, the *Daily News* and Clinton's office, with the help of the rest of the delegation, had invented a heroic role for Borja, a role his family had been either unable or unwilling to dispute. The Borjas felt betrayed by the *Times* article and the outrage it triggered. Ceasar Borja told other reporters that his mother had innocently believed that Chan was writing an upbeat article that would portray her husband positively. That's why she had been so willing to open up his record books, even though she thought it was unusual for the reporter to have focused on such small details. She spent a considerable amount of time with Chan, but the only words attributed to her in the long article were "It's not true," referring to the account in the *Daily News*. Borja said he didn't ever try to correct the misimpressions in the *Daily News* articles because he didn't know firsthand what had happened at ground zero. His father had told him he'd worked on the pile, and Borja had believed him with the same conviction with which he would have believed in a sign from God.

It is unlikely that the Borjas had tried to deceive anyone. By the time the original *Daily News* story was published, Borja was lying in a hospital bed at Mount Sinai, hooked up to tubes. The only journalist who had actually spoken to him was Edmund Silvestre, an editor and reporter at *The Filipino Reporter*, an ethnic paper where the younger Borja had once had a journalism internship. Silvestre had interviewed Borja before his condition had worsened for an article that was published January 5. This piece was not an attempt to make a hero out of Borja. In fact, the word *hero* never appeared in it. Instead, Silvestre portrayed Borja as a veteran cop who had become deathly ill after being assigned to ground zero and now needed a new set of lungs. He did make several errors of fact, most importantly in placing Borja at the pile immediately after the collapse. When asked about the discrepancies in the officer's story,[2] Silvestre explained that Borja had told him from his hospital bed that he had volunteered for duty at ground zero and had been there early enough to have retrieved human remains, including severed fingers. Silvestre said that Borja would not have recorded the time he had spent volunteering there in his memo book.

But the details of his story were not as important as the symbol that Borja had become, and Silvestre's article provided the raw material on which the tabloids, and several Capitol Hill offices, had constructed the heroic image of Borja rushing down to ground zero. That version was retold—and continually embellished—right up to the meeting with President Bush.

The other members of New York's delegations had not been able to check out Borja's story before Clinton invited him to Washington. To all of them, the *Times* article about Borja was embarrassing, but they insisted that it didn't change the fact that Borja had worked in the contaminated zone and had come down with a serious respiratory illness that doctors at Mount Sinai linked to his work there. In other words, whether or not the dust actually caused the disease, Borja's ground zero duty had exacerbated the damage to his lungs and led directly to his death. Even if Borja had been sick before 9/11, he wouldn't have died when he had if the dust had not worsened his condition. Clinton continued to defend Borja, despite attacks from critics. Her office put out a statement that said she "knows that sacrifices were made by so many, whether it was in the hours, days, weeks, or months after the attacks of September 11th and believes that they all deserve our help." *The Filipino Reporter* and the Borja family also refused to back down. But the *Daily News* admitted that it had gotten a number of facts wrong.

A year after Borja's death, his widow remained bitter about the way her husband's memory had been tarnished. Again, Silvestre and the *Filipino Reporter* were the only ones the family opened up to, and she blamed the *Daily News* for building her husband up to be a hero, and the *Times* for tearing him down. She said that the *Times* had ignored many of the facts she had given Chan, including the information about Borja finding the body parts. "They just chose the facts that made us appear bad." she told Silvestre. "But how are we going to fight a powerful press? I felt like my family was used as a pawn in a media war."

At about the same time Eva Borja was reliving her ordeal, Dr. Charles Hirsch's office was completing its investigation of the circumstances surrounding Officer Borja's demise. On his official death certificate, the cause of death was listed as idiopathic pulmonary fibrosis, without comment on what had triggered the disease.[3] The manner of death, a critical classification for making a link to 9/11, was listed as natural, not as a homicide. The results were dutifully recorded by Hirsch's office, and the Borja family did not attempt to challenge the findings or bring them to public attention.

Officer Borja, like James Zadroga, had put a human face on the troubling issues swirling around ground zero, and for a time, he had managed to draw national attention to the condition of the rescue workers. The Bush administration had responded with money and a promise to do more. The *Daily News'* ground zero campaign had proven embarrassing to Gov. George Pataki, who eventually gave in to the public scolding and pressed for changes to workers' compensation laws and pension regulations that provided more advantages for ground zero workers. And despite the blowup over the Borja story, the *Daily News* went on to win the 2007 Pulitzer for its editorial campaign on 9/11 health issues. But the whiff of controversy and scandal had started to settle over ground zero the way the dust had initially filled the air, and eventually it would thicken into a wall of opposition that threatened to halt all ground zero aid.

❁ ❁ ❁

The Borja story set the stage for a confrontation based not on science, but on perception, and would highlight a most nettlesome

aspect of the 9/11 aftermath. Until then, it had been sufficient for editorial writers and reporters to simply write *believed* after a responder's name to connect an illness or a symptom to the dust. But the two
sides of the issue were hardening. Those who doubted the dust was
dangerous refused to willingly suspend their disbelief; while those
who believed refused to willingly accept any doubt. Asking for hard
evidence meant risking repudiation. John Feal, who became one of
the most outspoken advocates for injured responders after half his
foot was sliced off while working on the pile, wagged a pious finger at
doubters. "Shame on everybody who opposes helping us," he
declared more than once.[4]

But doubts persisted, and with time they increased. In at least
one way, it was inevitable. With the exception of the fire department
and its baseline medical records, almost every other bit of information was self-reported. Workers told doctors at Mount Sinai and
researchers at the trade center registry how they felt and when the
symptoms had started. There was little downside to claiming to be a
9/11 victim, and the lack of scientific evidence made it possible to
include just about every illness, common or rare, in the list of reactions. But the Borja story raised the question of whether anything that
was self-reported could be trusted. Thus, the self-reporting that had
started as an unavoidable weakness of much clinical research grew
into a discomfiting contest between science and the truth itself. And
the *Daily News* was not alone in exaggerating the impact of the dust.

Within five years of the attacks, there was a steady outpouring of
heroes-turned-victims. A platoon of people who had spent any time at
ground zero and become sick with any illness or ailment freely told
their stories to reporters, TV correspondents, and movie producers
from around the world. The cycle of 9/11 anniversaries created a
great appetite for new ways to keep the story going year after year,
and the volatile mix of alleged government misdeeds in withholding
information from responders, along with the truly tragic conditions
many workers found themselves in, became a journalistic trap few
editors or reporters could avoid.

These news stories often turned out to be a blend of science and
health, with a strong dose of gumshoe whodunit. Reporters latched
on to vague theories and searched for experts to advance scientific-
sounding scenarios that explained how exposure to the dust had, in a

few years, triggered diseases that usually took decades to develop. Or they simply allowed the responders to link their illnesses to the dust, as though there could be no doubt. Formal science lagged behind those spot stories and had no definitive answers, but researchers put out tantalizing clues that were easily manipulated. Although epidemiology is based on long-term observations, several studies had already been produced by the fifth anniversary in 2006 indicating that the negative health effects of being exposed to the dust were lasting longer than expected and, in some cases, were more serious than initially anticipated. Although the studies focused on different groups—some looked at residents, some at pregnant women, some at recovery workers themselves—they consistently showed that those who had been exposed to the dust plumes in the moment of the towers' destruction suffered from the most serious symptoms.

The studies were consistent in one other important way. As mentioned earlier, with the exception of research coming out of the fire department, the work on ground zero responders was based on self-reported data. The people being studied provided their own testimony about the state of their health before 9/11 and what had happened to them since. There were no baseline reference points like those Dr. Prezant had started with, based on the department's yearly physicals. Most studies were built on personal recollection, which can be spotty. Without an individual's documented medical history, screening doctors could not know whether asthmalike conditions had just begun or were the recurrence of earlier bouts that patients had forgotten or misremembered. And as sympathetic coverage in the media continued, it was not surprising that more people came forward to claim that they, too, had been hurt by the dust.

Other factors also cut into the credibility of the studies. One is known as selection bias. Tens of thousands of recovery workers had come from the uniformed services and the building trades, which expected their employees to be in good physical condition. This gave them a particular perspective in responding to questions about their health prior to 9/11. Iron workers, operating engineers, and even police officers and detectives, tended to think of themselves as being in great shape, even when they weren't. Their inaccurate recollections would skew post 9/11 studies. At the same time, because most of the studies were voluntary, they did not necessarily cover a scien-tifically valid sample of responders. Instead, it was expected that those who were having health problems would have been among the first to come in for screening, while those who felt fine might be inclined to stay home, stacking the numbers in a way that showed a higher prevalence of disease. The authors of the studies usually reflected these drawbacks and acknowledged the possibility that this could distort their results. Certainly, these phenomena were not unique to 9/11 studies, and they did not completely invalidate the data. But they were important factors to consider.

Because the complete universe of responders was unknown, there was no easy way to get a representative sample of those who had worked at ground zero. Were there 40,000 responders, or 80,000? Eventually, Mount Sinai settled on 60,000 as the best esti-mate. Combining the fire department personnel with the 26,000 who had been screened at Mount Sinai generated a sample of about two-thirds of the total, which Dr. Philip Landrigan of Mount Sinai came to believe was large enough to counter any selection bias.

Critics said some of the 9/11 studies were unreliable because they had been conducted by institutions seeking funds to treat the very illnesses they claimed to be uncovering. This is not an uncommon complaint, but no evidence suggested that the data was being manip-ulated in that way. Such an effort would have required a master plan, and there never was one. The research effort had been pieced together over time, the unavoidable result of the stop-and-go funding and the reluctance of the labor unions to be used as "lab rats."

Despite the studies' limitations, they provided a trove of informa-tion that helped shape the monitoring and treatment programs. They also kept the medical community alert for negative health trends. The studies constituted an imperfect early warning system, and they helped guide policy makers as they continually assessed the severity of the problem and the adequacy of the response. They also contributed indirectly to the haze of misunderstanding.

As the fifth anniversary of 9/11 approached in 2006, John Howard urged Dr. Landrigan and the doctors at Mount Sinai to have a major study ready for release. Without such data, getting Washington to pay attention—and eventually provide the money for monitoring and treatment—would be a losing battle. Until that time, Dr. Stephen Levin and Dr. Robin Herbert, a codirector of the trade center program, had produced a limited number of research papers. One of the earliest was a preliminary analysis of the first 250 responders who had come in for monitoring. That 2003 study showed a pattern of respiratory problems, some quite severe, but it was an extremely small sample. A larger study by the Centers for Disease Control and Prevention released in 2004 closely paralleled the earlier Mount Sinai report. Mount Sinai's doctors authored several other studies and reports within the first five years, but none had yet carried the kind of weight that Howard wanted to bring to the debate.

As it tried to satisfy Howard's demand for a substantive report, Mount Sinai was in a most difficult position. It had heroically stepped forward in the early days of the disaster to screen workers when no one else had been willing to do so, relying on its own expertise and limited resources to cobble together a program, even as the number of people who needed the services grew exponentially. By the fifth anniversary, more than 15,000 workers and volunteers had been screened. The clinic also had access to medical data on another 5,000 workers who had gone to other hospitals and clinics in New Jersey, on Long Island and across the nation. Each worker and volunteer had been asked to provide a medical history, to describe how their health had changed since 2001 and to indicate whether they suffered any persistent symptoms. The sample was far from perfect and was clearly slanted toward people with medical issues, while undercounting workers without symptoms who stayed away. The drawbacks were obvious to everyone involved, but so were the potential benefits. Much could be learned from the clinical experience of those workers and volunteers, the biggest and most varied group of ground zero responders receiving medical attention.

Mount Sinai released its most comprehensive study a few days before the fifth anniversary of the attacks.[5] At an elaborate press conference managed by one of the largest commercial public relations companies in New York, Landrigan and Herbert, by now the head of the data collection unit, provided reporters from around the world with the intensely awaited results of their big study. They found that many individuals had suffered severe respiratory distress, which was not surprising. The caustic nature of the dust, and the pulverized concrete it contained, had turned throats and nasal passages cherry red, which made damage to lungs expected. What was surprising was how long the symptoms persisted. Several years after they had finished working on the debris pile, many individuals still were bedeviled by the same lung, throat, and nasal irritations. To determine the extent of the damage, the doctors conducted lung capacity tests. Although there was no pre-9/11 baseline to compare the results to, these tests laid a foundation for future study. They also provided a snapshot into the medical legacy of the dust.

Landrigan and Herbert explained their study methods at the news conference, being careful to disclose the limitations of their work. Then they delivered a startling statistic. They said that 7 out of 10 of the 9,442 ground zero workers in the study had severe respiratory problems that had persisted far longer than expected. Herbert brought the whole issue into a broader perspective, taking into account all that had happened since 2001. "There should no longer be any doubts about the health effects of the World Trade Center disaster," she said. "Our patients are sick. Our patients were very, very highly exposed and are likely to suffer health consequences as a result of that for the rest of their lives." By stating that there no longer should be doubt, she had tacitly conceded that doubts had persisted for as long as had the symptoms of some responders. It was a candid admission of the difficulty that Mount Sinai, the New York congressional delegation, and the responders themselves had faced, because doubts are raised more easily than they can be erased.

The study made dramatic headlines all over the world, and "seven out of ten" became the favored shorthand way of conveying the severity of the medical threats facing thousands of workers and volunteers. Seven of ten was something that would shake up even the most hardened Republican from the midwest who thought that New Yorkers were money grubbers and malingerers.

The report successfully focused attention on a potential health problem. "This study, I hope, puts to rest any doubt about what is happening to those who were exposed," said Senator Clinton. But a careful review of the results suggested that the situation may not have

been as dire as "seven of ten" suggested. In a last-minute editing decision before submitting the paper for peer review and eventual publi-
cation in *Environmental Health Perspectives*, Landrigan had
combined the most serious respiratory symptoms, such as shortness
of breath, with relatively minor common ailments, such as a runny
nose, to get to the 70 percent figure. Separately, the figures still represented serious levels of impact. Sixty-two percent of the workers in
the study reported persistent upper-respiratory symptoms, typically
the sinusitis, nasal dripping, and dry cough that plagued people who
worked at ground zero. Those who reported lower-respiratory symptoms, such as shortness of breath, which can be an indicator of a serious and possibly chronic respiratory problem, were just 15 percent of
the total. Given the size of the study and the even larger number of
responders in the New York region who could have been battling the
same symptoms at that time but hadn't yet been seen by Mount Sinai
or included in the analysis, either number warranted attention. But
by combining the two in the report and accounting for duplication,
Landrigan could say at the big news conference that 70 percent of
responders had reported "new or worsened respiratory symptoms."

Because Mount Sinai's findings had become the bible of ground
zero health issues, the 70 percent figure would be repeatedly mentioned in the following months and years. It became the catchphrase
of the health issues, and it was often misinterpreted and exaggerated
by those who did not bother to repeat Landrigan's full explanation. In
my own page 1 article in *The New York Times* following the news conference, I wrote, "Roughly seventy percent of 10,000 workers tested
at Mount Sinai from 2002 to 2004 reported that they had new or substantially worsened respiratory problems." Others went much farther.
"Seventy percent of the ground zero workers suffer from respiratory
illnesses," NBC reported. The front page of the *New York Post* was
expectedly graphic: "Air Sick" was the banner headline. Beneath it lay
the heart of the message that came out of Mount Sinai that day. Using
the bluntest terms, the *Post* declared, "Study: 70% of WTC are
Deathly Ill."

One of the few restrained responses to the new figures came
from City Hall, where Mayor Michael Bloomberg expressed reservations about Mount Sinai's findings. Bloomberg challenged Herbert's

statement about putting an end to doubts by raising some of his own. "I don't believe that you can say specifically a particular problem came from this particular event," he told reporters. "There is still much we do not know about the full nature and long-term health effects of the destruction of the World Trade Center."

Those doubts notwithstanding, Bloomberg announced at the same news conference a $16 million program to screen and monitor people exposed to the dust. The money would be spread over five years and was expected to provide enough services to take care of up to 6,000 students, residents, and office workers from Lower Manhattan who, until then, had not been part of any screening program. After stating his lingering doubts about the extent of the health impact, Bloomberg acknowledged that some people had been hurt and did, in fact, need help.

Mount Sinai clearly had no control over the way either City Hall or the tabloid editors interpreted its data. nor was it unheard of to combine upper- and lower-respiratory symptoms. But neither was doing so standard practice in peer-reviewed medical journals. Scientists disagree all the time. Some independent experts saw no scientific reason for combining the two and felt that they should have been kept apart, as the early versions of the Mount Sinai report had them. Others agreed with Mount Sinai's way of handling the data. Questions also were raised about selection bias and the reliability of self-reported symptoms. But Landrigan, who oversaw the writing of the report, staunchly defended it, arguing that the last-minute change was the trademark of a fussy writer who continued to edit right up to the moment the piece was submitted. He also maintained that upper-respiratory symptoms such as the runny nose and watery eyes of sinusitis are conditions that could cause prolonged misery for those who had them. He said they often are precursors of more serious lower-airways problems, such as shortness of breath. Moreover, both sets of symptoms had arisen from the same source of exposure, the dust, which justified combining them.

Nothing in the report suggested that the collection of the data had been manipulated in any way to produce a particular set of results, nor did any critic imply that. In the body of the study, and in the *Environmental Health Perspectives* article, Mount Sinai doctors clearly distinguished upper-respiratory symptoms from lower-respiratory ones and made no attempt to gloss over the difference. But in the summary of the article, in their presentation to reporters, and in the press release issued by the Howard Rubenstein Public Relations agency on behalf of Mount Sinai, the distinctions were lost.

Howard, who had urged that the study be done, was not at all disturbed by the way the findings were presented. "I was surprised they didn't say that 100 percent of the people have x, y or z," he once commented. As someone who had suffered severe sinusitis all his life, he sympathized with the idea of combining upper- and lower-respiratory symptoms. And he firmly believed that runny noses and watery eyes that develop simply because someone goes to work the way the responders did ought to be viewed as an important public health issue. He said it is not unreasonable for employees to expect to return from their jobs without being made sick by the work they do. But Howard also knew he couldn't go to the Bush administration asking for millions of dollars for 9/11 health programs on the basis of a study that said workers had runny noses. Including the lower-respiratory ailments was important for making the point to Congress and the White House. He said he expected that, over time, Mount Sinai would be able to refine its studies, establish strong baseline health data, begin to narrow down chronic symptoms, and catch early signs of a rise in life-threatening illnesses.

Other physicians and scientists were less understanding, and they expressed concerns that by presenting the results in an unclear way to an overly anxious cadre of reporters, who then further minimized the differences and exaggerated the seriousness of the symptoms, Mount Sinai had made its case stronger than it actually was. There was no suggestion of venality, or willful distortion of data. But given the importance of the study and the manner in which the results could only have been expected to be interpreted, combining the two to come up with the larger, more attention-getting figure invited overstatement at a time when precision and restraint were most needed.

However, from the perspective of forcing Washington to pay attention, the study succeeded. The reality of occupational illness is that there is often a need to act before all the evidence is in. Doing so gives medicine a fighting chance of aiding the workers who are already sick, not just those who might become sick in the distant future, when long-term epidemiological studies can be neatly wrapped up. Mount Sinai was caught in a vicious scientific Catch-22. It believed that ground zero represented a growing public health threat, yet it could not direct the attention of skeptical government officials to the plight of the sick responders until it had ample proof. And it couldn't make a convincing presentation of evidence until it had sufficient funds for the screening, monitoring, and treatment programs. Something needed to break the log jam. In many ways, Mount Sinai's 2006 study did that, despite the questions it raised in some quarters.

Since that report was issued, Mount Sinai has gone on to do precisely what Howard predicted it would do. Taking the results of that report as a starting point, Mount Sinai's doctors have continued to refine their message, building on the information they have collected through their clinical work to come up with a more comprehensive and finely tuned sense of the dust's legacy. In more recent studies, it found that the rate of asthma among the 20,000 ground zero responders who had been screened between 2002 and 2007 was twice as high as in the general population.[6] Up to 8 percent of the uniformed services and construction workers reported an asthma attack after September 11. The average rate for adult asthma in the United States is about 4 percent.

And in a disturbing, though admittedly limited, piece of research, Mount Sinai reported in 2009 that it had found a higher than expected number of cases of multiple myeloma in responders who were younger than 45.[7] In the entire population of more than 28,000 workers and volunteers in the screening program by then, doctors detected eight cases of myeloma. That is higher than the 6.8 that would have been expected in a group that size. Mount Sinai said the finding was significant because four of those cases of myeloma had occurred in men younger than 45. The disease most often strikes people who are decades older. Three of the four were law enforcement officers who had arrived at the trade center on September 11 and were exposed to the heaviest concentration of dust. The doctors also noted that the latency period for these cases was significantly shorter than expected for myelomas in people exposed to environmental hazards. In particular, they pointed out that the latency period for multiple myeloma linked to benzene and other solvents ranged from 10 to 20 years in several peer-reviewed studies done at other institutions.

When the "case series" was released to the public, Landrigan and Dr. Jacqueline Moline of Mount Sinai cautioned that it was an extremely limited number of cases and urged people not to overreact. But they said the results were so striking that they felt compelled to alert doctors throughout the region to be on the lookout for multiple myeloma in any responders they might treat. "Although it is too early to say whether the risk of multiple myeloma is truly increased among WTC responders, we felt it is important to report these cases, particularly because multiple myeloma is unusual in individuals younger than 45 years," they stated.

But Mount Sinai's findings, and their release to the public, again were questioned. The myeloma study included such a small number of cases that it couldn't be considered conclusive in any way, as Landrigan and Moline had cautioned. But one of the four highlighted responders younger than 45 was identified as not having undergone any examination by Mount Sinai's medical monitoring and treatment program. He had gotten in touch with one of the program's doctors in spring 2007, nearly three years after his myeloma had been diagnosed, and was subsequently enrolled. Two other cases were added in June 2007, years after their diseases had been diagnosed. Some epidemiologists and statisticians consider adding cases like this an unacceptable violation of scientific standards. And the four myeloma cases in responders older than 45 was actually less than the 5.6 that statistically would have been expected in this group.

While Mount Sinai's forward-thinking advocacy can keep the medical community on top of newly emerging diseases, it also shows the dangers of aggressive advocacy. Despite Landrigan's efforts to be precise about the limitations of the myeloma report, those reservations were not always incorporated into the message the public received. The *Daily News* again was out front, and in an editorial days after the myeloma report was released, the newspaper proclaimed in its headline that Mount Sinai had found the first proof of the higher cancer rates that many had dreaded (and that Herbert had years earlier publicly speculated could be "a third wave" of ground zero diseases). The headline was "New Horror for Heroes," confirming what thousands of workers had suspected about cancer all along. While the case studies are likely to achieve Mount Sinai's stated goal of warning clinicians about a possible threat, their immediate impact was to create greater stress and more anxiety for the thousands of responders and their families, who feared the worst.

Despite such controversies, Mount Sinai's most basic findings and conclusions were being corroborated by Prezant and the city's Department of Health and Mental Hygiene, which analyzed the medical information collected by the World Trade Center Health Registry. Their individual studies focused on different groups, but their results, like Mount Sinai's, held that the most harmful exposures had occurred during the first few days after the towers crumpled into themselves.

The world trade center screening program continued to face challenges. New participants kept signing up, making it difficult to define the size of the study population. Mount Sinai and the other hospitals in the consortium still had to fight for permanent funding to last the decades-long lifespan of the monitoring program. Despite those obstacles and the obvious weaknesses, the clinical data Landrigan's crew collected remains an invaluable source for understanding the aftermath of the dust.

Science itself was challenged after 9/11, so deep were suspicions planted in the first fearful days of the response. As details grew ever more complicated, even the most basic facts were undermined by doubt, the most noble intentions weakened by skepticism, the most tragic of times undercut by confounding evidence.

True to his word, after reversing himself on the death certificate of Felicia Dunn-Jones, Hirsch reconsidered other cases that were brought to his attention by surviving family members who, like Joe Jones, believed that their loved one's name belonged on the official 9/11 memorial. Given the growing awareness of the tragic death of James Zadroga and his wife, and the role that Zadroga's name was playing in Washington's efforts to get more assistance for injured responders, Zadroga's case became a priority.

The customary way for a coroner to determine the manner of death is the autopsy, which can reveal many secrets. But in Zadroga's case, it was far too late for Hirsch to conduct his own. He was forced to reconstruct the physical trail. Among the most important findings was the death certificate from the Ocean County, N.J., coroner, who had found "with a reasonable degree of medical certainty" that Zadroga's death could be linked to ground zero dust. And Zadroga had received help from the September 11th Victim Compensation Fund, the same entity that had recognized the connection between Dunn-Jones's death and the dust. By going over the documents in both those proceedings and reconstructing as best he could the time between the detective's work at the site and his death just over four years later, Hirsch hoped to reach his own science-based conclusion.

Zadroga had first called in sick before 2001 ended, and he had deteriorated so rapidly afterward that he was able to apply for help from the victims' compensation fund before the cutoff date at the end of 2003. Kenneth Feinberg reviewed Zadroga's medical records and determined that his worsening condition had likely been caused by his exposure to the dust. Using the standard of a preponderance of evidence, Feinberg judged that Zadroga, who had been 29 on 9/11, a former football player and weightlifter, was unlikely to be able to work again or support his family. Zadroga was given an award of more than $1 million. By then, he had moved to central Florida with his wife, Ronda, and their baby, Tyler Anne, who had been born just three weeks after September 11. The police department had put him on long-term disability, and his doctors believed the warm air would do him good. His police career over, he bought a 15-acre mini ranch with six longhorn steers and a bull not far from his wife's parents. He wanted to get as far away from New York and the dust as he could.

Zadroga could not run far enough, and tragedy followed him to Florida. The family lived in a comfortable house surrounded by the open spaces that Zadroga had been looking for. Ronda, who had been brought up in Florida, was happy to be back and living only a mile from her mother and father. But by fall 2003, when she was only 29, Ronda, a slender woman with shoulder-length dark blonde hair, was going through a bad time and decided to spend time with her parents, though Zadroga visited. Her parents have consistently refused to talk about what happened, but police records paint a disturbing picture. After one of those visits from Zadroga, Ronda's parents found a black purse under her bed. In it were several hypodermic needles, a bottle containing different types of pills, and two spoons. Her mother, Rosalie, also found needles under the bedspread and on the floor. When Rosalie asked what they were doing there, Ronda replied, "It's nothing, Mom." Two days later, Ronda had to be taken to a local hospital. She was later transferred to a county hospital, where she died on October 12, 2003.

When Zadroga called his parents in New Jersey to tell them what had happened, they were at a garage sale looking for items to stock their new family dream. Arcadia, Fla., where James and Ronda had lived, was becoming a hot new center for antiques, with several dozen thriving businesses. The plan was for the entire Zadroga family, including Zadroga's older brother, John, a furniture restorer, to open an antiques shop there. After hearing about Ronda's death, Joseph and Linda Zadroga got in their car and drove overnight to Florida.

While the Zadrogas were making the long trip, Ronda's family was meeting with the DeSoto County, Fla. Sheriff's office to express their concerns about her death. According to files from the sheriff's office, Ronda's father, Roger Byrd, told a detective that his son-in-law had admitted that both he and Ronda were abusing drugs and that they had shared intravenous drugs shortly before her death. They told the detectives that Zadroga was a heavy prescription drug user with an "alleged disability" who couldn't take care of himself or his daughter.

When Joe Zadroga arrived at his son's house, the place was a mess. James's three dogs had been left inside for days, and urine and feces were everywhere, including on some of the baby's toys. Zadroga's father quickly cleaned up. Soon two detectives from the county sheriff's office, along with an investigator for the state Division of Child and Family Services, showed up. Zadroga was out making funeral arrangements, and his father identified himself as a former police chief, a cop with 27 years of experience. He thought they had come to take the baby away. "We have nothing to hide," he said, and let them in. The detectives later reported that the house had clearly just been cleaned, and they had noted spots on the rugs. They asked who was going to take care of the baby, and Joe said he and his wife planned to bring her and their son back to New Jersey. The detectives and the investigator then left.

Despite a request from Ronda's parents, the local medical examiner's office refused to perform an autopsy. The official cause of death was listed as a massive staph infection, which could have come from the hospital or from dirty needles, but nothing definitive was noted. The medical examiner did observe multiple needle puncture marks on both of her arms, and a urine test showed traces of methadone, which is used in treatment programs for drug addicts.

Zadroga and his baby daughter moved back to New Jersey after the funeral, leaving behind the dream of ranching and antiquing for the reality of the New Jersey shore. With the money from the compensation fund, he helped his parents buy a large house in Little Egg Harbor, where the hotels of Atlantic City are visible in the distance across the salt marsh behind their backyard.

The extended Zadroga family moved into the big house at the end of a cul-de-sac in January 2004. Zadroga and the baby took an upstairs bedroom, where he spent much of his time. Joe Zadroga administered his pills four times a day and generally oversaw his medical care. When his son developed a serious infection that had to be treated with antibiotics, a shunt was put in his arm and he used hypodermic needles to flush out the tubes. Zadroga still had an IV attached when he died, and his body was brought to the Ocean County Medical Examiner's office to be autopsied.

A little over a year later, Joe asked Hirsch to review those findings. He said he did so only for one reason. He wasn't interested in suing the city. In fact, he couldn't because of the money from the 9/11 compensation fund, which prohibited such lawsuits. He simply wanted was to see Zadroga's name inscribed on the 9/11 memorial. For a tough-as-nails former police chief, that was something worth fighting for, an honor retrieved from the horror of losing a son. Hirsch asked Joe to send his son's complete medical record, from Breton's autopsy report to the documents that had been presented to the 9/11 fund and the police pension board, along with anything else that would help him retrace what had happened. If Hirsch could link Zadroga's death to the dust as the New Jersey coroner had, he could classify the detective's untimely death as another homicide, making him the 2,751st victim of the terrorist attack on New York.

In reviewing the material that Joe provided, Hirsch, who had lasted 18 years in the hothouse of the New York City medical examiner's office without scandal, had to rely on the results of an autopsy he had not supervised, something that made a belt-and-suspenders kind of man like him uneasy. He knew well the difference between the expertise of his office, which had handled more than 100,000 autopsies during his tenure, and the one in Ocean County, with its aging suburban population, where most autopsies would find a narrow range of heart disease and cancers. Hirsch and his team understood death to be a creative demon filled with mystery and mischief, always willing to make the obvious unfathomable. He had become a detective of the human body, assessing all available medical evidence but looking beyond that to social background, personal habits, travel, and other bits of personal information to help provide the answer to what he routinely referred to as the state of being "inconsistent with continued life."

Hirsch ended up with a substantial amount of material on which to base his decision. Among the most complete portfolios was that of the medical board of the Police Pension Fund. Zadroga had applied for a line-of-duty disability pension in 2002. The board had found that Zadroga was unable to work, but it had not determined that his symptoms were job related. The ruling had an impact on Zadroga; a line-of-duty pension would have provided substantially more money for him and his family. In 2004, Zadroga had applied to the board again, this time presenting more documentation. Among the records were the medical opinions of several private doctors who believed that his respiratory problems were related to his work at ground zero. Unlike the questions surrounding Borja, there was little doubt that Zadroga had been at ground zero the first day. He submitted attendance and overtime records showing that he had arrived on September 11.

Hirsch also had in front of him the report of Breton's one-hour autopsy. Zadroga's body still had an electrode sticker pasted on his right side. He had weighed 216 pounds, far below his normal weight of close to 300. Breton had noticed multiple tattoos on both of Zadroga's arms, as well as on both legs, on his neck, over his right chest, and on his upper back. He also described slight, barely discernable scars from stab wounds on his stomach.

Breton's report indicated that Zadroga had serious health issues. His heart was markedly enlarged, as were his lungs. Breton described the lungs as brownish colored, somewhat fleshy, and finely granular. Under the microscope, he had found countless small cysts, or granulomas, throughout the lung tissue. Cutting them open, he had found foreign material he couldn't identify but that he described as being "consistent with dust." He sent samples to the Armed Forces Institute of Pathology, which had reviewed the lung tissues taken at Deborah Hospital several years earlier. Breton consulted with other doctors who had treated Zadroga, and also spoke to his father. Putting that history together with the autopsy results, Breton wrote in the final report that "it is felt with a reasonable degree of medical certainty that the cause of death in this case was directly related to the 9/11 incident."

Without the body itself, the records were all Hirsch had to confirm or contest Breton's findings. But he did have one important document that Breton apparently had not had when he made his final report. The Armed Forces Institute of Pathology analysis of the lung tissue had been sent to Breton on November 2, 2006, months after the autopsy report was completed. When he finally did see it, Breton did not find anything that required a revision of the death certificate. But the two-page report contained the kind of information that was a starburst signal for someone with Hirsch's background and experience. When the tissue sample slides were exposed to supersensitive light microscopy, they sparkled brightly. "I do not exaggerate," Hirsch recalled. "It's as bright as the sky is going to be on the night of the Fourth of July." He recognized the material causing the flashing light as talc and cellulose that the biopsy analysis had identified.

Hirsch then compared the slides to the biopsied tissue samples that had been taken at Deborah Hospital in 2003, which were included in the documents from the pension board. The 2003 biopsies had not shown any talc or cellulose crystals. If Zadroga had breathed in the materials at ground zero, they should have been present in his lungs in 2003. But the record showed they were not.

The dead speak to Hirsch and reveal secrets that otherwise would be lost forever. For him, talc was a telltale sign of a junkie habit of grinding up prescription painkillers like oxycontin, mixing them with water, and injecting them directly into the bloodstream. This put the drugs in overdrive, making them work both faster and more power-fully. The drugs could be absorbed quickly, but the talc, the inorganic material that pharmaceutical companies use to hold together the med-ication in the shape of a pill, cannot easily be absorbed in the blood. It usually has to be broken down in the stomach and then passed through the waste system. When pills are injected, the talc can clog blood ves-sels in the lungs, triggering an inflammatory reaction. Ultimately, some of the material works its way through the walls of the blood ves-sel into surrounding air sacs, causing the lungs to fail. The condition is known as "mainliner's lung."

On October 16, 2007, five months after he reversed course on Felicia Dunn-Jones, Hirsch sent a letter to Joe Zadroga. Trying to be both judicious with his words and straightforward with his message, Hirsch wrote that after studying the medical records and supporting documents, he had come to a conclusion that was "markedly differ-ent" from the one the New Jersey coroner had reached. Hirsch said, "It is our unequivocal opinion, with certainty beyond doubt, that the foreign material in your son's lungs did not get there as the result of inhaling dust at the World Trade Center or elsewhere." Hirsch had said what he believed had not caused Zadroga's fatal lung problems, but he had not laid out what he thought had been the cause. Hirsch invited Joe to a personal meeting where he would provide the details of his investigation, apologizing in advance for what he understood would be a shocking conclusion. "We regret that we cannot agree with your belief, but we must interpret the facts as we see them, with-out regard to personal considerations," Hirsch wrote, a statement that summed up his attitudes toward the difficult work of the medical examiner and the strict code by which he had run the office for nearly two decades.

Hirsch had not revealed anything to anyone but the family. He is famously averse to the kind of high-intensity buzz that an office like his, in a city like New York, can provoke. In all his years as chief med-ical examiner, he never held a news conference, and he did not intend to make an exception in this instance. However, Zadroga's father was so upset by the findings that he had released Hirsch's letter to reporters. After his long career in law enforcement, he knew when something bad was going down. He drove to New York so Hirsch would have to tell him face to face about what he had found. When he, his wife, and their lawyer, Michael Barash, talked to Hirsch, Zadroga first placed a framed portrait of his son on the conference room table. "While you're talking, look at Jimmy," he told Hirsch. "I want you to understand that Jimmy was a person and not just an object."[8] The news was worse than Joe had expected. Hirsch told him that he believed Zadroga had been injecting himself with painkillers, just as the Florida detectives had been told four years earlier. Hirsch said the slides from the Armed Forces lab were definitive. "Certainty beyond doubt," the phrase he used in his letter, essentially means the alternative is impossible. Joe was devastated, as shocked as he was angry. "I never saw needle marks on his arms. I was a cop for 27 years—I would have seen needle marks." His wife rushed out of the conference room, upset. "I'm lucky that Barash was there," Joe said. "Otherwise, I would have lost my temper." As the Zadrogas drove off, Barash talked to reporters. "We got an explanation," he said. "We just don't agree with it."

Despite Hirsch's firm defense of his conclusion as having "certainty beyond doubt," his explanation did not satisfy everyone. Among those who remained suspicious was his predecessor, Dr. Michael Baden, who had reviewed the tissue slides and doubted that they showed what Hirsch said they showed. Since serving as medical examiner, Baden had become a media star, with his own cable television program about forensic pathology. He was not afraid to critique the work of others. Baden said that when he checked the tissue samples and saw the 2006 report from the Armed Forces Institute, he concluded that the talc and cellulose were among the many materials loosed by the collapsing towers. He also said that when he examined the slides, he saw glass fibers and other particles that could not have come from pills, but had been inhaled at the trade center site. He took issue with Hirsch's argument that the foreign material had been found in the blood vessels of the lungs. Baden was familiar with mainliner's lung and decades earlier had written about the effects of injecting prescription drugs in a classic medical text. But in this case, he concluded that the areas in question on Zadroga's slides were packed so closely together that it was just as likely that the dust was in the alveoli of the lungs as in the blood vessels laced between them, meaning they had been inhaled, not injected.

Hirsch strongly disagreed with Baden and those who asked what difference it made—after all, Zadroga unquestionably had been exposed to the dust:[9]

> "The lesson exemplified by Zadroga is very clear cut. Decisions that we make cannot transcend the information that they are based upon. I believe that the doctor who did Zadroga's autopsy, and then also his consultant, failed to take into consideration the entire history. Zadroga allegedly inhaled foreign material in his lungs when working at the site of the World Trade Center in 2001. Zadroga retired and had lung biopsies done in 2003. They were extensive lung biopsies. They were generous. I've read the reports. There isn't a question of sampling error or anything like that. There were appropriate samples taken from more than one part of his lung. In 2003 there was no cellulose and there was no talc in his lungs. He died and was autopsied in 2006, and his lungs are full of talc and cellulose. Furthermore, it got there by way of the bloodstream and not by way of the air passages. But that's a matter of technical interpretation how it got there. I believe that it's categorically, unequivocally demonstrated in the autopsy that it got there by way of the bloodstream. But even forgetting that, if his lungs are full of talc and cellulose in 2006 and it wasn't there in 2003, how can you opine that it got there because he inhaled it in 2001? I don't see how the pathologist could have concluded that those crystals got there because of his work on the site of the World Trade Center. I don't think they took into consideration the fact that his lungs were free of those crystals in 2003. It's impossible."

Not unexpectedly, Hirsch came under intense criticism, with Clinton, Maloney, and Nadler leading the pack. Maloney publicly raised the question of Hirsch's independence and the city's conflict of interests in deciding how Zadroga died. Although she had initially called on Hirsch to review the deaths of all responders who died outside of New York, a position she took after the reclassification of Dunn-Jones's death, Maloney now called for limitations on Hirsch's power: "The history of 9/11 should not be decided behind closed doors by one person." There were calls for a commission to make sensitive decisions about the 9/11 memorial. For the very first time in all his years in office, Hirsch felt direct political pressure. "Let me make perfectly clear, no New York

City official has ever attempted to influence my judgment on any case," he noted. "Mayor Bloomberg has been unfailingly supportive, no elected official, nobody who works for an elected official in New York City has ever attempted to influence my judgment in any case of any sort. The only time in my career, and I would point out to you that I've been doing this work for 44 years, the only time in my experience that political pressure has been exerted on me is associated with the World Trade Center, and it has come from people elected to Congress and to the Senate of the United States of America. I'm not going to get any more personal than that. And I can tell you that it doesn't make any difference. It hasn't had any influence on me whatsoever."

Hirsch was born in the Midwest, and despite his many years in New York City, he still can look and sound like the old-fashioned country doctor that his mother had wanted him to be. Tall and lanky, he speaks slowly and carefully, punctuating sharp remarks with piercing gazes. He has a tendency to quote aphorisms, a habit that even he realizes can go too far. He'll say, when dealing with bereaved families who come to his office looking for answers, that "the truth hurts, but it also heals." On the lobby wall outside his office is a Latin saying that he quotes often and that he translates, "Let laughter and conversation cease. This is the place where the dead come to nourish the living." When talking about the outcome of the ground zero injury cases, he concedes that "it is easier to be a historian than a prophet." He insists that if he had been given an ultimatum about changing his scientific decision on Zadroga or James Godbee or Dunn-Jones, he would have been prepared to accept the consequences of saying no rather than compromise his standards.

"Another aphorism, please forgive me." His long, bony fingers start to point. "Beware of someone who is willing to compromise his standards. Because if his standards go, the principles will not be far behind. And then you become a very dangerous person."

Autopsies can tell a lot, but they do not speak with a single language and their results are open to interpretation. That is one reason Howard had formed a task force in 2006 to draft a uniform set of autopsy reporting guidelines to help make sense of the increasingly tumultuous ground zero aftermath. Howard knew that as the thousands of ground zero workers began to die off from a variety of causes not necessarily related to their exposure, there would be questions about their lives and their deaths. With workers spread out all over the country, the kind of differences in approach and execution that arose between Hirsch and the New Jersey medical examiner could be multiplied many times over. Howard worried that there would be doubts about the dust far into the future. He wanted a single set of national guidelines so that, in every death involving a ground zero worker, the same standards of examination and interpretation would be applied.

Howard consulted several forensic experts, including Hirsch. Hirsch's main concern was that slides and tissue be preserved for future examination, when more information might be available. He proposed building a database that would be useful for testing contemporary samples with prior ones. He knew from experience that "if you don't have it, you can't test it." But the federal government pulled the plug on the project before a final set of guidelines could be reached. The formal reason given was that officials were concerned that results could end up being misused in lawsuits that ground zero workers and their families filed against their employers. No autopsy guidelines or reporting requirements were ever issued. The closest Howard came to achieving what he had set out to do was providing financial assistance to the New York State Department of Health to maintain a registry of the deaths of ground zero workers. By collecting such data, it was believed, the state would be able to act on erupting health issues before they could escalate into a crisis.

Hirsch's conclusion about Zadroga's drug use was stunning. Instead of the hero cop whose name symbolized the dedication of first responders, Zadroga was labeled as a drug addict and, by implication, was anything but a hero, further confounding New York's understanding of what had happened at ground zero. Bloomberg commented, "We wanted to have a hero, and there are plenty of heroes. It's just that, in this case, science says this was not a hero."

Zadroga's father was furious at Bloomberg and publicly slammed him for attacking his son. Joe simply refused to believe that his Jimmy, who had wanted to be a cop since he was a kid, was a drug addict who had been shooting up while living with him. Bloomberg later apologized publicly to the Zadrogas but did not change his mind about what had happened. "I believe that James Zadroga was a hero for the way he lived, regardless of the way that he died," he said, "and although the medical examiner has made an independent determination as to the specific cause of death, there should be no doubt in anyone's mind that James Zadroga served this city with distinction." The mayor added, "I certainly apologize for my comments, and I committed to the family we will find a dignified way to honor his son's sacrifice."

As with the Borja incident, and the questions that had been raised about Mount Sinai's reporting of symptoms, the convoluted tale of Zadroga's death reinforced the notion in the minds of some people that the entire issue of 9/11 illnesses had been fabricated or overblown, and that many people were taking advantage of public sympathies for their own gain. New York's congressional delegation was left in a particularly uncomfortable position. The massive bill they had introduced to establish a national program to screen, monitor, and treat 9/11 responders had been dubbed the "James Zadroga Act." Because of Hirsch's ruling, Zadroga's name would not be added to the city's formal list of 9/11 victims. But there it was on the bill that the Bush White House had given no indication of supporting. Maloney and her staff knew the Borja and Zadroga setbacks had hurt the efforts to get support for ground zero workers, but because so little progress had been made under the Bush administration, they felt that the setback could be overcome. And as Senator Clinton had done in defense of Borja, the delegation continued to defend Zadroga, regardless of the unflattering evidence that had been uncovered. They argued that no matter what had happened to him at the end, Zadroga most likely would still be alive if he had not needed to take pain-killers so he could breathe after spending three straight weeks at ground zero. Even his father came around to that way of thinking. Years after his son's death, now with a bold tattoo on his forearm of a crucifix, his son's name, and the words "Not Forgotten," Joe was realistic about his son's death.

"Even if he did, what does it matter?" Joe asked. "He was dying at that point. Nobody knows how much pain he was in." He said his son's lungs had become hard as leather and so enlarged that they had pushed up against his rib cage. Every breath hurt. Every breath was a fight. And a deteriorated disc made every movement agony. Zadroga was taking twelve 100-mg tablets of oxycontin a day toward the end of his life, "enough to kill a horse," Joe said. "He was in so much pain, that's why he did it. If he did it."

Hirsch's findings spurred plenty of outrage, both from people who felt he was disgracing the name of someone who had dedicated his life to protecting the city, and from others who believed Zadroga had tried to manipulate the system. The stark differences between the New Jersey coroner and Hirsch regarding his death added to the confusion, and deepened suspicions that had been building in the city since the earliest days and 9/11's aftermath. It seemed that even though all the world had watched the towers come down and had seen the dust rampage through the streets, even though the dangers of being exposed to the dust without proper protection had been clear from the first day, and even though response plans had been drawn up and government agencies had responded to the disaster in myriad ways, nothing was certain about the aftermath of 9/11 except that uncertainty reigned.

In October 2008, just after the seventh anniversary of 9/11, Commissioner Raymond Kelly of the New York Police Department presented Distinguished Service medals to the families of eight officers who had died after being exposed to ground zero dust. Among them were Officer James Godbee and Detective James Zadroga. Their names would not be inscribed on the official 9/11 memorial, but they were added to the department's wall of heroes at police headquarters in Lower Manhattan. Joe and Linda Zadroga keep a framed copy of their son's commendation on the wall of the home they shared with him, right near the front door so they see it every time they come in or go out. And as the Obama administration took over in Washington and the Democrat-controlled Congress took a more open and welcoming look at providing steady long-term funding for the care and monitoring of ground zero workers, HR 847, the bill laying out that program, continued to bear the name of the "James Zadroga 9/11 Health and Compensation Act."

Endnotes

[1]Chan, Sewell and Al Baker, "Weeks After a Death, Twists in Some 9/11 Details," *The New York Times*, 13 February 2007, p. 1. Available at www.nytimes.com/2007/02/13/nyregion/13health.html?_r=1&scp=1&sq=Chan%20and%20Borja&st=cse.

[2]Personal interview, 29 December 2009.

[3]Interview with Ellen Borakove, Office of the Chief Medical Examiner, 17 June 2009. Borja's death certificate was officially filed 9 January 2008.

[4]Sisk, Richard, "FEDs Blasted over 9-11 Aid Shortfall," *The Daily News*, 22 July 2005, p. 32. Available at www.fealgoodfoundation.com/original_web/Articles/Shame%20on%20feds%20for%20not%20giving%20911%20aid.pdf.

[5]Herbert, Robin, Jaqueline Moline, Gwen Skloot, et al., "The World Trade Center Disaster and the Health of Workers: Five Year Assessment of a Unique Medical Screening Program," *Environmental Health Perspectives* 114, no. 12 (December 2006): 1853–1858. Available at http://ehp.niehs.nih.gov/docs/2006/9592/abstract.html.

[6]Data presented at the 2009 annual assembly of the American College of Chest Physicians.

[7]Moline, Jacqueline, Robin Herbert, Laura Crowley, et al., "Multiple Myeloma in World Trade Center Responders: A Case Series," *Journal of Occupational and Environmental Health* 51, no. 8 (August 2009): 896–902.

[8]Personal interview, 15 September 2009.

[9]Personal interview, 30 June 2009.

12

Assaulting uncertainty

New York City was slowly being blinded by a habitual opacity about the aftermath of 9/11 and ground zero that blurred images and hid some things in plain sight. After the Zadroga flare-up, many New Yorkers shared Rep. Carolyn Maloney's conclusion that Charles Hirsch should never have been in the position of determining who was a victim of the September 11 attacks. They looked askance at his decision to contradict James Zadroga's autopsy and to draw a seemingly arbitrary deadline around James Godbee's death, usually overlooking the fact that Hirsch also had agreed to add Felicia Dunn-Jones's name to the list of victims. His strict adherence to science and logic counted for little; the denigration of belief that began in the immediate aftermath of the attacks had grown steadily more corrosive. For many, finding that Zadroga's and Godbee's untimely deaths, though tragic, were not related to their work in the recovery effort was a cynical move to protect the city from charges that it had acted with reckless disregard for the responders' well-being.

The contradictions went all the way to City Hall. After succeeding Giuliani, Mayor Bloomberg had to deal with the consequences of his predecessor's decisions. The controversy surrounding Zadroga's death underscored the city's, and Bloomberg's, greater conflict. The same mayor who would expend political capital attempting to ban smoking in public places and trans fat from restaurant menus might have been expected to readily side with those who became sick after working on the pile. But the potential liability for the city had grown too enormous to ignore.

As tales of sickness and death added up, the $1 billion insurance policy provided by Congress seemed to be all that stood between the city and a looming financial disaster. But it awkwardly positioned the city against some of the very people who had, on September 11 and afterward, come to its aid. Bloomberg's own thinking about ground zero illnesses had evolved slowly and taken tortuous twists and turns. When the first lawsuits were filed, he was clearly unwilling to acknowledge that damage had been done. "There's been a lot of controversy and different studies," he told reporters then. "Those that I've seen recently said that, generally speaking, people that worked there did not have any long-term detrimental effects. But it's something you have to keep monitoring." Bloomberg repeatedly urged caution and even expressed skepticism about links between the dust and chronic diseases, rightly pointing out—as he had on the day the big Mount Sinai study was released in 2006—that definitive studies had not yet made the case. But as the legion of responder advocates continued to grow, Bloomberg was less inclined to defend that position. And with Dr. John Howard increasingly lobbying for a greater federal role, Bloomberg came to realize there had to be another way.

The attention to fact that Bloomberg showed in 2006 was not unfounded. He was right to point out that big studies can show trends, but linking a particular disease to a specific exposure in an individual requires a whole different level of certainty. Nonetheless, this was a politically untenable position. At around the same time he had announced the $16 million screening program for residents, office workers, and anyone else who had been exposed to the contaminated air but was not eligible to be seen at Mount Sinai, the mayor revealed a change in strategy that essentially reversed his previous position. Five years after the attacks, he set up a task force to assess the full scope of the disaster, estimating the number of people who were exposed and the medical uncertainties they faced. When the report was released in February 2007, the city was no longer denying that the dust had harmed New Yorkers. Instead, it was building a case for a city stricken. Rather than trying to minimize the impact of the dust, the city now sought to maximize it. The panel concluded that more than 680,000 people who had been exposed to the dust might seek treatment. That figure included firefighters; police and city employees; and office workers, students, and residents of Lower Manhattan, Brooklyn, and New Jersey who lived within a 2-mile radius of ground zero. The potential cost of providing services for those people was calculated at $392 million per year, which the panel recommended the city aggressively seek from the federal government. Another of the panel's recommendations was to press Congress to reopen the September 11th Victim Compensation Fund, which would effectively wipe out the city's legal liability, obviating the need for the $1 billion in insurance, which could then be funneled into the reactivated fund.

That set the city on a contradictory track. While it was providing millions of dollars in assistance to people it acknowledged had been hurt by exposure to trade center dust, it continued to draw down millions from the federally funded insurance policy to challenge the accounts of sick responders who were suing the city for failing to keep them from harm. That titanic confrontation quickly escalated into one of the largest and most expensive legal proceedings New York City had ever been involved in—a mountainous and, in many ways, unprecedented courtroom offensive that would tax not only the city's resources, but eventually also its moral fiber. Some of the most contentious issues surrounding the aftermath of the terror attacks—the questions of certainty, responsibility, and what had been said and done—along with the clashes between perception and truth that had kept the city under a confounding cloud for years would be confronted in their entirety in the polished wood-paneled walls of a federal courtroom in Lower Manhattan.

The legal assault began inconspicuously enough in the middle of 2003 with phones calls from the parents of students at Fox Lane High School in suburban Bedford, N.Y., the same school that attorney David Worby's children attended. Those parents called Worby looking for a favor. The school's popular hockey coach, New York City police detective John Walcott, had taken the boys into the regional finals of the state championship and put Fox Lane hockey on the map, earning honors for several of his players and a Coach of the Year award for himself. The parents told Worby that Coach Walcott had been diagnosed with acute myelogenous leukemia and was having trouble getting his disability pension from the New York City police department. "Do us a favor," they said. "See this guy."

Walcott was just 36 when he spent five months at ground zero and the Fresh Kills landfill in 2001 and 2002. In 2003, he felt worn out, which he at first thought was because he was running himself ragged by coaching the hockey team while also putting in long shifts on the job. When just walking left him short of breath, he finally went in for tests. About 18 months after he put in his last day working with the trade center debris, a doctor drove a long needle into his hip to extract enough bone marrow for a biopsy that confirmed his worst fears. Leukemia had sent his white blood cells on a rampage. They were growing so ferociously that they were squeezing out normal red blood cells, which his body needed. Left untreated, he was told, AML could lead to death in weeks.

His doctors weren't sure why he'd gotten sick, but they knew about his exposure to the dust and they thought there was a chance that the toxins—particularly benzene—that he had been exposed to at the site might have triggered something. Walcott had to undergo a brutal course of chemotherapy and a bone marrow transplant in which he nearly died.

After he became too weak to work, Walcott applied to the Police Pension Fund for a line-of-duty disability, which would have given him a pension equivalent to three-quarters of his annual salary. Such a designation was a critical part of his plan to put his life back together. It would acknowledge that his illness was indeed linked to the work he'd done as a detective—in this case, long duty at ground zero and Fresh Kills. When the board turned him down, Walcott contacted a number of lawyers. But none would help. Then he heard from Worby.

Worby wasn't looking for additional clients. In fact, he was no longer even practicing law full-time. He had a wildly successful personal injury practice in suburban White Plains and made lots of money. At one time, his previous firm, Worby Delbello Donnellan and Weingarten, had been among the largest in suburban Westchester County, with a lucrative zoning, corporate, and commercial practice. He also handled big personal injury lawsuits, winning record settlements for his clients. With his confident, easy manner, he was a natural for television, and he experimented with a local program of his own that he called *It's Time to Sue*.

Things changed after he and his wife, Cynthia, divorced in 1994. He scaled back many parts of his life, spending less time at the office and carving out more time to be with his children. He kept his hand in personal injury litigation, thinking he could do an occasional trial while still helping to raise his kids. On 9/11, he asked his former wife to bring the children over because he wanted them all to be together in those most difficult hours of that most uncertain day. Worby remembered the day President Kennedy had been assassinated in 1963 and the fear that had pulsed through him then, although he had only been a boy. He vowed on the morning of September 11 that he would do everything in his power to ensure that his own children did not have to bear the same kind of burden. He spent the rest of that day and several more with his children at the family home in White Plains.

By the middle of 2003 when Walcott approached him, Worby was spending ever more time on his first love, composing music. He'd written a catalogue of pop and country songs, tunes such as "Wishful Thinking" and "Did You Ever Believe?," and was then working on an array of creative projects that tapped his abundant musical ambition. On the day Walcott called him, he was flying back from a business trip to pitch an improbable movie idea about a dyslexic black youth who raps backward. On the way home, he had also stopped in Nashville to record two new songs.

Music was a Worby family tradition. Both Worby's brother and sister became symphony conductors and directors. Worby himself plays the piano and can perform his own compositions, although he usually prefers to have someone else sing them. He has been an over-achiever since he was a kid. He brags that the first few books he read on his own were about Clarence Darrow, and he was the kind of dreamer who could watch *Inherit the Wind* and then prepare a sample summation of the case. He picked up Ivy League credentials at Cornell and then Villanova law, where he made the *Review* and collected offers from big firms in New York and Philadelphia. But Worby longed to be in the courtroom, making the kind of dramatic gestures and sweeping statements he had read about. "I was told, if you wanted to be a trial lawyer and get into court, to go to a small firm," he recalled. And that was how he started, though he didn't stay small for long, and he never abandoned his passion for music.

He had finally managed to strike a comfortable balance between his two loves when the Walcott case fell into his lap. At the outset, he was wary. His years as a trial lawyer had taught him to distrust the information clients convey when he meets them. Worby had learned to cross-examine them from day one, to avoid surprises in the courtroom later. He also had adopted an inviolable set of rules: "Know what you don't know" and "Don't take a case unless you can recover your costs" were two of the principal precepts he lived by. But because of his personal connection to Walcott, and a gut feeling from the first time he met the detective that his leukemia had something to do with ground zero, he broke both rules and took the case. At first, he planned to keep it simple by just writing a letter to the pension board. When that didn't work, he began the process of suing the city, filing the required notice of claim. "I'll worry about if it's going to get expensive some other time," he remarked then.

Shortly after the notice of claim was filed, Walcott called to say he had a friend, former partner Richard Volpe, whose kidneys had gone on the blink. Volpe had no family history of kidney problems; he had graduated from Fox Lane High School and, at 5 feet, 9 inches and 230 pounds, had been a model of strength. Now he was looking at a kidney transplant. Then another case came to Worby, this one also a 9/11 cop whose lungs were shot. And then more. Worby got permission to talk to their doctors. He asked whether they believed the illnesses could be linked to their work at ground zero. They didn't rule it out. They said they just didn't know for sure. Exposure seemed the probable cause, but they kept tripping over a basic discrepancy. Although there was a well-established connection between environmental exposures and certain diseases, it usually took a long time for those diseases to develop. For Walcott's leukemia, for instance, the normal latency period was between five and ten years, although there were exceptions. In Walcott's case, however, just 18 months had elapsed from the last day of work at ground zero and his diagnosis. Was it the dust or coincidence? After all, leukemia strikes otherwise healthy people all the time. Ground zero responders had cough and maybe asthma. But cancer was a different story, and researchers were not yet talking about cancer except in the vaguest way as a potential future threat. Similar latency discrepancies in other responders kept their doctors from making a link that otherwise, based on the conditions they observed, seemed to be a natural conclusion.

Worby needed to know more about chemicals and exposure. He started with basic Internet searches about toxins, particularly benzene. He then reached out to other people who were worried about the effect that exposure at ground zero might be having. He talked to Suzanne Mattei, who then headed the Sierra Club's New York office and who had worn a face mask when she went back to the organization's Lower Manhattan office a few weeks after the towers were destroyed. Worby also spoke to Juan Gonzalez of the *New York Daily News* and to Kate Jenkins, a whistleblower at the EPA who had uncovered documents she said proved that the agency and the city of New York had withheld air-monitoring results that showed contamination far worse than the agency reported. The EPA distanced itself from her, arguing that Jenkins had never been assigned to work on any part of the ground zero response and, therefore, was not privy to the critical information. Still, she had used the files that Joel Kupferman had obtained through the Freedom of Information Law to show how the EPA had concealed damning information, charges that the agency and the city repeatedly denied.

Worby didn't give up there. He kept searching for an answer, ignoring the limitations of generally accepted science in favor of an unorthodox solution. Going back to one of his golden rules, he now knew what he didn't know, and he felt that actually gave him an advantage. He conceded that he didn't have the same level of scientific knowledge as the doctors and researchers who publish in scientific journals, but he felt this actually freed him from certain constraints: "I was incapable of thinking inside the box. I ruled out nothing."[1] A trained doctor of medicine would not link Walcott's leukemia to the dust because research and scientific literature said the latency was too brief. But Worby didn't know enough not to do that. He continued to research cause and effect, exposure and disease. He had failed chemistry in high school, but he wasn't looking for an answer that had been arrived at long ago. What happened at the trade center was unprecedented. So, he reasoned, how could an answer lay in a book somewhere? He searched for a theory that could explain what the doctors were telling him was inexplicable. He found that chemicals interacting with each other changed the way they affected the body. It was a well-known aspect of Dr. Irving Selikoff's work on asbestos. Asbestos workers who smoked were more likely to get asbestosis than those who didn't smoke. If the contaminants in cigarette smoke could have a multiplying effect on the toxicity of asbestos fibers, why couldn't the witches' brew of materials in the dust, ash, and gasses have had an accelerating effect on the benzene and other toxins and, consequently, the unprotected workers who breathed it all in? And if exposure to hazardous materials in a factory typically had taken place eight hours a day over many years, what would be the impact of more intense ground zero exposure, where responders worked 12-, 18-, or 24-hour shifts for days or weeks at a time without adequate protection?

Worby eventually moved away from his theory about accelerated latency in favor of a broader interpretation, basing this hypothesis on studies of firefighters suggesting that continual exposure to harmful elements in smoke and soot increased the incidence of disease. Worby argued two separate points. First, he held that all the responders had, in effect, become firefighters. Working on the pile simulated the cumulative impact of years of a firefighter's normal exposure to fires, which led to a higher rate of disease. Second, he argued that uniformed emergency responders, including police officers who spend significant time during their careers securing the perimeters of fire scenes, arrived at ground zero with accumulated loads of contaminants already in their bodies. What this signified, he posited, was that latency periods had actually begun long before September 11.

His theories were not widely supported by the scientific community. Even though science is based on probability, not certainty, researchers were not comfortable with his leaps of logic, no matter how temptingly they answered the rescue worker's personal conundrums. Worby insisted that scientists who agreed with him would appear as expert witnesses at trial, although he did not identify them. Under the so-called Daubert Principles that will guide any trials, the presiding judge will be the scientific gatekeeper, determining which evidence can be presented. The defense will challenge Worby's theories about "synergistic effects" and "accelerated latency," and Worby will have to prove to the judge that his theories are based on sound data that respects the scientific method. The judge will rule on the reliability of scientific evidence and on its relevance, and determine whether it is allowed to be entered as evidence; then a jury will have to decide whether such proof credibly explains what happened.

As Worby continued his amateur detective work, sick responders kept showing up at his office. The number of cases quickly outstripped his ability to handle them. As he became more involved in defending the workers, Worby realized that the fight had not gone completely out of him. He was ready to defend these men and women against what he felt was a terrible injustice. He firmly believed that the dust's hazards should have been recognized almost immediately. He also thought there should have been much firmer enforcement of rules on wearing protective gear. The city and its contractors had let down those who had come to the rescue. The single mechanism that had been available for the responders to seek some kind of justice had been the September 11th Victim Compensation Fund. But the Fund had gone out of business at the end of 2003, before Worby's clients knew they were sick. The courts were the recovery workers' last hope.

Worby realized that his resources were limited and that if he intended to represent the growing number of responders, he needed help. He would have to form a business association with another law firm, one with more experience in handling big personal injury cases and the logistical capability to take on a potentially huge—and costly—class action. It would take phone banking; document ware housing; and the ability to collect, photocopy, file, and distribute hundreds of thousands, if not millions, of pages of records. The reward was substantial, but so was the risk, because the lawyers would have to pay for all the groundwork before they could collect a cent.

In summer 2004, Worby visited the offices of Paul Napoli at 115 Broadway in Lower Manhattan, a turn-of-the-century Gothic office tower adjacent to venerable Trinity Church. From Napoli's corner office on the 12th floor, there is a classic view up Broadway, past the apartment of Catherine McVay Hughes, toward City Hall, the EPA headquarters, and Kupferman's office. This is the historic parade route for presidents, popes, and sports heroes as they glide beneath a blizzard of tickertape. And off to the west, just one long block away, was the immense hole in the heart of the city that was ground zero. After the towers fell, the office building had to be closed for several weeks because power was interrupted, forcing Napoli to temporarily move his legal operation to another space.

Napoli had a track record of winning cases that ground zero responders would find encouraging. But he also had a history of judicial scrutiny that could raise questions for those who knew about it. Napoli is several years younger than Worby, but he has a big reputation in New York City's heavyweight legal circles. "Love me or hate me, I'm going to do my job" could be printed on his calling card. He was a street kid compared to Worby—no Ivy League degree or fancy contrast-collar shirts. But they did have in common the same timbre of self-confidence that made them want to shun corporate law and favor instead the precarious life of a trial lawyer. Napoli initially went to work for a small Long Island law firm, where he asked for the toughest cases. He became known as the lawyer who would take on unlucky clients nobody else wanted, and somehow win. His first personal liability case was a medical malpractice suit against the Mount Sinai Medical Center on behalf of the family of an admitted drug addict who had died after he was given the wrong medication. The addict's family was almost destitute and hadn't been able to find a lawyer willing to help. Napoli agreed to help the family, and he won a quarter-million-dollar settlement for them.

That victory gave him a taste for being a trial lawyer. He got involved in breast implant cases that other law firms wouldn't take. He had a knack for getting to the heart of an issue and proving his case to win big settlements. He was so successful in the field that, by 2004, he and his wife, Marie, also a lawyer and, like Paul, an alumnus of St. John's University Law School, were able to donate $500,000 to renovate a lecture hall, which subsequently was named for them.

That was a fairly substantial drop in the collection basket for a man who had not yet turned 38. One case in particular had helped catapult him from scrappy kid to wealthy legal powerhouse. Trolling for new business one day in 1997, Napoli had read about several women who had been treated at the Mayo Clinic for heart trouble after taking a combination of prescription drugs (fenfluramine and phentermine, which was later changed to dexfenfluramine) that went by the common name fen-phen. For a time, the drugs appeared to be a magic solution to the country's diet craze, a surefire way of suppressing appetite that could shed pounds quickly. Doctors prescribed the fen-phen duo for roughly six million people, the bulk of them women. Among its side effects were pulmonary hypertension and an increased risk of injury to heart valves.

After reading about the Mayo Clinic study, Napoli and Marc Bern, an aggressive trial lawyer who had joined Napoli's firm, decided to run a newspaper ad soliciting clients who had been taking the drug and who had subsequently developed heart problems. Luckily for them, the advertisement coincided with a decision by the Food and Drug Administration to take fen-phen off the market. That action had the same effect on personal injury lawyers that waving a red flag has on a bull. Until then, a few lawsuits challenging the diet drugs had been filed around the country. Now thousands poured in.

Some fen-phen users needed open-heart surgery to repair or replace sensitive heart valves. Most, however, claimed to have developed a leaking heart valve that caused a condition known as mitral regurgitation that ranged in severity from mild to life-threatening. In August 1999, a jury decided against the drug maker, American Home Products (later Wyeth Pharmaceuticals Company), and awarded the plaintiff—whose heart valve damage was mild and who suffered from shortness of breath and fatigue—more than $20 million. Thousands of similar suits were underway, along with several class-action lawsuits seeking prolonged medical monitoring for millions of people who had taken the drug. In October 1999, Wyeth agreed to a settlement with an anticipated payout of $3.75 billion to put an end to the litigation.

That did not end Wyeth's problems. The company's willingness to pay so much money with so little testing (Wyeth had waived the statute of limitations and did not ask for conclusive proof that fenphen had caused heart valve problems) set off a legal feeding frenzy. The burden of proof was reduced to a simple echocardiogram to show blood flow, a documented history that the plaintiff had indeed taken the drugs, and a doctor's affirmation that some damage had been done. Still, many lawyers opted out of the settlement, preferring to take their chances in court.

Napoli formed a professional partnership in July 2001 with another New York firm, Hariton D'Angelo, to round up more fenphen claims. The partnership bought its own echocardiogram machines, hired its own professionals to administer the heart flow tests, and paid around 80 cardiologists across the country to analyze the echocardiograms for the tell-tale signs of mitral regurgitation that could be blamed on the diet drugs.

Napoli eventually amassed 5,600 clients, including many that had been signed by other firms called runners. He was convinced that by threatening to go to trial, he could win greater compensation for his clients than by accepting the original settlement. His gamble was successful, and before he went to trial, he won a separate settlement for his clients estimated at nearly $1 billion, with a reported payout for the lawyers of around $350 million, making Napoli a very rich man.

But the way the fen-phen case had been handled, and the possibility that forcing Wyeth into a huge settlement just to be rid of the legal hassles would make it possible for undeserving clients to receive compensation awards, raised fundamental questions about the fairness of the mass tort system in America and the way federal courts could be bowed when huge numbers of clients are brought before them. One federal judge in the fen-phen litigation had accused the Napoli partnership of running a medical mill that lured in clients and turned out diagnostic tests whose reliability was questionable. The judge eventually threw out more than 75 cases that he found to be "medically unreasonable"[2] and gave Wyeth the right to audit every echocardiogram that the plaintiffs produced. Napoli insisted that the tests had been done properly, and he did not back down. He challenged the judge's findings about the alleged inaccuracy of the tests and eventually got all the dismissed claims paid. "We brought a little New York to Philadelphia," he boasted.

Napoli also got into a protracted dispute with another law firm that had referred several hundred fen-phen clients to him in 2001. Those lawyers claimed Napoli had manipulated the settlement in a way that cheated them out of a substantial portion of their fees. Napoli argued that legal experts had reviewed the settlement before it was put into place. He insisted that he had done nothing wrong and that the other lawyers were being greedy. A New York State Supreme Court judge then raised questions about Napoli's handling of the settlement itself and ordered a trial, which incorporated the dispute between lawyers. At the beginning of 2010, the complicated case was still moving forward.

Napoli was no stranger to controversy or to fighting against tall odds. He seemed to thrive on the challenge. He belonged to a legal family used to dealing with bad press. His father, Joseph Napoli, had been part of a personal injury law firm in Queens that gained a reputation for suing the city for damages from accidents, potholes, and the like. The law firm grossed as much as $20 million a year from such personal injury lawsuits. But in the mid-1980s, federal prosecutors began a racketeering investigation that turned up evidence of an audacious disregard for the truth. The lawyers at the firm were found to have used their relatives as eyewitnesses to phony accidents. They were accused of keeping a supply of doctors' stationery to write up reports of injuries that never occurred. And they were not beyond creating evidence. In one instance, an accident investigator working for the firm was accused of using a pickax to make a small pothole into a larger, deeper one before submitting a photograph of it as evidence. A federal jury found Joseph Napoli and several associates guilty of racketeering. He was sentenced to four years in prison and was disbarred in New York.[3]

Paul Napoli doesn't like to talk about his father's past, and clearly his father's transgressions have nothing to do with his own work. But when the subject comes up, he concedes that although the troubles made it more difficult for him to get his start, they helped shape his attitudes about the law. His father was disbarred in 1992, the same year Napoli graduated from St. John's. The experience sobered him and has led him to scrupulously avoid ethical conflicts whenever possible. "I look at it as an experience to help me do better," he said.[4]

When Worby first visited in 2004, Napoli's firm was tying up the loose ends of the fen-phen class-action suit and beginning other potentially lucrative legal proceedings. As Worby laid out his theory about ground zero dust and the accelerated latency caused by the synergistic effect of all the compounds and elements it contained, Napoli had his doubts. "I, for one, wasn't sure about the nature of the injuries," he said. He also knew that the law firms in New York that usually handle the affairs of cops and firefighters had declined to take on most of the cases stemming from ground zero. Then Worby told Napoli that the doctors treating John Walcott and Richard Volpe had changed their views and now believed that their ground zero exposure probably had caused their illnesses. Napoli started his own investigation, beginning with the book Juan Gonzalez had written about the dust in 2002. As he looked over the medical records of Worby's clients, he was convinced enough to bring on additional lawyers to review documents and begin laying the groundwork for suing the city of New York over the dust.

While the fen-phen experience certainly helped Napoli captain the massive ground zero litigation, substantial obstacles besides the accelerated latency periods needed to be overcome. Although most of their clients complained of respiratory problems such as those that Mount Sinai and the fire department had already reported—asthma, sinusitis, chronic obstructive pulmonary disease—or digestive issues caused by the high alkalinity of the dust, the workers also claimed to have other illnesses, including several different cancers that had not yet been linked to ground zero. The lawsuit would have been stronger if every claimant had had the same disease that could be traced to the same environmental hazard. In the fen-phen case, the effects of taking the drug were mostly limited to damage to heart valves. All of the clients had taken fen-phen. What differed from person to person was the severity of the injury. For the ground zero dust exposure cases, Napoli and Worby were facing a medical encyclopedia of symptoms and illnesses. Each new one sent them back to the list of hazardous materials in the dust, looking for known and suspected links.

Worby and Napoli eventually represented most, though not all, of the 10,000 responders (more than half of them firefighters or police officers) who sued the city claiming hundreds of different sicknesses. They agreed on a way to divide the work. On this personal injury dream team, Napoli provided the logistical guts but would mostly remain hidden from public view. Napoli's voice is tattooed with a slight Brooklyn accent, and he has a boyish, wise-guy grin that makes him seem like he's trying to pull off something that he shouldn't—a trait that opposing lawyers, and sitting judges, can find exasperating. Worby, on the other hand, is so used to performing that he can appear both tough and sensitive at the same time. He tends to favor bright cufflinks and white-collar blue shirts, his sandy hair slightly long over the ears and in the back, so that he can flow easily between the court room and the stage where he performs his music.

On September 13, 2004, at the Marriott Hotel near ground zero, it was Worby who had announced the filing of a class-action lawsuit on behalf of public and private employees involved in the long cleanup at ground zero. The suit initially named the four big private construction companies that had handled the work for the city, as well as the Port Authority of New York and New Jersey and Larry Silverstein, the owner of Number 7 and leaseholder of the twin towers. Worby explained to reporters that the city would be added to the list of defendants once procedural requirements were met. He was flanked by Walcott and a dozen recovery workers, many of them Latinos who had cleaned offices without personal protective equipment, not even gloves or a dust mask. The lawsuit cited safe workplace laws in New York State and claimed that the companies had ignored their responsibility to provide suitable working conditions.

Clearly comfortable in front of the television cameras, Worby concisely laid out the heart of his arguments: The city had been in a foolhardy rush to move ahead. He insisted that after the first few days had passed and the chances of recovering any survivors was nil, the job should have been shut down until proper safety precautions were put in place. "There was no rush on September 15, or on October 15," and so on, Worby told reporters. And for the first time in public, he made a dire prediction: More people would die as a result of being exposed to the trade center contaminants than had died in the attacks on 9/11, an assertion he would make repeatedly as the litigation inched forward. Not afraid of being considered alarmist, Worby called ground zero the greatest toxic contamination in the history of the nation, rushing through the list of hazards in a verbal sprint that added to the sense of urgency and gave the impression of unassailability.

The dust, he asserted, contained these elements:

- Two hundred thousand pounds of lead from the estimated 50,000 personal computers in thousands of offices
- Mercury in the towers' more than half a million fluorescent lights
- Dioxin from oil and fuel
- Two thousand tons of asbestos

- Benzene from more than 91,000 liters of burned jet fuel
- Cadmium, PCBs, and up to 2 million pounds of toxins known as polycyclic aromatic hydrocarbons

Worby was accompanied by an expert witness, forensic toxicologist William Sawyer, who called the debris pile a "giant toxic waste site" and pointed out that the incomplete combustion created by the long-smoldering fires had churned out harmful emissions until the fires were extinguished in December. Workers such as Walcott breathed in this toxic soot while working around the pile, and in many instances, the level of contaminants to which they were exposed exceeded federal standards. Worby said he would not be seeking punitive damages against the employers. His goal was to win enough money to establish a system of screening and tracking exposed workers for decades, to detect early warning signs of disease. When asked about his own remuneration, he conceded that, in such cases, lawyers' fees could amount to a third of any settlement, but he was quick to point out that bringing the class action to court required a substantial outlay without any guarantee of return (a violation of his second golden rule, or an acknowledgement of his confidence that the case was winnable).

The news conference announcing the lawsuit was a carefully choreographed production designed to lay the groundwork for a sympathetic public response to the plight of the responders. Creating that positive perception of the workers would turn out to be a critical part of the Worby–Napoli team's legal strategy. "They were all our WTC heroes then," Worby told reporters. "And now they're our WTC victims." The dozen workers who flanked him silently during his presentation were made available to reporters afterward and were instructed to be cooperative. At least one accompanied a television news crew to ground zero to be filmed. Worby made a DVD of the news conference available to reporters afterward, and it contained, apparently inadvertently, a kind of director's cut video exchange that showed just how much of a staged production it was. After the news conference concluded, the producers tagged on a short hallway interview with Dan O'Connell, who was then president of Kodora Communications, which had put the production together. On the video, O'Connell, who jokingly identified himself as the minister of propaganda for the event, was asked by an off-camera interviewer how the news conference went. "Given the amount of time we were given to pitch the story, we did well," he replied, likening Worby's performance to hitting a three-run home run in the seventh game of the American League Championship series. Image and perception remained the ultimate goals.

Few of the ground zero workers in the lawsuit knew much about Napoli's history with fen-phen. Most, in fact, didn't know anything about him at all, even after they had joined the lawsuit and were being represented by him in court. Worby had been the very public face of the litigation from the beginning, and he was the central figure of the news conference in 2004. But when the workers called the toll-free number that Worby gave out then (1-877-WTC-HERO), they were connected with Napoli's office.

The litigation landed in the tightly disciplined courtroom of Judge Alvin K. Hellerstein, an experienced and impatient jurist who handled other 9/11 litigation, including the cases of the families that declined to accept a settlement from the September 11th Victim Compensation Fund and insisted on suing the airlines over the deaths of their relatives. He also heard the cases of the families of dead firefighters who had tried to sue the city over the decision to issue an internal communications system that had failed disastrously on 9/11. Long after the debris had been cleared from ground zero, the 9/11 tragedy elicited raw emotions in his courtroom on the 14th floor of the Daniel Patrick Moynihan Federal Building at 500 Pearl Street near Chinatown, less than a mile from ground zero. (That is the same building where the Obama administration proposed putting the mastermind of the 9/11 attacks on trial. Bloomberg initially saw merit in the idea of forcing the suspected terrorist to face a jury just blocks from ground zero. But when the cost of security was estimated to exceed $200 million a year, he pressured Washington to move the trial outside the city.)

Hellerstein initially tried to pare down the number of cases by redirecting most of them to the state courts, arguing that only events directly related to the crashes were covered by the federal legislation (the Air Transportation Safety and System Stabilization Act) Congress had passed in the immediate aftermath of the attacks. He argued that the federal court was not the proper venue for the cases involving respiratory injuries that took place after the rescue phase ended and the recovery and cleanup officially began. He also wanted all injuries that were linked to any location but ground zero—the Staten Island landfill, the riverside transfer station, or the medical examiner's office—remanded to the state court. But in 2005, the Second Circuit Court of Appeals reversed his decision, saying that the federal court was the appropriate place to hear all litigation related to the attacks. That suited the city, because responders and volunteers had come from all over the country. Keeping the cases in federal court ensured that the city would not have to defend itself in many different state courts.

With the venue question settled, Napoli and Worby continued to enlist clients, swamping the court with hundreds of new cases each month. The maneuverings for such a massive legal confrontation are dense and archaic. When Worby and Napoli were forced to move the claims from state court to federal court, they had to pay to have each of the 10,000 plaintiffs listed separately, although they all were eventually consolidated under a master complaint with a single docket number: 21 MC 100. In another move designed to keep him in sure control of the litigation, Hellerstein refused to certify this as a class action. Unlike fen-phen, in which the triggering agent was a single combined drug and the most prominent resulting injury was heart valve damage, each ground zero plaintiff was exposed at a different time and in a different way, depending on arrival, deployment, and time spent at the site. The ways that the dust affected individuals differed so greatly from one to another that hundreds of diseases were potentially involved. Lawyers in huge class actions can bring so many cases that they can tip the balance of power in court to their side and away from the bench. Hellerstein wouldn't have it. By consolidating the individual claims into a joint action, Hellerstein hoped to maintain control, maximize efficiency and speed up resolution of the cases. It did not turn out exactly that way.

Worby and Napoli's strategy covered a combination of claims, including reckless disregard and dizzying incompetence that they would say bordered on criminal action by the city and its contractors. They wanted to show that, in the 48 hours after the first plane struck, firefighters had not had access to adequate personal protective equipment. Their air tanks had been practically useless because they lasted no more than half an hour, while the fires at ground zero would burn for 100 days. From that particular aspect, ground zero more closely resembled a forest fire than an urban blaze, and New York never adequately reacted to that reality. Instead of adjusting its procedures to take that long duration into account and slowing things down to impose long-range controls, the city continuously sacrificed safety for speed.

Worby and Napoli conceded that it may not have been possible to provide adequate personal protection to firefighters or the construction workers who poured in to help them during the frantic search for survivors. But they insisted that once the chance of finding survivors ended, the rescue turned into a recovery and removal operation. At that point, they contended, the city should have regrouped, issued strict safety guidelines, enforced them aggressively, and otherwise acted as though worker safety was at least as important as clearing away the debris.

For five years after the news conference at the Marriott, the lawsuit moved ponderously through the legal system. Despite a full calendar with the other trade center litigation, Hellerstein worked to maintain control over the case, ensuring that the massive litigation was not stalled while logistical issues were being resolved. The city asked to review basic medical documents, and as they started to come in, Hellerstein had to referee a gigantic battle of strategy and tactics between the city and the workers. Every aspect of the case was oversized. Just calling up the legal documents on the federal court's computerized system could freeze a computer terminal, so massive was the record. Any day Hellerstein called a case management session, his courtroom was packed with dozens of lawyers representing the city, the four prime contractors, and dozens of subcontractors, along with attorneys who represented a few rescue workers who had not signed with the Worby–Napoli team. They filled every place on the public benches and were allowed to spill over into jury seats.

Napoli personally handled most of the courtroom pleadings at this stage of the case, constantly pushing back against the city. Hellerstein grew impatient with the legal wrangling and occasionally seemed peeved with Napoli, whose brashness sometimes peeked through the courtly veneer the federal bench expected. Hellerstein more than once threatened Napoli with sanctions unless he provided all the medical records the city requested. Napoli had argued with the judge that the city's request was overly broad. Hellerstein was reluctant to leave out anything and ordered that all medical records, whether or not directly related to the claimed trade center injury, should be produced for each plaintiff dating back to 1995—and longer, if warranted. That would include information from doctors that the clients had not seen for years, doctors who had died or moved, and records from dentists and podiatrists and other specialists that on the surface seemed to have nothing to do with 9/11. Many of the clients did not have the records, which forced the lawyers to negotiate with busy medical practices that already were buried in insurance company paperwork. When the documents were produced, they had to be reviewed by medical professionals, collated, and filed accordingly. Napoli and Worby used a Long Island warehouse to store the quickly expanding mass of documents.

Hellerstein made it abundantly clear that he intended to push for settlement of the cases. Well before the first trial was ready to be heard, he appointed two independent legal experts to act as special masters, or adjuncts to the court, to ensure that his orders from the bench were followed and to take on other tasks designed to help move the litigation along. The two experienced jurists Hellerstein selected, James A. Henderson of Cornell Law School and Aaron D. Twerski, former dean of the Hofstra Law School (who had earlier been involved in the Agent Orange case on the side of the veterans), were given a broad mandate to analyze the range of illnesses and symptoms that Napoli and Worby had reported. They helped categorize the illnesses into six broad groups and the symptoms of each into four classes of severity. This way, if the chance for a settlement arose, they could refer to an already agreed-upon grid to distribute the biggest awards to those who were most ill. Hellerstein felt time breathing down his neck. "Unless we do something now," he warned both sides seated before him in the courtroom, "this case will drag on and it will be left to our children, and our children's children, to settle."

For Worby and Napoli, the lawsuit's unwieldy nature became a strategic advantage. As the number of clients grew and amount of medical records and other documents that had to be collected exploded, the prospect of ever going to trial became less likely. They did not have to restrict themselves to the most serious cases. To build their numbers, they took in many cases, even those of responders with minor illnesses and those whose only complaint was that they were worried about what might happen to them in the future. The lawyers' strategy was hitched to the idea that a settlement would mean that the difficult questions— proving that there was a causal link between the dust and disease, challenging the good faith aspect of the city's response, deflecting the responsibility of the workers to have protected themselves—and all those medical, legal, scientific, and social policy dilemmas that had confounded the city and clouded its vision, would never have to be answered conclusively. The problems would be resolved by money, and the issues would simply go away, if only the city agreed to a settlement.

But the city dug in its heels and would not agree—at least not until it got the terms it wanted, including a cap on future liability, terms that no one had expressed any intention of offering.

Endnotes

[1] Personal interview, 13 February 2007.

[2] Bartle, Judge Harvey III, Memorandum and Pretrial Order No. 2640, United States District Court for the Eastern District of Pennsylvania, 14 November 2002.

[3] "Lawyer Napoli Disbarred," *Newsday*, 28 February 1992, p. 33; and Bernstein, Nina, "No Holds Barred for Guilty Lawyer; Disbarment Proceeds Slowly," *Newsday*, 11 February 1992, p. 7.

[4] Personal interview, 7 February 2008.

13

Science on trial

When James E. Tyrrell Jr. is not around, other lawyers in the wide circles of power and privilege he travels in sometimes refer to him as "the master of disaster," with a precarious balance of both antipathy and respect. *Super Lawyers* magazine was one of the first to use that sobriquet to describe Tyrrell, an admiring nod to his work representing corporate clients enmeshed in some of the nastiest legal calamities of the last century. Tyrrell is widely known as a fierce and precise opponent, a champion debater who knows the law and how to use it to the advantage of his clients, who, not surprisingly, love him and pay mightily for his services. The same is not true of his opponents and critics, who accuse him of being rapacious and underhanded. In many ways, he resembles his namesake, Sir James Tyrrell, a fifteenth-century English knight who was a hero to some but a villain to others. Tyrell's story is a vivid one, immortalized by Shakespeare in *Richard III*. An honorable nobleman in the House of York, Tyrrell became master of the king's henchmen after the Duke of Gloucester assumed the throne as Richard III, following the mysterious death of two princes who were in line to become king. After Richard was killed in the Battle of Bosworth in 1485, Tyrrell successfully switched loyalties for a time to Henry VII and again gained positions of power. But he later was accused of treason and imprisoned in the Tower of London. Under torture, Tyrrell was said to have confessed to having had a hand in the murders of the two young princes, but he would not say where their bodies were hidden. Tyrrell's head was chopped off on May 6, 1502.

James Tyrrell the lawyer doesn't believe he is related in any way to Sir James. "We're hardly noble," he says of his family.[1] He didn't even know about Sir James until a family trip to the bloody tower in

2000, when he was traveling with his son's college lacrosse team. Tyrrell's own ancestors came from Ireland by way of Jersey City, and he figures they probably were chased out by the British. But he, too, is honored by some and considered a scoundrel by others (who no doubt would call for his head, had they the chance). Tyrrell is a fierce litigator, defending big corporations in product liability suits. He started out representing Monsanto in the Agent Orange case brought by Vietnam War veterans exposed to the herbicide, and he represented General Electric against women who had been injured when breast implants filled with the company's silicone ruptured. He is careful, cautious, and unrelentingly polite, rarely making a mistake and almost never doing anything that antagonizes the judges before whom he appears. Yet when it comes time for the kill, he does not hesitate to finish off his courtroom opponents.

Nothing about his rapacious nature can be divined from his outward appearance: neatly parted hair, courtly manners, impeccable tailoring, and controlled demeanor, even in the middle of a courtroom cat fight. A top competitor in national debate tournaments in high school, and a moot court champion at Harvard Law School who served briefly in the Navy Judge Advocate General's Corps during Vietnam, Tyrrell presents a striking contrast to Paul Napoli's streetwise persona. But Tyrrell is in the unenviable position of defending the city of New York and its contractors and subcontractors in the high-stakes fight against the thousands of workers who are repeatedly referred to in the courtroom and in the media as "heroes." Napoli and David Worby, with the help of sympathetic tabloid media and a legion of responders—including a few who had devoted their lives to persecuting the government for its perceived 9/11 sins—managed to create a public image of the city as callously sending workers onto the pile without regard for their safety. In the court of public opinion, Tyrrell was a bad guy from the day he was selected to represent the city in federal court. The *New York Post* dubbed him "the devil's advocate," which, for Tyrrell, was something of a relief because they at least had not called him the devil himself. On the other side of town, the *New York Daily News* relentlessly criticized Tyrrell and the captive insurance company, which, by the end of the decade, had burned through $200 million in administrative costs and legal fees defending New York City. At the same time, the city, through the captive, had paid less than $300,000 in claims to workers with orthopedic injuries, and not one cent to anyone who had developed a respiratory illness or cancer.

Bringing in hired legal guns was a departure for New York. For the physical work of stabilizing Lower Manhattan and removing the debris at ground zero, the city had assumed quick and sure control, believing its own expertise was more perfectly suited to the job than the accumulated experience of the federal agencies. At the very outset, New York had also defended itself, putting together a trade center task force within the office of the city's corporation counsel. The possibility of facing lawsuits from the extremely dangerous work of the cleanup had been apparent within the first month after the attack. The city was being advised by its lawyers—and the legal staffs of the four prime contractors—that workers, volunteers, and residents could eventually file lawsuits for a wide range of injuries. Within a few weeks of the attack, a deputy mayor in Giuliani's office was being warned that the city faced as many as 10,000 liability claims connected to 9/11, "including toxic tort cases that might arise in the next few decades."

The special captive insurance company created to defend the city against 9/11 lawsuits operated like any other insurance company, with a board of directors, salaried officers, and requirements for maintaining enough reserves to meet its obligations for the next quarter-century. Once it was established, the captive looked around for a firm to handle the city's defense. It held a legal beauty contest to pick someone to take on the whole mess—handling the city's defense and also defending all the private companies that had done work for it during the cleanup. The captive decided that it would be more efficient to deal with one legal team than a squadron of lawyers individually representing each one of the defendants. Speaking with a single voice, especially one that commanded the kind of attention that could counter the plaintiffs' public relations advantage, was expected to strengthen the defense's position. The request for proposals went to the top 30 toxic tort law firms in the country. At the time, Tyrrell worked for one of largest of them, Latham & Watkins, with more than 300 lawyers in its New York office and a newly formed office in New Jersey that Tyrrell led with Michael Chertoff, the future head of Homeland Security in the Bush administration. In October 2004, just

weeks after Worby filed the class-action lawsuit, Tyrrell was picked to
lead the trade center case. Two years later, he was recruited by Patton
Boggs, a powerful law firm in Washington, to open offices in New
York and New Jersey. He did, taking many of the lawyers, and the
trade center case, with him.

The $1 billion in reserves deposited by the federal government
quickly became intoxicating fiscal catnip that neither plaintiffs nor
defense seemed able to resist. Before New York State had passed the
legislation it needed to charter the captive, only about 130 trade center lawsuits had been pending. All the others that had been filed till
then had been resolved by the September 11th Victim Compensation
Fund. Once the captive opened shop at the end of 2004, lawsuits
poured in hundreds at a time, with everyone hoping to reach into that
$1 billion pot. But as in so many of the conflicts that had arisen since
the towers crumbled, the issue was clouded by misunderstanding or
deliberate misinterpretation. Even members of Congress who voted
for the $1 billion fund insisted that it had been designed to compen-
sate injured and ailing workers, just like the original fund. In truth,
Congress could have decided to reopen or extend that fund, but it
hadn't. Instead, it had deliberately channeled the issue to the courts,
setting up a system for covering the city's liability and defending the
private construction companies that had pitched in to help—a logical
move for an administration that had insisted there was no danger in
the air. The state-chartered insurance company would cover the costs
of indemnifying the city, just as any home insurance policy would
cover the cost of defending a homeowner facing a liability lawsuit.

Some of the confusion about the fund's purpose stemmed from
willful disregard of the facts, an overt attempt to sway public opinion
against the captive and, in turn, the city's defense. But the law itself is
straightforward. It calls for providing $1 billion "to establish a captive
insurance company or other appropriate insurance mechanism for
claims arising from debris removal, which may include claims made
by city employees." Nonetheless, Sen. Charles Schumer and others
who had pushed for it repeatedly insisted that the money was
intended to compensate the "heroes" who had been injured in the
recovery operation, and it should be used that way. (In 2007, Napoli

and Worby sued the city and the captive in state court for misusing and wasting the money Congress gave them. When Mayor Bloomberg told reporters that the lawyers "just don't know the facts," the lawyers responded testily, "[I]t's the mayor who doesn't know the facts.")

Although the New York City Law Department no longer controlled the case, the lawyers there had strong ideas about how it ought to be handled, and they didn't always agree with the outsiders. Used to dealing with the barrage of legal attacks against the city's day-to-day operations, these lawyers believed that, for the city to be held liable for injuries to the workers, Napoli and Worby would have to prove that the city had acted recklessly and without regard to the health and safety of the people working there. And that meant proving not that masks hadn't been given to everyone on the pile, but that the city hadn't bothered to hand out any masks at all. The lawyers knew that no matter how imperfect the handling of ground zero might be portrayed, there was plenty of evidence to show that the city had attempted to do the right thing. They also knew that more than 130,000 respirator masks had been distributed to workers during the cleanup, and that the city, the uniformed services, and the contractors all had repeatedly urged workers to wear them. The message had been conveyed at daily safety meetings, through signs and posters at the site, and even through the Department of Design and Construction's early surveillance plan of using digital cameras to identify violators. The city's lawyers had a sense from early on in the fight that some of the workers' claims of injuries and ailments related to 9/11 might not hold up in court. Experience with pothole claims and broken sidewalks had taught them to be suspicious.

The lawyers also relied on an aspect of city law that requires anyone intending to sue the city to first file an initial notice of claim within a short time of the incident that caused the injury. That notice usually triggers a pretrial questioning session to determine whether there is sufficient basis for the suit to move forward. The first batch of these proceedings, designated 50-H hearings, left city lawyers with the impression that the symptoms listed in the lawsuits had been exaggerated. In some instances, the workers were unable to provide any corroborating information about the symptoms that they themselves had earlier reported. Other times they contradicted the information about the amount of time they had spent at ground zero. And under questioning by the city, some conceded that their troubles had been temporary and that, at the time of the hearings, they felt fine.

Some lawyers thought the city's best bet for putting a quick end to the litigation was to file a motion for summary judgment and to ask the court to reach a quick decision based on the undisputed material facts of the case, which they believed were firmly on their side. This kind of a "so what?" motion can be successful as long as both sides do not disagree on important material aspects of what happened. Then if the plaintiffs tried to second-guess the city by arguing that the recovery should have been handled differently, the city felt confident it would win. In the early phase of the litigation, Napoli and Worby did not dispute the fact that air monitoring had taken place at ground zero at some point, that thousands of respirators had been handed out (although responders weren't always properly trained in how to use them), and that the fire department's daily Incident Action Plans included advisories about wearing respirators but didn't do much to make sure the advisories were followed.

The city's attorneys believed that even if Napoli and Worby could prove that there were not enough respirators for everyone at ground zero or that enforcement was lax, it wouldn't matter, because the city had tried to make working at the site safe, and the court would be reluctant to overrule the city's actions during an emergency. With the monumental chaos of the cleanup and worries about the slurry wall collapsing, of biological contamination, or even of another attack in Manhattan, the city was willing to concede that its efforts had not been perfect. And that, it argued, was a far cry from reckless disregard for the safety of the workers.

But Tyrrell and the Patton Boggs team saw summary judgment as too risky a strategy because it let everything rest on the judge's interpretation of undisputed material facts. "A summary judgment motion can be lost because there is a genuinely disputed material fact. That is the Achilles heel of a summary judgment motion," Tyrrell noted. In a complicated case such as this, with many possible points of dispute, the plaintiffs could ask the court to look at disputed facts, such as when the respirators were available or how consistently the city supervisors enforced safety rules, and deny the defendants' motion for summary judgment, at least for the moment. Plaintiffs could also claim they did not have enough time to obtain all the necessary documents and testimony related to the case to show that a material fact is disputed, again forcing the court to deny the motion.

Judge Alvin Hellerstein allowed limited discovery to take place so that facts about the rescue and recovery at ground zero would be laid out clearly. The lawyers deposed dozens of responders, city officials, and expert witnesses. They often strayed from the court's order to strictly limit questioning to the immunity issue, providing detailed insights into what had happened after the towers were destroyed. The plaintiffs' team grilled Michael Burton, executive deputy commissioner of the Department of Design and Construction. When Burton was asked whether he had considered shutting down the project when compliance with personal protective equipment dipped below 30 percent, he responded, "I can't recall anybody telling me, even with the vast array of experts out there, I don't think there was one individual that ever made that recommendation to me. So, no I don't think I considered it." Beyond that, Burton said, if he had told fire department brass that the job ought to be stopped because people were working on the pile without the proper respirators, "I think they would have looked at me like I had three heads."

Under questioning, executives from the four principal construction companies testified that they had initiated their own safety plans or had drawn up plans with others, and that they had tried to get workers to wear proper respiratory protection from the start. They acknowledged the difficulty of getting workers to keep the hot, uncomfortable masks on all day long for weeks on end, when they had hardly ever worked with the respirators before. They discussed the complicated issues affecting safety at the site and generally agreed that strict enforcement by the Occupational Safety and Health Administration (OSHA) or the city's health department might have been effective, but it could have wasted a lot of time and, in the end, might not have made any real difference in worker safety. They also said that, in the latter stages of the project, they did begin to fine or suspend workers who consistently flouted the rules, but that didn't do much to improve compliance rates.

James Abadie, the senior vice president in charge of the New York office for Bovis, one of the four big contractors, testified that one of his supervisors had been let go in November 2001 after being reprimanded repeatedly for ignoring safety rules. "He didn't want to wear his mask," Abadie said during his deposition. The supervisor wasn't being contrary or unruly; instead, Abadie said, "He was very gung-ho on the fact that he was saving America."

Safety monitors patrolled the site, taking note of people working without their respirators on, Abadie said. But after a while, construction workers realized that they were not going to get fired if they flouted the rules. They also watched firefighters come back to the pile day after day without wearing their masks, so they left theirs off, too, despite Bovis's best efforts at compliance. When Abadie said that, he got under Napoli's skin. "You're blaming the workers that work for you for not wearing respirators, is that what you're telling us?" Napoli snapped. Abadie said, no, that wasn't it. "Well, who are you blaming?" Napoli countered. Abadie said that a more effective enforcement plan would have helped a lot, but he didn't think they could ever have gotten to 100 percent compliance on such a large and busy site.

Napoli did not challenge the veracity of the accounts given by city officials or the construction company supervisors. What emerged was a portrait of a flawed response in which sometimes all the choices were bad choices. City lawyers thought that the stage had been perfectly set for the "so what?" summary judgment motion.

But Tyrrell was convinced that the stronger strategy was to press for a motion to dismiss, based on the claim that provisions of state law provided the city with broad immunity when responding to an attack or a civil defense emergency. It was a tactic that Tyrrell would have gleaned from the monumental Agent Orange case, in which the federal government was shielded by its assumed sovereign immunity.

"It is not a difficult question as a matter of law," is how Tyrrell framed the immunity question in court documents.[2] He conceded, however, that it is a complex public policy question that balances the harm done by eliminating the public's right to sue with the benefits of unleashing the powers of government and its contractors to respond to crises without the fear of being sued. Tyrrell cited the New York State Defense Emergency Act, enacted during the dark days of the Cold War in 1951, when the possibility of a nuclear attack on the United States seemed very real. Responding to such an unthinkable act would be an unprecedented challenge, and the legislature did not want government hobbled by worries over liability, as long as it acted in good faith to protect the public interest. Tyrrell also pointed to the precedent set by another state law, one that extends immunity to government and its private contractors when responding to natural or man-made disasters.

The two sides wrangled over the issue, weighing both options while considering the consequences of making the wrong decision. If Tyrrell's strategy worked, they would be able to get the court to put an end to the litigation before the city was dragged into a bruising legal battle. However, if they were wrong, they were certain to be caught in legal quicksand, a costly and distracting conflict that would go on for years, just as the Agent Orange litigation has continued for decades. Tyrrell was convinced from the beginning that the immunity argument was the right way to go; eventually, after broad discussions about tactics, the city reluctantly agreed to proceed that way.

Besides the technical legal maneuvering involving pleadings and motions, Tyrrell had a sensitive argument to make that required great finesse because it could be seen as supporting the plaintiffs' position. In court, he acknowledged that those who had rushed down to help and who worked at the pile under exhausting and dangerous conditions were, in fact, true heroes. He also acknowledged that the city of New York had managed, under unspeakably difficult conditions, to raise itself back up. When another calamity strikes the city, or any city, and government reaches out to the private sector for help, those who will be expected to respond need to be able to do so without fear of financial ruin if they are sued for the work they do. Tyrrell argued that allowing the suits to go forward would poison this atmosphere of civic involvement, hampering future rescue efforts and endangering countless lives.

Napoli and Worby wasted no time launching their counterattack. In court, they criticized the city's efforts during the rescue and recovery operations as being woefully inadequate and, in some instances, fraudulent, and not constituting a "good faith effort," as outlined in the statutes, especially after compliance rates for respirator use plummeted and there was little attempt to improve them. They cited state labor laws requiring employers to provide safe workplaces, regardless of the exigencies of the moment. They argued that the contractors were "doing nothing more ... than engaging in [the] regular course" of their day-to-day business activities, and that this should not be construed as responding to a civil defense emergency.

They also tried to convince Hellerstein that the city's claim of immunity did not hold up to congressional scrutiny, arguing that if the members of Congress had believed that the city and its contractors could not be sued, they would never have felt the need to create a $1 billion insurance fund to help the city defend itself against such lawsuits.

Hellerstein was mindful of the great public interest in the suit and the huge number of people involved. He did not believe that a dry courtroom deliberation on the issue of whether the city—and, by extension, the private construction companies—could be sued would satisfy the public need for airing perceived injustices. He had learned from the volatile emotions unleashed by the other trade center cases he was hearing (particularly the ones involving the radios) that the pain caused by the events of 9/11 ran very deep and that the years that had passed had done little to dull them.

In late 2006, Hellerstein ruled that the city did not have unlimited immunity, although he did find that at particular times and places during the rescue, recovery, and cleanup operations, the city and the contractors could have had immunity. It seemed logical that the initial response by the fire and police departments constituted civil defense and would be covered by the city's immunity, but what about the routine removal of steel and concrete in February and March? The ironworkers who cut their way through the tangled beams so a victim's body could be recovered were doing essential government work, but what about the laborers who had been hired to sweep the perimeter? Even after dozens of depositions had been taken and thousands of pages of documents had been provided, Hellerstein ruled that he still didn't have enough information to determine the limit of the city's immunity. He declared it to be a question of fact that could be settled only at trial. Whether the city and its contractors were covered by the immunity statutes would have to be decided on a case-by-case basis, and that would entail gathering even more information before a single trial could begin. The city had to continue producing an endless stream of documents for a case that might not have any legal basis, depending on the way immunity was finally determined. And the plaintiffs continued putting together countless records for trials they firmly believed would be supplanted by a settlement.

The city appealed Hellerstein's ruling, and the Second Circuit issued a stay on all proceedings until it reached a decision. The court held on to the appeal for more than a year. Finally, early in 2008, the Second Circuit upheld the spirit of Hellerstein's decision, finding that the city did not have blanket immunity but that under some circumstances the city and its contractors were protected from lawsuits.[3]

For all the conflicting details and abstract legal theories argued in court, one confounding truth emerged from the confrontation: The deeper the litigation proceeded, the farther it got from providing the kind of justice that the responders, and Hellerstein, were demanding. The period of gravest danger—the first weeks after the collapse, when the environmental hazards were greatest and the rescue operation was in full swing—corresponded most closely to the definition of civil defense and response to disaster outlined in the immunity statutes.

Thus, it was achingly apparent for much of the time that the litigation crawled along that the most seriously injured responders might not be compensated if their cases went to trial. The need for protection was greatest when the ability to provide it was most limited. The agonizing conundrum for the court, and for society, was that when science would be most able to prove the connection between exposure and higher risk of disease, the law would be least willing to assign blame. And the stronger the legal argument became, the weaker was the science.

With the immunity issue still rather vague, many questions remained. If the city was immune from lawsuits while responding to an emergency, at what point did the emergency response turn into more conventional municipal cleanup? Precisely when should the city have slowed things down to ensure that everyone on the pile had proper protective equipment—and was wearing it—instead of moving with full haste to recover the remains of dead firefighters and office workers? The sheer number of plaintiffs, and the variability of their arrival at ground zero and the time they spent there, made comprehensive answers impossible. Each case would have to be judged on its own merits.

That prospect distressed Hellerstein, who clearly was losing patience with the litigation. He understood the city's argument that a negative ruling could have a chilling effect on future rescue efforts. But Hellerstein, who had been appointed to the federal bench by Bill Clinton in 1998 after a long and successful career with one of New York's old-line law firms, Stroock & Stroock & Lavan, had a keen sense of wanting to do the right thing. He was determined to uphold the oath he took as a federal judge to "administer justice without respect to persons, and do equal right to the poor and to the rich." It was apparent that he felt the overwhelming public interest in ground zero demanded that something be done to help the responders who had been injured. In his rulings on procedural matters and in the comments he made from the bench, it was clear that he knew he was expected to provide more than a technical legal decision. The people deserved justice, not legal niceties. And many of the injured had already waited too long.

Because of the range of cases he handled, Hellerstein probably knew more about the anguish of 9/11 than any other judge in the Southern District. The families that did not go before the victim compensation fund because they insisted on trials came before him. (Eventually, all but one family settled instead of going to trial.) The relatives of firemen who died in the collapse had come before him with claims that the two-way radios they had carried had not worked properly, preventing them from responding to an order to evacuate. He listened to the tearful arguments of the families who longed for the microscopic remains of the deceased to be removed from the Fresh Kills landfill and transferred to a fitting memorial.

Hellerstein had been 67 when New York City was attacked, the son of working-class Jewish immigrants. He had grown up in the Bronx speaking Yiddish at home and had made his father, a shopkeeper, intensely proud when he had graduated from Columbia University in 1954 and then Columbia law school two years later. Similar to Tyrrell, he had served in the Judge Advocate General Corps—in his case, for the U.S. Army. A lifelong New York Yankees fan, he celebrated his 60th birthday by attending the Yankees fantasy baseball camp.

Hellerstein's up-from-the-ground life story imbued him with a profound sense that fairness and justice were as essential to life as are water and air. In those other 9/11 cases, his rulings had shown that he understood how the law itself, no matter how noble, could not always provide a remedy for those who had suffered injustice. This was particularly clear in the cases involving the firefighters' radios. The families had already accepted compensation from the Feinberg fund, which prohibited them from pursuing any other legal recourse. Burdened by their decisions, and furious with the city over its handling of the radios, they came to Hellerstein hoping to find a way to press their case. The law was clear, and the families didn't have a strong argument. But Hellerstein believed that justice would not have been served by summarily dismissing them; fairness required more. Although he eventually ruled against the families, he offered them ample opportunity to tell their stories in court, in front of city officials, the radio manufacturer's lawyers, and reporters who would publish accounts of the families' tragedies.

A federal courtroom was far from an efficient setting for resolving the responders' demands for justice. The burden of proof, the rules of the court, and the unassailable exigencies of science and epidemiology were often at odds there. Delay, protracted negotiation, and legal minutiae would always conspire to keep the court from delivering satisfactory answers in time to compensate those who had legitimately been injured at ground zero. But there they were, in Hellerstein's courtroom, month after month, anxiously awaiting some resolution. At one point, Hellerstein had suggested that the $1 billion that Congress had appropriated for the city's legal protection go into a fund that would compensate people for injuries they had suffered while in service to the city without dealing with issues of fault. But Tyrrell said the city could agree to such a plan only if it had protection from future lawsuits. His experience with Agent Orange had taught him how difficult it could be to draw a line under this kind of toxic tort; decades after the Vietnam War ended, new diseases were still being added to the list of those linked to Agent Orange exposure.

Hellerstein, too, was mindful of the precedent set by the Agent Orange litigation and the decisions made in that case by District Court Judge Jack B. Weinstein, who had been one of his professors at Columbia. Facing many problematic issues in the Agent Orange litigation, Weinstein had used the power of the court to create conditions that convinced the parties to settle, which they eventually did, although for a far lower amount than the plaintiff lawyers had sought.

When the idea of settlement was raised in Hellerstein's court, Napoli and Worby argued that $1 billion would not be enough to adequately compensate all 10,000 clients and those who might become sick in the future. They wanted the court to also take into account the separate liability insurance that the private contractors had, in addition to the captive policy. When Tyrrell and Napoli argued over the terms of the settlement, Hellerstein got testy. "Forget about the law. Forget about the analyses. Ask yourself the most basic practical question that you have to ask as a plaintiff's lawyer: What can I do for the people who have entrusted their most precious asset to me as a lawyer? How can I bring about a return so they can enjoy it and their children can enjoy it in their remaining lives?"[4] The judge then warned them what would lay ahead if they could not find a way to deal with each other. "This case will not be a boon to you. It will be an affliction that will consume your practice and the practice of your colleagues, and you will never see the light of day. That is the understanding you have to get. It is not easy."

As Hellerstein ushered the massive cases forward, he kept pushing both sides toward a settlement, and Napoli and Worby took steps to be prepared in case a settlement was reached. Plaintiffs are not obligated to participate; they can pass up their percentage of the offered settlement and choose instead to go to trial, where they, of course, stand the chance of losing everything or having to wait years for a verdict. In 2007, Napoli and Worby asked all their clients to sign contacts authorizing them to negotiate a settlement for which they would receive compensation of a third or more of whatever the award might be. They were criticized for using strong-arm tactics, which they denied.

With the city continuing to pursue its immunity defense, the court, with the help of the special masters, assembled a severity chart based in large measure on the medical records that Napoli and Worby had gathered for thousands of responders, including Ernie Vallebuona, Mike Valentin, John Walcott, Marty Fullam, and Sarah Atlas, who were part of the lawsuit. Both plaintiffs and the defense agreed on a range of respiratory illnesses and gradations of severity from the least serious, such as runny noses, to the most serious, which included some cancers and, ultimately, death. Hellerstein ordered Napoli and Worby to provide medical records for each client, a massive undertaking. At regular intervals, documents were sent to the city for review.

After spending a year collecting and reviewing the records, the city released an analysis in 2008 of the health claims of the plaintiffs, as portrayed in the documents. It was the first time that anyone besides the Napoli–Worby team had evaluated the responders' medical records (although, at that point, the city had not been permitted to conduct its own examinations or tests). Until then, Worby had the stage all to himself. In countless interviews, he used the rapid-fire delivery he had perfected to rattle off chemical contaminants and the diseases they caused in his clients, with an emphasis on cancer. The links were always inferred, and scientific proof was never given. Worby simply said these workers had been exposed to these chemicals, and now they had these diseases—and a growing number of them had died. When asked about incidence rates compared to the population-at-large, Worby promised to reveal everything in court.

With access to those preliminary medical records, Tyrrell finally had a chance to flesh out what the city's own lawyers thought they had detected in those early 50-H hearings. Tyrrell prepared a detailed analysis and summarized the findings before Hellerstein. Several surprises cropped up, but nothing created more of a stir than the revelation that more than 300 responders had admitted in papers submitted to the court that they were not sick at all and had suffered no persistent symptoms following their work at ground zero. They said they had joined the suit because they were worried about the future. Around 3,000 of the plaintiffs claimed to be suffering from symptoms no more serious than a runny nose or a cough. In all, the responders had listed a remarkable total of 387 different diseases. The list included high blood sugar, deviated septum, and Bell's palsy, which have no known connection to dust exposure, as well as cancers and blood diseases, which have latency periods from exposure to onset of 15 years and longer.

When the results of the city's preliminary analysis were made public, the notion of several hundred uninjured people suing the city for negligence fed into the ever expanding climate of doubt above ground zero. Just as the unfolding developments in the cases of Detective James Zadroga and Officer Cesar Borja had strengthened those doubts, so did these revelations, which temporarily overshadowed the plight of the responders who truly were sick, sometimes too sick to be heard.

In response, Worby and his team promised that no one who did not deserve compensation would receive a dime. They insisted that it was legitimate for healthy workers who worried about getting sick in the future to join the lawsuit because so much about the effects of the dust was still unknown. Science could someday define precisely the connection between dust and disease, and, as Agent Orange and other previous environmental exposures have shown, the list of diseases could be very long.

In the years since the attacks, there seemed to be no end to the ways in which people tried to use ground zero to further their own schemes. People who claimed they were New York City firefighters turned out not to be; people who said they spent time volunteering in Lower Manhattan turned out to have never actually touched the pile. As the scientific studies increasingly linked a long list of respiratory problems to the dust, more people claimed that their exposure, no matter how brief, had caused their illness because, well, what else could it be? And without conclusive evidence, there was little downside to claiming that any illness that had developed in anyone even remotely connected to the cleanup was the result of exposure to the dust. Filmmaker Michael Moore got a lot of attention when he brought several responders to Cuba for medical treatment of illnesses they claimed were connected to ground zero. One had unspecified respiratory problems, and another needed a new set of teeth. Standing up for those who were sick became an industry in itself. In one case, Michael Bellone, a former nightclub bouncer who showed up to volunteer at ground zero, was arrested years later for impersonating a New York City firefighter and illegally possessing fire department gear that he used to promote a book he wrote about his experiences after 9/11. In another, Scott Shields enchanted many people with stories of how he and his golden retriever, Bear, had found numerous victims in the pile. But those tales were eventually debunked. Bear was not a trained rescue dog, and Shields was later arrested for taking thousands of dollars in rental assistance money from FEMA after fraudulently claiming he had lived in Lower Manhattan on 9/11.

Exaggerated claims also showed up in workers' compensation courts. In one instance, a Merrill Lynch assistant vice president filed for benefits under a special provision of the New York state law that extended coverage to ground zero volunteers. The executive claimed she had suffered post-traumatic stress after she volunteered to help direct bank workers to the ferry that took them to safety in New Jersey on the morning of September 11. The executive claimed to have been a recovery worker because she had recovered her office laptop, and insisted that she had been involved in cleanup operations because she had cleaned up her apartment to use as a temporary office. Her claim was denied.

In interviews after the city challenged the veracity of the rescue workers' claims in court, Napoli and Worby accused Tyrrell of unfairly presenting the plaintiff-heroes as "liars, cheats, and malingerers." But the lawyers themselves had not completely resisted the temptation to overstate things. In a document presented to the court, they asserted that a New York State Department of Health study had determined that 128 responders had already died because of their exposure to trade center dust, a sobering statistic that would have lent great weight to Worby's predictions about the dust's deadly traits. Napoli and Worby referred to the health department's mortality registry, which tracked deaths among ground zero responders. The department hoped to compare the rate at which responders died to national mortality rates and, in so doing, determine whether the responders were at greater-than-normal risk for certain illnesses. But reaching such conclusions would take years, and far more investigation, especially without the kind of autopsy guidelines Dr. John Howard had proposed or that Dr. Charles Hirsch had recommended in order to save tissue samples for future reference. The department simply noted deaths among responders, regardless of cause.

At the time Napoli and Worby put together their brief for the court, 128 responders indeed had died. But the health department had not connected any of the deaths to the dust, nor had it ruled out the possibility that the dust had caused some of the deaths. The number simply reflected how many of the 60,000 workers at ground zero had passed away from any cause at all, including traffic accidents, assaults, and suicides. When confronted about their misrepresentation of the data, the lawyers admitted that they had gone beyond what they knew at the time and had inadvertently misstated the nature of the health department's figures.

Advocates for the rescue workers regularly repeated the same kind of mistake. As the number of deaths invariably grew, so did the advocates' outrage, but the mistake was rarely corrected. In the following years, tabloid accounts of the health department's growing death list continued to present the results as a tally of the dust's deadly toll. And the fact that the numbers came from the state health department was seen as endowing the figure with a degree of independent confirmation and welcomed certainty.

Judges have been criticized for being overly eager to recommend settlements in mass torts, pushing for a comparatively speedy resolution to avoid complex and lengthy trials focused on gnarly points of law. In many instances, the private companies being sued accept the settlements to put an end to the conflict and move on, even when there is inconclusive scientific evidence that their products caused any damage. Judges have been known to take the position that smoothing out technical details is less important than achieving justice, which can sometimes require finding the sweet spot between noble law and the messy facts of life. And in the 9/11 cases, it was increasingly clear that some people had indeed been severely injured. Even if no scientific proof could show how many had been harmed, justice would not be served by turning away the injured, no matter what the law said about immunity.

Ironically, the very existence of the $1 billion insurance fund may have ensured that none of the responders, no matter how sick, received timely compensation. As Hellerstein observed in his 2006 decision on the limits of the city's immunity, "The availability of a one-billion-dollar fund authorized by Congress should not serve as encouragement to lengthen and complicate these proceedings. The scar to the public interest needs to be cleansed, speedily, in good time." The captive insurance company spent money at a ferocious pace to pay for the city's French-cuff legal defense. Napoli and Worby wanted to get their hands on it for their clients, and inevitably for themselves, after spending millions on the litigation. And Tyrrell understood that there was no advantage to mounting anything less than an all-out defense of the city, during which time he and his associates kept the billing meter running. Tyrrell saw the city as having a responsibility to the workers, but also to other Americans, who had provided the $1 billion and expected it to be handled judiciously, not simply meted out to those who had put their hands out to ask for some. In 2009, he filed a motion to dismiss lawsuits by police and fire-fighters on the grounds that uniformed city employees have other recourses and are not covered by the state's labor laws. The move enraged responders but would have significantly winnowed the number of those eligible for some kind of court-ordered compensation, if a settlement were to be reached.

Hellerstein tried several ways to short-circuit the process so that a settlement was possible, but it was a stretch to say that his efforts were successful. The notion of allowing limited discovery leading up to the motion to dismiss based on the city's immunity defense allowed Napoli and his team to open new avenues of attack based on the millions of pages of documents they had requested. Hellerstein's limited immunity decision did not scare the defendants into settling. Even the appointment of James Henderson and Aaron Twerski as special masters and their compilation of a severity chart did not lead to the settlement Hellerstein had envisioned. By 2009, after he had turned 75, Hellerstein still vowed to see the cases through. He then decided to up the ante.

With the help of the special masters, Hellerstein devised a system for culling the thousands of cases into a manageable sample of benchmark lawsuits that could be brought to trial comparatively quickly. He hoped that if the cases were selected properly, the laborious preparation for the trials and the reality that arose from the intensive discovery process would convince both sides that a broad settlement was a much better option than going to trial with expert witnesses, scientific debate, and detailed investigation of each of the 10,000 responders.

To begin with, Hellerstein ordered Napoli and the plaintiff team to eliminate duplicate cases and any clients who rightly belonged to a parallel litigation involving the owners and tenants of buildings surrounding the trade center. That reduced the number to 9,090—still huge, but it was a start. The 9,090 cases were divided into five groups. Napoli was given 40 days to provide the records pertaining to the first 2,000 cases. The cases then were to be classified by severity, using the chart already developed by the special masters, and culled to just 225. Finally, Napoli and Worby were to choose 2 cases out of the 225 that they wanted to bring to trial. Likewise, Tyrrell and the city picked two to be tested at trial. And the court itself, with the help of the special masters, selected two cases.

Every 40 days, another 2,000 or so cases were similarly documented, culled, and then picked over. In the end, when all five groups of cases had been reviewed, a select core of 30 cases would be subject to extensive discovery leading up to a limited round of trials. In these benchmark proceedings, basic questions would be raised about who did what on the pile, who wore what, what was tested, what was said, and what was required. After those were dealt with, the science of causality itself could end up being on trial, with scientific evidence and expert witnesses expounding in court. The medical conditions of the individuals would be picked over carefully, each symptom challenged, each diagnosis held up to scrutiny. Responders would have to undergo extensive medical examinations to document their illnesses, and the testing, which would be videotaped, could end up being shown to jurors. At times, it might seem that grand rounds from a teaching hospital had passed through the federal courthouse.

Tyrrell picked cases that involved implausible medical claims or that helped frame the immunity issue by focusing on individuals who were present only during the earliest days, when the city was responding to a civil defense emergency. Napoli and Worby honed in on their strongest cases, in which the link between the dust and disease was most tangible and had had the greatest impact. One of those involved Lieut. Marty Fullam, who continued to recover from his lung transplant. The court itself looked for a range of cases that were likely to raise issues that neither Napoli nor Tyrrell had brought up.

One of the first cases the court selected was that of a veteran firefighter, Raymond Hauber, who had died of esophageal cancer in 2007 when he was just 47. Tyrrell did what he had vowed to do, scrutinizing each plaintiff's medical history looking for indications that the health problems predated 9/11 or were unrelated to ground zero. In doing so, he and his team questioned Hauber's doctors, asking about the firefighter's weight, his eating habits, and even a sexually transmitted disease he had contracted. The information was leaked to the New York tabloids, which ran outraged articles about the city's attempts to besmirch a hero, an early indication of how nasty the trial process could turn out to be.

Months later, as Hellerstein decided to narrow the 30 cases to a more manageable 12, more disparities arose, further impairing the credibility of some cases. An investigation by the Associated Press showed that one worker who claimed to have developed respiratory problems, skin rashes, and acid reflux after working on the pile had been ill for several years before 2001. In another case, a police officer whom the lawyers listed as having lung cancer turned out not to have cancer, but rather chronic asthma. She claimed that the lawyers had submitted incorrect information.

In addition to these embarrassments, Napoli's team suffered other setbacks as a few of their responder clients, including some who were involved in what had been positioned as strong cases, backed out, and decided not to continue to participate in the litigation.

The prospect of these benchmark trials coming undone threatened Napoli's original strategy of accumulating as many cases as possible. The weakness of some of the cases severely undercut the plaintiffs' credibility and further strengthened the position of critics who claimed that although some legitimate responders had been seriously injured, the overall number of those affected was significantly smaller than Napoli and Worby had claimed.

Even as Hellerstein worked hard to bring the cases before him to a satisfactory conclusion, there were indications that ground zero litigation could go on for much longer. In September 2009, in time for the eighth anniversary of the attacks, New York Gov. David A. Paterson signed Jimmy Nolan's law, named after a carpenter from Yonkers who became ill after working at ground zero. The bill gave thousands of rescue and recovery workers additional time to file lawsuits for injuries sustained in the aftermath of the towers' collapse. The city's chief lobbyist in Albany claimed the new law would revive some 3,000 old cases, intensifying the legal battle in federal court, laying an additional financial burden on the city, and frustrating Bloomberg's efforts to reopen the victims' compensation fund.

Hellerstein kept putting pressure on both sides. As 2010 began, serious settlement negotiations were underway. At the first court hearing in the new year, Hellerstein forced Napoli and Tyrrell to acknowledge the existence of a draft settlement document more than 70 pages long, which some of the lawyers in court representing small groups of responders said they didn't even know existed. Hellerstein put Napoli on the spot, asking him to report on the negotiations. "You put me in an awkward position," Napoli said as he rose from the plaintiffs' table.

"When haven't you been in an awkward position?" Hellerstein retorted.

Neither Napoli nor Tyrrell was willing to divulge any specifics of the proposal in open court. They couldn't because they had signed a confidentiality agreement. But after the court session ended, Hellerstein called them into his chambers for an off-the-record discussion, undoubtedly to drive home his strong desire for a settlement agreement, and soon. In court, Hellerstein reminded both sides of the looming trials, which were scheduled to begin in little more than three months. After he did so, Robert H. Riley, a lawyer for the Port Authority, which was a defendant in the case but was not represented by Tyrrell, went right to the heart of the litigation, attacking the biological plausibility of the plaintiffs' case and asking the judge to do what he had so far refused to do: order the plaintiffs to produce scientific evidence that the dust plausibly could have caused cancers in just a few years, even though the scientific literature held that latency periods were decades long. It was a put-up-or-shut-up motion, aimed directly at what Hellerstein knew was the weakest point of Napoli and Worby's claims.

If Hellerstein had ordered Napoli and Worby to produce their evidence on cancer before the trial began, and then had found the proof unconvincing, he could have summarily dismissed those cases. But Hellerstein wasn't interested in doing that. It would have been seen as a legal technicality that denied many their day in court. He rejected the Port Authority's motion for an advance ruling and said that questions of proof would be handled as each case came to trial, unless a settlement came first.

Endnotes

[1]Personal interview, 16 October 2009.

[2]Memorandum in Support of Motion for Judgment on the Pleadings Based on State Statutory and Common Law Immunity, 17 February 2006.

[3]Docket no. 06-5324-cv, argued 1 October 2007; decided 26 March 2008.

[4]Court transcript, 28 November 2006, 26–27.

Part IV

Reality

14

Missed opportunities

On a blustery late summer morning in 2007, with heavy rain and flashes of lightning across the city, Joseph Jones finally had the chance to hear his wife publicly acknowledged as the 2,750th victim of the terrorist attacks of September 11. Felicia Dunn-Jones was just one of so many, yet six years after the fires at ground zero were extinguished, she was the only person till then whose death had been officially attributed to exposure to the dust. With his daughter, Rebecca, at his side (son Joe junior was too emotionally distraught to be there), Jones, along with Kiki and Rick Bennett, the lawyer who had helped him get Dunn-Jones's death classified as murder, listened intently as a New York City firefighter intoned "Felicia Gail Dunn-Jones," in a stout voice that tore through the hearts of her family.

The events of September 11 then flashed through Jones's mind—the nightmare of locating his wife, rounding up their kids, and then bringing them all back home safely to Staten Island. Try as he might, he couldn't help but dwell on the unfathomable mystery of what might have been. Had she just decided to head to the Hudson River and the ferry to New Jersey, instead of hiking to the East River and the closed Williamsburg Bridge, would she have avoided breathing in the cloud and its entrails for hours that day? If she had been allowed to leave the Education Department's building after the first plane struck and had made it to Brooklyn before the towers had disintegrated instead of being forced back upstairs by a security guard, could she have avoided the dust that killed her?

Those missed opportunities have haunted him ever since. "There's always that doubt in your mind, that 'what if,' and *if*—it's such a big word," he recalled.[1] On a gold chain around his neck hangs the engagement ring he gave to Dunn-Jones after she proposed to him, along with the simple gold wedding band she wore for 18 years. He doesn't say more, but his eyes carry on the story. The events that reshaped his life were so monumental that it was hard to comprehend how he, a drug store assistant manager, had been caught up in them. The only way to reduce it to comprehensible size was to think of the minute dust and to imagine it spreading in every direction, covering everything—and everyone—in its path. Some just brushed it off and moved on. Not him. And surely not his family, most especially not his son. Although Joe junior had not been able to link his mother's death to environmental contamination, he did connect her disappearance with the attacks that had brought the towers down. He didn't have a clue what sarcoidosis is, or what it did to her. In his mind, there had to be a person to blame, not a disease, an act of war, or a government agency that screwed up. In his moments of greatest grief and frustration, he sometimes yelled out, "Bin Laden killed my mother!"

The persistent need for answers is often accompanied by a twin desire to rearrange fate. As the years following the disaster have accumulated, it has become clearer not just to Jones, but to many others touched by the dust, that opportunities for minimizing the post-9/11 tragedy were repeatedly missed. Enough scientific evidence has been collected to leave no real doubt that exposure made many people suffer, though certainly not everyone who breathed the dust. The recovery of Lower Manhattan was a complex operation—spontaneous yet long-lasting—marked by thousands of small decisions that were based on thousands of simple assumptions, each one defined by a certain logic that, independently, would not lead toward the sickening of thousands of people who came to help. And yet....

Each one of the decisions represented a turning point where, had someone or some agency acted differently, a whole series of events might have radically changed course. Individual actions were all interrelated so that, as with a nuclear reaction, one event led in a direct line to another, and then another, in a powerful chain reaction. The cumulative effect of all the individual acts helped open the door to disaster. Such critical moments as these arose in each aspect of the disaster response, and they can be divided into distinct groups of decisions: those that were mostly political; or scientific; or related to health, legal, or basic issues about safety on the site.

Much of what happened in 2001 and 2002 has been second-guessed, and a mythology has grown up around some of it. One issue in particular is raised perhaps more often than any other, and that is the decision by the Occupational Safety and Health Administration (OSHA) not to enforce its own workplace safety rules. Instead, the agency entered into a cooperative agreement with all who were involved in the recovery to voluntarily comply with safety regulations. Ground zero became the biggest project the agency ever undertook, and it lasted longer than any other. More than 1,000 OSHA employees were involved, and they distributed 130,000 respirators. Still, the argument usually plays out along these lines: If OSHA had aggressively enforced the rules, workers would have been cited for not wearing safety gear, and their employers would have been fined so much they could not have afforded to ignore the rules. But evidence suggests this is not necessarily so.

The cooperative agreement marked one of the few instances in which labor, management, and government agreed to work together at ground zero. Although a spirit of cooperation overcame the nation after 9/11, on the ground, the old jealousies and competition remained very much alive. The labor agreement was notable in not having been shaped or distorted by the climate of doubt that had been created at the outset of the disaster. And it was not without precedent. The agency had had similar arrangements with contractors on some of the biggest construction projects in New York just before 9/11. The idea of working with the private sector instead of holding a hammer over the companies was a reflection of the Bush administration's *laissez-faire* approach, but the results had generally been accepted as satisfactory before 9/11. And at ground zero, despite the hellish conditions, not one life was lost during the cleanup. Much smaller and more orderly construction sites in New York have not matched that record.

The alternative to the cooperative agreement would have meant OSHA inspectors issuing citations, which would have led to hearings and, eventually, fines against employers for noncompliance. But that process could have taken months and would have had limited impact. Work was done on a time-and-material basis. Fines would have been built into the fees they charged (especially with the city demanding that the job be completed as quickly as possible). In essence, the city would have ended up paying the fines itself. OSHA also would not have had the power to enforce workplace safety rules over the fire-fighters, police officers, and other uniformed workers, further weakening the agency's ability to keep everyone safe through enforcement.

Still, many insist that because OSHA acted in an advisory role, unnecessary problems arose, especially after the rescue phase ended in late September. Compliance with respirator rules dropped then and kept dropping when laborers saw there were few or no consequences to leaving off the sweaty masks that made difficult tasks even more difficult.

In other moments, political decisions stole opportunities for limiting the damage the dust caused. One such moment came when perception trumped science. The early responders on the scene, taking stock of the incredibly diverse mixture of elements in the debris, and with an understanding that the buildings had imploded with pulverizing force, knew that the dust would be dangerous to breathe. There was a clear expectation that once there was no one left to rescue, ground zero would be declared a Superfund hazardous waste site. In fact, a scientist for the Environmental Protection Agency (EPA) had recommended it. That would have imposed the kind of work safety rules that apply to all designated contaminated sites, including hazardous waste landfills. There was no doubt that the debris contained asbestos, benzene, and highly caustic cement dust, among other dangerous elements. The detection of any one of the toxic materials could have triggered orders to wear special protective gear. But in the minds of some officials, declaring 16 acres of Lower Manhattan a Superfund site would have blighted that part of the city the way the infamous Love Canal poisoned the name of Niagara Falls, New York. And that possibility was considered absolutely unacceptable while the city was attempting to regain its footing. The city applied the same thinking years later to cleanup projects at the Gowanus Canal and Newtown Creek in Brooklyn, where New York officials resisted Superfund designation because they feared it would drive off private developers. Even so, the Gowanus officially was added to the Superfund list in 2010.

Making ground zero a Superfund site would not have doomed Wall Street. With the right degree of scientific data, the city could have established a core area, or "hot zone," and set up aggressive monitoring while cleanup proceeded. That core could have been surrounded by a transition zone. Beyond that would lie the remainder of Lower Manhattan, where the air might truly have been "safe to breathe" for most people, excluding the sick, the young, and the elderly. This kind of action would have required transparency and a willingness to level with New Yorkers, but it could have been done. In 2001, around 38 Superfund sites existed in New York, but the city learned to live with them and, eventually, all but ignore them. In fact, ground zero has been behind barricades since 2001, and the toxic shell of the Deutsche Bank building has shadowed the area for most of the decade. Workmen disassembling the contaminated building were forced to wear respirators and Tyvek suits. But delis and pizzerias a block away offered their lunchtime specials as though nothing had happened. (Two firefighters who died in 2007 trying to put out a fire in the Deutsche Bank building that was started by careless workmen represented two more fatalities than occurred in the nine months of the ground zero cleanup itself). The ill-fated building still loomed over a mostly empty ground zero as a new decade began, a mocking tribute to the haste with which the trade center debris was swept away in preparation for the rebuilding that had yet to occur.

Had ground zero become a Superfund site as soon as the rescue phase ended, there might have been less confusion over Christie Whitman's statements concerning the safety of the air because care could have been taken to differentiate the site from the rest of Lower Manhattan. And Whitman might not have been so susceptible to the pressure from the White House's Council on Environmental Quality to downplay the hazards so that Wall Street could reopen. The danger zone, where the air was not safe, would have been clearly marked. Still, even without a Superfund designation, Whitman could have been much more precise with her statements. And the media could have pressed her for clarification. Had some reporter asked, "Where exactly is the air safe?" when she said there was no immediate danger, much confusion could have been avoided, and the entire storyline of the aftermath of 9/11 might have been different. Had the *New York Times* been as critical of Whitman's September statements as it would be of those made by officer Cesar Borja's family years later, or if the

New York Daily News had treated the Borja story with the same skepticism with which it viewed the statements of the EPA, there would have been more clarity and less misunderstanding all around.

The command structure for the rescue and recovery operation was never as clearly defined as it needed to be. After the rescue operation ended, command was split between fire department brass and the Department of Design and Construction. Even the super-efficient forest fire service team could not help then because of the shared command's unavoidable inefficiencies and confusion. In large measure, this situation arose because of the rush of emotions directed toward firefighters and the tragic losses they suffered. Respecting them prevented a proper command structure with a single head from being put into place. Such conflicts were largely avoided at the Pentagon. Although that was a significantly smaller and less complex recovery operation, it presented some of the same dangers and challenges as those at ground zero. But the response there was managed so that the command structure shifted as the workload changed.

At first the Arlington County Fire Department was in charge of putting out the fire and making sure it didn't start up again while the bodies of 184 victims were recovered. After ten days, the fire and rescue phase ended and the FBI assumed command of the site, initiating a crime scene investigation. Finally, when the FBI was finished collecting evidence, the Pentagon's own construction management team, backed by private contractors, came in to complete the cleanup in just a month and a day. There never was more than a single incident commander at a time. Work rules were clear and the phases of the project were universally understood. The entire area was secured the very first day, and entry into the zone was tightly controlled. Although recovery workers were exposed to dust and incinerated building materials, they were fortunate in that a recent renovation of that section of the Pentagon had removed asbestos, lead paint, and other hazards. Nonetheless, worksite safety rules—requiring Tyvek suits and respirators at all times—were universally enforced, although some FBI agents complained that they were more appropriate for industrial operations than a crime scene investigation.[2] Still, not one of more than 3,500 people who worked on the recovery there became sick.

In New York, the enormous emotional stakes of the disaster made command far more difficult. But the reality came down to this: Responders risked their lives to recover the remains of the victims, a task that was supremely noble but that, in the end, did not require such haste. Only one person had the moral authority that could have divided the operation into the same kind of distinct phases as at the Pentagon, providing the opportunity for properly addressing safety issues. Mayor Rudy Giuliani had earned the respect of the city—and, in fact, the whole country. It was up to him to make the case that the city had already suffered enough and would not allow one more person to be injured. But he didn't. His supporters deny that this was possible, pointing to an ugly incident in early November when police and firefighters scuffled near ground zero, leading to a few black eyes, a number of arrests (charges later were dropped), and a lot of frayed emotions. But the brawl did not occur because the mayor tried to shut down the site to impose stricter safety regulations.

Firefighters had amassed that morning to protest the mayor's decision to reduce the number of firefighters on the job from 64 to 25. Most of the firefighters still on the pile worked as spotters, keeping watchful eyes for signs of human remains. Only 91 of the 343 missing firefighters had been recovered by then. The firefighters, already antagonized by Giuliani over the issue of the malfunctioning walkie-talkie radios, saw the move not as an expression of concern about their safety, but as an attempt to accelerate the cleanup before Giuliani's term ended, replacing firefighters with mechanical cranes that could dig faster. As the angry firefighters, some in their turnout coats, marched toward the trade center site that morning, they pushed over police barricades. Police pushed back, and the scuffle quickly got out of hand. In comments to reporters later that day, Giuliani revealed how much of a sore point the firefighters had become. "Firefighters will continue to have a role," he said. "But what they're not going to be allowed to do, and they were doing it in the past, is to take over the whole site."[3] The brawl said more about firefighter hubris than about any lack of respect for the sacrifice of those who died. And those same hoary traditions that prevented firefighters from listening to outsiders who tried to protect them did great harm to the firefighters and to their families, though few in the city dared say so at the time.

The Bush White House missed several opportunities to minimize the risk to workers and residents in Lower Manhattan. Some were simple, such as forcing the conga line of dignitaries who came after the President to send a different message by wearing even a small N-95 paper mask while touring the site. But the White House, in cooperation with City Hall, stuck to a single message: There was little to worry about. That unwillingness to level with the public sowed misunderstanding, which turned into obstacles when Congress made decisions allocating money for monitoring and screening programs. It became extraordinarily difficult to lobby for medical monitoring before a Congress that believed there was nothing hazardous in the dust.

Even when Congress came up with money for the September 11th Victim Compensation Fund, the mixed signals coming from ground zero led to a lack of clarity about what was happening. The fund compensated responders whose injuries and illnesses arose before the fund expired at the end of 2003. Had Washington consulted with someone such as Dr. Stephen Levin of Mount Sinai, they could have gotten a better understanding of the medical consequences of exposure and a more forthright evaluation of the risk. Then it would have made sense for the fund, with its unlimited budget, to have operated for several more years, covering the bulk of the people with legitimate claims who would eventually go on to sue the city. But without that insight, the fund expired just as many responders were realizing that their hacking cough was not getting better. This set up a vastly inequitable situation in which some responders were compensated but others were not, even when the injuries and illnesses they suffered were the same. Neither science nor medicine determined who received awards; instead, it was an arbitrary date and the random act of when the illness made itself known.

Washington did eventually reach out to help ailing responders who got sick after the fund expired, but instead of reviving the fund, Congress channeled most of the injured workers into the federal courts, one of the least efficient ways of compensating people with difficult-to-prove exposure injuries.

The Bush administration and Congress missed the chance to get ahead of the health crisis several times, with potentially dire consequences for responders. The government waited unconscionably long to provide money for screening and monitoring. Only after the doctors at Mount Sinai, working with labor unions, devised their own plan, rounded up political support, and made a strong case for funding did Washington reluctantly make limited emergency appropriations. But the money always trailed the need. It ran out quickly, and the screening programs were not nearly as comprehensive as they could have been, especially when they were needed most. The prohibitions on research and treatment became substantial obstacles with oversized consequences. By the time treatment money was available, thousands who needed help had simply given up.

Some public health officials believe that New York City missed an opportunity to make safety and health a central part of the recovery when it failed to award Bechtel the contract it had sought for a comprehensive health and safety plan to cover the entire site. The New York City's health department passed up an opportunity in the early days after the attacks to provide guidelines for physicians throughout the region who treated injured responders, instead waiting until the fifth anniversary, in 2006, to do so. And when Mayor Bloomberg in 2007 announced the appointment of a city coordinator for 9/11 programs who would do in New York what Dr. John Howard was trying to do in Washington, he named a public relations specialist, Jeffrey Hon, to the position. The office immediately slipped into bureaucratic oblivion.

Words can be extremely powerful, and restraint by the responders' lawyers likely would have reduced anxiety among sick workers and kept many of them out of federal court. Each time David Worby or Paul Napoli recited the long list of ailments and diseases they believed were linked to the dust, responders everywhere anguished over their chances of getting the illnesses themselves. Cancer headlines and sound bites whipped up fear in all responders and their families, who hardly ever asked for details or proof. Many undoubtedly acted on those fears and joined the lawsuit against the city, but the sheer volume of plaintiffs so engorged the litigation that it defied simple solutions and denied those who were truly sick a timely resolution.

But perhaps nowhere were more opportunities missed than in the basic science of determining what had occurred in the immediate aftermath of the towers' collapse that morning, and what effect the resulting dust, ash, and gasses had on the tens of thousands of people who were exposed to it all. Time and again, simple decisions were made that took the research and analytical work down a meandering path that limited what science could achieve. And the absence of solid evidence unleashed confusion, distortion, and towering plumes of anxiety.

The investigation got off to a bad start by focusing almost exclusively on a single contaminant: asbestos. Previous incidents, notably the Con Ed explosion in Chelsea, had made people more wary of the dangers of asbestos, and critics such as Joel Kupferman and Juan Gonzalez demonized it, undoubtedly increasing the worries of New Yorkers. Although no amount of asbestos is considered safe, the near-exclusive focus on it as an indicator of risk was misdirected because other hazards that proved far more pervasive, such as the dust's caustic nature, were ignored or overlooked. Authorities reported that asbestos had not exceeded standards, but they said little about the dangers of the dust itself.

The EPA says that the information about the alkalinity of the dust would not have changed its response in any way. But industrial hygienists believe that if the information had been made public earlier, it could have forced authorities to determine exactly how far the dust had traveled and the extent to which it had managed to contaminate interior spaces. And that information, in turn, would have made a proper cleanup of indoor spaces imperative. Instead, the arbitrary boundaries that the city and the EPA set led to the ultimately futile voluntary cleanup. And that imperfect response was followed by the technical panel and its aborted effort to bring peace of mind to New York.

Finally, the federal government missed an opportunity to consolidate the hard work and good science that had been done till then by not reappointing John Howard when his term ended in mid-2008. The outgoing Bush administration, clearly tired of Howard's advocacy and the growing burden of the health programs that he helped put into place, sacked him, despite fierce lobbying by New York's congressional delegation. Thus, as happened with the EPA technical panel, the federal government seemed to throw up its hands, declare victory, and walk away from the problem.

Without Howard at the helm, the program drifted for about a year. But then in September 2009, nine months after the inauguration of Barack Obama, Dr. Thomas Frieden, New York's post-9/11 commissioner of health, took charge of the Centers for Disease Control and Prevention. Frieden reappointed Howard national coordinator for 9/11 health issues, reviving hope in the long-term future of the monitoring and treatment program, and providing what many wished would be an additional push for passage of the Zadroga bill.

Endnotes

[1]Personal interview, 5 August 2009.

[2]*After Action Report on the Response to the September 11 Attack on the Pentagon*, prepared for Arlington County by Titan Systems Corp. Available at www.arlingtonva. us/departments/Fire/Documents/after_report.pdf.

[3]Lombardi, Frank and Michele Mcphee, "Bravest vs. Finest in WTC Melee," *New York Daily News*, 3 November 2001, p. 3.

15

Afterclap

When the voices of the doomsayers who predicted an environmental holocaust matched the rhetoric of the deniers who were unwilling to acknowledge any serious illnesses linked to the dust, the city and large parts of the nation were unable to come to any conclusions about what had truly happened at ground zero. New York's government turned schizophrenic, fighting against the sick responders in federal court even as it begged Washington to fund screening, monitoring, and treatment programs for them. Complex litigation dragged on for years, even as more people fell ill and died. Scientists and medical experts were pushed beyond the limits of their expertise as they were badgered to prove a link between dust and disease that could not be proved—not yet. Then they were denounced for giving incomplete answers to those questions.

Ground zero was contaminated not only by dust, but by a cascade of errors—some well meaning and unavoidable, others driven by arrogance or neglect. Those misjudgments broke down the trust that existed by mutual consent between government and its people and set the stage for a confrontation between perception and truth that dragged on long after the towers came apart. Not just the environment had been poisoned. The dust seemed toxic for the relationship of officials to those who elected them, for the trust between science and the public, for the integrity of the news media, and for the power of the courts to deliver justice. This breakdown could be seen as an artifact of that particular moment in history, a distortion of reason that seemed to parallel the growing distrust in an administration that had started a war on what turned out to be a false pretense and then declared victory when there was none to be had. Or it could be a testament to the passing of the age of belief.

As public trust faltered, people on both sides of the ground zero health divide began to doubt each other, which then led them to exaggerate as they tried making points above the din. This process is not limited to ground zero, but is a reflection of the way much public debate now occurs: The truth gets mangled in the attempt to convince or persuade. Exaggeration about the dust provoked even more confusion and less understanding. Hubris, political correctness, and turf battles for influence and the high moral ground all contributed to the fog. It became almost impossible to say anything about ground zero and its impact on health that was not tainted by rancor or fear.

As each anniversary of the attacks came and went, the city remained deeply divided. Some of those who were sick did not receive the help they needed, while some who were not sick stood to get help they didn't deserve. And questions lingered about whether we had learned anything from the tragic experience of ground zero that would prepare us for the next time we would be forced to respond to an unimagined disaster.

The recovery operation at ground zero was by no means a failure. It was a tragic success, a delicate balancing act involving different, and sometimes conflicting, interests. Just as thousands of workers cleared away the 1.5 million tons of twisted steel and concrete in record time to reveal the bedrock foundation of the twin towers, their struggle with disease and doubt in the aftermath of 9/11 exposed contradictions in the nation's approach to acceptable levels of risk. At its most basic, this was a story of managing risks and calibrating expectations.

If epidemiologists do their jobs well, the raw numbers contained in their studies can begin to reveal the parameters of a large tragedy, the outlines of a looming health crisis or the roots of a medical false alarm. In the wake of 9/11, data helped shape the response of public health agencies and created a degree of public understanding and sympathy—though not always. As the studies mounted along with the years, epidemiologists presented a clearer image of the real respiratory damage that had been done to those who had been exposed to the initial plumes of contaminated dust. They also suggested that some of the most acute initial aftereffects could turn out to last, as once was predicted, "for the rest of their lives."

But we faced severe limits on what we could know and how we could learn it. Most of the data had been derived from clinical studies, such as those done at Mount Sinai and the fire department. Little in the way of laboratory research, with sample doses and control groups, had been conducted. Replicating the dangerous conditions that had existed in the first days after the attacks would have required knowledge of what was in the smoke and gasses that had covered the pile then. But such measurements had not been taken. Besides, the funds simply weren't available to support that kind of research in any significant way. Dr. John Howard recognized this fault long ago and planned to address it once the funding for monitoring and treatment was secured. But after the Bush administration shifted from apathy to outright resistance following Howard's proposal in late 2007 for a service contract· that would have institutionalized the responder health program, the idea went nowhere. Howard fought hard to keep the research going. He feared that if momentum were lost and the cohort of responders in the various programs dispersed, "we'd lose the science and we'd never know how the population was affected." In that case, Howard predicted, "the ultimate victory would go to those who do not want science to come out of this."

Laboratory studies would have supported the raw numbers, but they would not have captured the entirety of the suffering that continued long after 9/11. It is important not to lose sight of the individual lives that were darkened by the dust—or the hardships that people like Marty Fullam and his family will have to face for the rest of their lives. His combination of pulmonary fibrosis and polymyositis might turn out to be too specialized to be included in any study, a rarity that would not show up in any statistically significant way even in a sample of 60,000. Yet it is more than real every single day at Fullam's Staten Island home.

The aftermath of the collapse of the twin towers underscored the limits of what epidemiology can do. Given enough time, the studies could provide a reasonable degree of medical certainty. But Fullam and so many others simply did not have that much time to wait. For them, "We won't know for 30 years" simply was not an acceptable response, though it may, in fact, have been accurate. Neither would the benchmark cases selected by lawyers and the court have provided definitive answers about the real level of risk the responders faced.

Instead, their outcomes would be a reflection of legal strategy and public perception, regardless of the science.

Most of the researchers working on the 9/11 impact were medical doctors, and most personally saw the patients who constituted the data in their studies. For some, it became impossible to separate individuals from gross numbers, or to forget how the needs of some might not reflect the reality of many. As scientists, they strived for the most significant results, coming as close as they could to showing, with a high degree of certainty, the connection between cause and effect. But even then, the elusive 95 percent confidence interval that researchers strive for is recognition of the absolute limitations of dealing with the intricacies of the human body. Nothing is black-and-white. But when it comes to environmental triggers and the emergence of future diseases, can society afford to wait for absolute certainty?

"Hardly anything anyone does is 100 percent certain," Dr. David Prezant told me once, in a long conversation about the interaction of science and advocacy. "How about nothing that anybody does is 100 hundred percent certain."

In the end, all of them—from Prezant and Paul Lioy to Charles Hirsch, David Worby, Paul Napoli, and James Tyrrell, along with the thousands who are worried about their futures because they once breathed the dust—were looking for certainty. It became clear that there are different standards of certainty, depending on who is trying to find it and where. Medicine has one definition; science and the courts have others.

What they all sought—evidence that a definitive scientific link between dust and disease either exists or does not—is the ultimate proof, but it may not have been a realistic expectation for dealing with an environmental and health catastrophe like ground zero. Even the most convincing study, done to the most exacting standards, could highlight increased risk but would be inadequate to prove that one individual contracted a specific disease after exposure to a particular toxin.

As our storehouse of useful chemicals has grown, we have been forced repeatedly to weigh their benefits against the increased risk and uncertainty they carry. Our industrial past holds many tragic examples of how difficult it is to provide justice after the damage has been done. One case, in particular, involving nuclear workers in upstate New York, casts an eerie shadow over ground zero. We now know that workers' labor with radioactive material for the Manhattan Project during World War II, and later simply working in the same contaminated buildings, sowed the seeds of many illnesses. It took half a century, until 2000, for the federal government to acknowledge its guilt in exposing the workers to excessive radiation without either warning them or offering adequate protection. Even when it had accepted responsibility for what had happened, Washington's response was so complicated that few workers or their survivors ever received adequate compensation. So much time had passed that work records no longer existed, and even the buildings where the men had worked had been torn down long ago. To replicate conditions that had existed then, the government developed an arcane system known as dose reconstruction, which uses old records and surveys to calculate how much radiation a worker was exposed to. Because such records are open to challenge by the victims, their lawyers, and the government, fair compensation can be delayed for years. That experience should stand as sufficient warning that waiting decades for scientific proof can steal even more from those who have been injured.

Science and research are working on solid ground that eventually will provide a set of answers about what happened in New York after 9/11. All three of the principal sources of data about ground zero—the fire department, the city health department's World Trade Center Registry, and the Mount Sinai consortium, including the residents' program at Bellevue Hospital—continue to do the long-term monitoring that should eventually shed light on the most vexing questions. The registry, with its post-9/11 baseline of medical information for 71,000 people, has already shown how the respiratory and mental health symptoms of those who were first on the scene have been the most severe and, in fact, have persisted longer than expected, pointing to a range of problems that will be around long after the trade center site is rebuilt. With additional funds from Washington, the registry has been verifying cancer and mortality rates, and someday might be able to determine whether the dust cut into life expectancy.

That, of course, is the question that has caused the greatest anxiety, no matter how it is answered. A "yes" or "maybe" about cancer can set off tidal waves of anxiety in a city where post-traumatic stress is probably the most pervasive legacy of 2001. Even a negative finding about the dust-to-cancer link triggers anger and sometimes scorn. In 2008, the World Trade Center Medical Working Group, which Mayor Bloomberg pulled together and included, among others, Philip Landrigan, Prezant, and Joan Reibman, reached a clear conclusion about cancer. "To date," the report found, "there is no evidence for or against a causal connection between trade center exposure and any form of cancer." When the group's second annual report came out a year later, it reached the same conclusion. Yet because of the doubt that had contaminated the air over New York for so long, many people refused to accept that finding, certain beyond doubt that a link exists and reminded of it by the tabloids every time a responder dies in a cancer ward.[1]

When three responders died within five days of each other in fall 2009, all from some form of cancer, their families, the advocacy groups they belonged to, and the tabloid press all saw it as proof that, despite the studies, the dust is a killer and deaths would surely continue to mount. On the anniversary of James Zadroga's death in January 2010, some rescue workers gathered at ground zero to read the names of those who had died, regardless of what science said about why. They read 103 names that day. Given the age of the responders, and the high rates of cancer that normally exist in the New York region, there is little doubt that the numbers indeed will continue to rise. But science will find it difficult to pry from that mass of data elements sufficient to form a causal link between cancer and the dust for many years to come.

Mount Sinai's data eventually became much stronger than it was in the unplanned first few years when the Selikoff Clinic had been inundated with wheezing responders and volunteers who gasped for breath after giving their names, although some of the old problems persisted. Doctors there continued to produce important research that covered both raw numbers and individual cases. They found a correlation between duration of exposure and severity of symptoms that was in line with fire department studies. As the decade ended, the consortium continued to register around 100 new patients a month, suggesting a stubborn persistence of symptoms or an inkling among the remaining responders that there's no harm in jumping on the bandwagon. Nearly 10,000 of the 27,250 who had been screened by then had received special medical care, with 71 percent treated for upper-respiratory problems, 46 percent for lower-respiratory problems, and 52 percent for gastrointestinal issues. Nearly a third needed psychiatric counseling for stress. Mount Sinai completed studies on anosmia among responders who had lost all or a portion of their sense of smell, and on sarcoidosis, with results comparable to the fire department's critically important research on the disease.[2]

Landrigan and the others understood the limits of epidemiology and of their own data in meeting the needs of the very people the program was designed to serve. So they continued to do what they had tried to do from the very first days: to make the world aware that something serious was going on and to be on the lookout for signs that it could get worse. And as they produced additional research, they again raised questions about the extent to which advocacy could be taken without compromising science. In 2010 they put out preliminary research findings claiming they were the first to discover potentially serious heart problems in responders. Mount Sinai immediately garnered headlines and was mentioned in nightly newscasts. However, the reality might be different. In a scenario similar to the release of Mount Sinai's multiple myeloma case studies, the researchers pointed out the many limitations of their own work—it was a small sample, there was no control group, and it was far too early to draw any conclusions. The results were presented at a medical conference, not in a peer-reviewed scientific journal. Press releases issued by Mount Sinai only nodded to those factors, and predictably, most news reports ignored them, increasing the worries of thousands of responders who now added heart failure to the list of potential health effects tied to the dust.

From the beginning, the most conclusive findings about the health implications of the dust came from the fire department, and that should continue. Drs. Kerry Kelly and Prezant were, in effect, company doctors, but because of their openness, transparency, and commitment, firefighters trust them. Prezant did not need to use early results to convince his people to come in for screening, nor did he have to advocate for them before reluctant funders the way Mount Sinai's doctors did. The thin line between medicine and advocacy was stouter at the fire department than elsewhere. And Kelly and

Prezant's work after 9/11 demonstrated to the firefighters that their faith in them and their program had been justified.

Prezant believed that he and Kelly might one day be able to use their data to link several autoimmune diseases to the dust, the way sarcoidosis and sarcoid-like granulomatitis were suspected of being connected. He intensively studied diseases such as Lt. Fullam's polymyositis, which he suspected might actually be an autoimmune response instead of simply a connective tissue disease, and thus could have a stronger link to ground zero exposure. Having established that firefighters lost the equivalent of 12 years of lung capacity in the first year after the attacks, Prezant pursued an important milestone: an eight-year study looking at the persistence of lung injuries to determine how many firefighters had recovered since that first year, how many had remained the same, and how many had deteriorated further.

The results of that study provided a revealing peek into the future. Prezant found that the passage of eight years had done little to improve conditions for many firefighters. Respiratory symptoms generally persisted with no meaningful recovery in lung function. That left a substantial proportion of workers—13 percent of the firefighters and 22 percent of the emergency service workers—with abnormal lung function. The long-term persistence of the conditions surprised Prezant, but he did not believe that it indicated disabilities were permanent. Improvement had not come with time, but he felt it could come with treatment. His next goal was trying to tease out whether those who took asthma treatments showed improvement, and if so, whether starting or increasing treatment could help others.

Cancer had been the area of greatest concern since Joel Kupferman and Juan Gonzalez had first raised that alarm. The fire department, the Mt. Sinai Consortium, and the Registry actively tried to find answers to whether cancer rates among the responders had increased. The fire department published cancer rates from its retirement disability database that raised some issues, but it was a limited study that did not include all its responders. When Kelly and Prezant did an exhaustive five-year study after September 11, the results were revealing but far from conclusive. Yet during an interview with me[3] in which he passionately described his research and its limitations,

Prezant insisted that if a statement saying there's no link to cancer is attributed to him, the sentence had to carry an addendum. "If you say that we haven't shown anything yet, you have to in the same sentence say that we may actually publish something different from that, not 20 years from now, but even in the near future, because cancer is a moving target with variable latency periods." In other words, nothing has been ruled out. "Everyone's work on cancer is just a start. It has to be carefully looked at. We have to age-control it, population-control it. It's much more difficult to do epidemiology on cancers." Every initial study will have to be repeated, he said, because cancers are notorious for taking a long time to develop after the initial environmental exposure.

Perhaps because he continued to see individual firefighters in his examining room every Sunday, Prezant was particularly sensitive to the impact his research had on them. He knew that once firefighters ask him "How'm I doing?", their next question invariably would be, "How're the other guys doing?" And because he talks to them frequently and knows them well, he knows how much easier he could make their lives if he were to just say that esophageal cancer, leukemia, multiple myeloma, or any other disease they are battling is linked to the dust, making them eligible for special treatment or additional compensation. But he also knows that if the results are not valid, countless numbers of people who were exposed to trade center dust may be needlessly worried. "For this vulnerable population, any additional stress without cause would be inflicting a second disaster upon them." Without solid science, the credibility of all the trade center programs would be undermined and would handicap the researchers' ability to advocate effectively in the future when answers do become available. Advocacy is most effective when it is based on scientific research that is careful, precise, and above reproach. "Rumors are tempting to embrace because they may be true, and, unfortunately, early on in advocacy efforts they can sometimes be more powerful than facts," Prezant said. "But in the long run, it is facts that provide the strongest basis for advocating real solutions to healthcare problems and providing a true path to recovery."

To help guide them through the very real temptations toward advocacy, and to overcome the limitations of epidemiology, ground zero researchers followed a well-worn path. Where they could find no definitive proof, they applied the criteria of evidence that were put forward by prominent British medical statistician Sir Austin Bradford Hill, who refuted the tobacco industry's claims that cancer could never be conclusively linked to cigarette smoking. Hill proposed nine criteria that, in the absence of absolute proof, could be used to determine a link between environmental sources and disease. Although all nine can be applied to the ground zero exposure, three are particularly significant. One is the strength of the association, which requires that an increase in dose or exposure result in a greater incidence of disease (known as the dose response curve). In his work, Hill looked at lung cancer rates in the general population and compared them with much higher death rates of lung cancer among cigarette smokers, clearly demonstrating the link. Various 9/11 studies have all shown that the closer responders got to the initial dust clouds and gasses, the greater their exposure was to the hazardous material, and the higher their risk of serious illness.

Another Hill criteria is consistency across studies, which the fire department, Mount Sinai, and the registry have shown again and again. Applying this to ground zero means that when a single study cannot provide absolute proof about linkages, consistent results from several different studies can effectively make the case for it. The third criteria is biological plausibility, which Hill tried to explain in a classic 1965 essay by quoting Sherlock Holmes. Holmes, Hill wrote, had advised Dr. Watson, "when you have eliminated the impossible, whatever remains, *however improbable*, must be the truth." The impact of caustic dust, fiberglass, and soot on respiratory systems is well documented and, without question, biologically plausible. The proofs are less solid when it comes to the dangers of asbestos, dioxin, benzene, and many other substances in the dust. Yes, they have been known to cause cancer and other serious illnesses. But latency periods have confounded the issue at ground zero, and reliable conclusions will require long-term monitoring.

Dust became an enduring trope for the emotions and perceptions that hovered over New York, changing the outlines of the city's reality. And in some ways, long after the dust itself was washed down and blown away, the city remained blinded, thrust into a prolonged battle for absolute certainty when such a standard simply did not exist. Large-scale disasters such as ground zero may call for another level of proof that recognizes a preponderance of evidence equally with a reasonable degree of certainty and a pragmatic acceptance of the human cry for help.

This inchoate concept sometimes goes by the name of presumptive proof. As a result of post-9/11 legislation, most of New York City's uniformed responders, as well as most of its municipal employees who were involved in the recovery operations at ground zero, were covered by presumption bills of some form that give them broad access to disability pensions or the workers' compensation system if they develop health problems (respiratory and sinus illnesses, post-traumatic stress, cancer, or even certain autoimmune diseases) that can reasonably be linked to the dust. The New York Workers' Compensation system gave everyone who worked on or near the pile nearly a decade to register their presence there, essentially leaving open the possibility of filing formal claims at some distant moment if an illness can be traced back to 2001.

The Zadroga bill also was outfitted with presumptions (and a shorter list of qualifying conditions), but its rocky legislative history made its passage uncertain. It fell victim to the financial crisis and the uncertainty and skepticism hanging over 9/11 claims, which intensified after Dr. Hirsch released his conclusions about Zadroga's death. With the election of President Obama and the revived Democratic majority, Carolyn Maloney's office worked overtime with other members of the delegation to revive the bill. In summer 2009, a similar proposal was introduced in the Senate for the first time. That version of the Zadroga bill[4] provided long-term funding for screening, monitoring, and treating tens of thousands of eligible responders in the New York area and around the country, along with residents of Lower Manhattan and parts of Brooklyn. It would have covered respiratory diseases, sinus conditions, mental health disorders, and certain musculoskeletal injuries, but it excluded cancer and autoimmune diseases. The bill also would have reopened the victims' compensation fund and kept it operating until 2031, enough time for the traditional latency periods to play out. The bill would even have included long-term liability protection for the city and its contractors.

After all the controversy surrounding the imperfect health studies that had been done—and not done—at ground zero, after the hysterical headlines and the misleading official statements, after all the legal maneuvering in federal court and the sharp elbows in Washington, and even after the shock of Hirsch's conclusions about what had really happened to Zadroga, the bill that still bore his name seemed to finally address every concern. Still, no consensus could be reached. The Patrolmen's Benevolent Association abruptly withdrew its support and campaigned openly against passage of the bill as written because blood illnesses and cancers were not included on the list of diseases linked to the dust. However, the Detectives' Union maintained its support because a provision in the bill allowed those diseases and others to be added later, if warranted. Then activist community groups that had long supported the idea of a federally funded program for responders came out at rallies against this new version of the Zadroga bill, asserting that it shortchanged residents, school children, and downtown office workers. Their calls for a substantial expansion of coverage were met with frustration and sometimes anger from responders who believed that tinkering with the bill might doom it.

As those internal squabbles within the ground zero community were being addressed, the Zadroga bill was overtaken yet again, this time by the President's healthcare overhaul and then the budget crisis. Once more, the bill's message seemed to fall on deaf ears. At a ground zero rally on the eighth anniversary of the attacks, Maloney, surrounded by labor leaders, firefighters, and cops, along with Joe Zadroga and Catherine McVay Hughes and so many other people who had been involved in the struggles since September 11, passionately pleaded for passage of the Zadroga bill. But the public address system at the temporary podium she used could not amplify her voice enough to be heard over the roar of construction machines in the ground zero pit. As she called for action, only those who were closest to her—and who already agreed with her—could hear. The new towers were going up right behind her, and the sound of their rebirth drowned out the cries for help.

A few months later, the Obama administration shocked Maloney and the rest of New York's congressional delegation by abruptly withdrawing its long-promised support for the Zadroga bill, saying that economic hard times made it impossible to back the bill and its price tag of $11 billion over 30 years. The administration did offer to double the yearly appropriation for responder medical programs to $150 million, which would keep them captives of the annual budget cycle. Deeply disappointed, Maloney and the others vowed to fight on, certain they could convince President Obama that the need was real and was not going away.

Resolving these matters is more than simply a medical or scientific challenge. It has to address the way society conceives of the truth. Public perception has shaped the dust as much as the obliterating force of the collapsing towers created it. The dust was transformed by turns from something harmless—which it clearly was not—to something heinous—which, in most cases, it wasn't either. Arrogant media hijacked the story, repeatedly distorting the disaster by either playing up or toning down the danger and ignoring science. An arrogant city government used fear to wrest money from Washington or to slough off its own responsibility. Politicians arrogantly used the disaster to further their careers. And in the end, even some responders acted with arrogance, claiming to have all the answers and intimidating those who dared question them. They all thought they knew best and watched out for their own interests, when the most sincere motivation in the face of disaster ought to have been ensuring the safety, health, and spirit of the city and its people. They were not courageous enough to relay the truth in all its complexity, to distinguish between short-term and long-term health effects, to be precise about what was known and what won't be knowable for a long time, to insist that the difference between safe and dangerous is a matter of data, not degree.

Many mistakes were made. Many opportunities were missed. After nearly a decade, the recovery of New York was still ongoing. Even as the gaping hole at ground zero filled with the concrete and steel of a new vertical port, and sad memorials took shape beside sacred places, the city did not return to what it was the morning of September 11.

As some of the distortions were swept away, the bottom line became somewhat clearer: Many people had been sickened by their exposure to the dust. Many others who had breathed in the dust had not become ill at all, or not in any lasting way. The 2009 report of the mayor's working group concluded as much: "While the vast majority of people exposed to the attacks on 9/11 and its immediate aftermath are healthy and symptom-free, thousands of exposed individuals continue to suffer from WTC-related mental and physical health conditions, and some of these conditions are likely to be chronic." This is what reporter Bob Woodward and Carl Bernstein once called "the best obtainable version of the truth." Those arrogant enough to claim otherwise—who used the tragedy to declare that everyone who breathed the air that Christie Whitman had called safe had become ill, or who contended that all those who had said they were sick were just trying to exploit the system—were guilty of manipulating the truth for their own purposes.

It is important to get this right. To figure out how to respond to an environmental disaster without first throwing environmental safety overboard. To devise a way to balance the economic needs of returning to normal with the need to ensure that the aftermath of a disaster not be allowed to claim more victims. For us to achieve this balance, we need to better understand the limits of science and the degree to which we can guarantee a safe environment. We need to acknowledge that we know what research can tell us, and when, and be prepared to make decisions on that schedule, not our own. We need to vow to stick to the truth, no matter where it leads. We need to strive for certainty, or as close to certainty as is possible or appropriate. And when such assurances cannot be given, we need to avoid temptations to play on public sympathies with weak truths and distorted realities. If the limits or our knowledge and capabilities can be truthfully explained, those who are most affected might comprehend that the efforts of science to provide solutions are constrained by an imperfect reality—but those efforts are better than no solutions at all.

It also is important that we know how to deal with another disaster so that we can limit its afterclap—to use an ancient but fitting word— more comprehensively than was accomplished at ground zero. An afterclap is the unexpected event that comes just when everyone believes something extraordinary has ended, as with the aftershocks that followed the 2010 earthquake in Haiti. In New York, the list of victims of the trade center disaster was not capped on 9/11. And it didn't end with the addition of Felicia Gail Dunn-Jones or with Dr. Sneha Anne Philip, a neighborhood resident who had disappeared on 9/11 and was declared legally dead by the courts in 2008, thus becoming victim 2,751. Hirsch also examined the death of Leon Heyward, a city employee who was swallowed by the dust cloud on September 11 and died of lymphoma-complicating sarcoidosis in 2008. After reviewing the record, Hirsch linked Heyward's death to the dust and, in 2009, declared his death a homicide, adding his name to the official list of victims. He is number 2,752. Surely others will follow.

Ground zero's afterclap itself has prolonged fears. Years after the attacks, subways riders in New York could still board a No. 1 train downtown and see it plastered with posters, paid for by the city's Health and Hospitals Corporation, asking the questions, "Lived There? Worked There? You Deserve Care," and directing them to call a 9/11 health hotline. Workmen removing air-conditioning units from the wall of a building on Greenwich Street in downtown Manhattan found the cavities coated with ground zero dust. Residents moving bookshelves and heavy desks regularly discovered the dust in those hard-to-reach places. Catherine McVay Hughes kept a half-dozen high-powered air purifiers humming in her apartment day and night. Tiny remnants of what once were the world's tallest buildings were probably tucked into corners all over the city. Paul Lioy still kept some of the strange mixture in his cold room, macabre tufts of catastrophe that could no longer harm anyone. The damage had already been done, though how much wouldn't be known for decades to come.

Even then, the true story will take shape only if strict standards of science are imposed, without emotion or pity, but with an under standing of what is technically possible. As compassion fatigue about ground zero set in, battle lines became blurred, and even some of those who suffered the most, such as Ernie Vallebuona and Dave Fullam, started to drop out, shunning the rallies and congressional hearings and wanting nothing more than to spend precious time with their families and start anew.

More interest has been focused on rebuilding the office towers and memorials at ground zero than on rebuilding the lives of those who were injured there. In many ways, building a skyscraper is easier than putting individual lives back together. Yet even the physical reconstruction efforts downtown have not been spared the misery of drawn-out emotional and economic battles. Except for the conspiracy fringe, no one doubts that the towers were destroyed by terrorists, and although disputes over how the rebuilding should proceed drag on, there's almost universal agreement that the World Trade Center should be rebuilt in that consecrated place. But no universal agreement arises over what happened after the buildings fell and what should be done for those whose lives were reshuffled by the dust.

Unlike the dust-covered tea set that became an unforgettable icon of the disaster, their lives cannot simply be rinsed and returned to normal. They may never be together in a single courtroom or congressional hearing or crowded hospital clinic, but they share a similar stake in the future. It will take a heightened sense of fairness and justice, not strict legal interpretations or bull's-eye scientific proof, to do right by those who were claimed by the dust and whose lives were never the same afterward. The courts won't resolve any of the legal puzzles about immunity, liability, or fault, even if a generous monetary settlement is ever reached. Lawsuits like this can go on indefinitely. Because the United States Supreme Court rejected attempts to cut off future claims in other cases, it is unlikely that any attempt to end the lawsuits against the city and the contractors would be successful here. New York is considered a second injury state, which means that even if a responder were to accept a settlement for respiratory injuries, there could be circumstances under which the courts would allow another lawsuit to be filed in the future if that same responder was diagnosed with another disease.

At best, the long, tortuous road taken by the litigation, the millions of pages of documents, and the vast complex of lawyers and doctors and researchers that consumed so much time and money over the years can lay down a map of how to avoid some of the same obstacles next time. But it cannot provide answers. And without such answers being resolved, the obscuring cloud that settled over these issues can never be lifted.

Trust collapsed with the towers, and dust buried the truth. To clear the air and set things right, certain absolutes need to be recognized. Those who are genuinely sick because of the dust should be given sufficient help, generously offered. Those whose lives have been shattered by the dust should receive fair compensation if the entitlements they are already receiving from insurance, pensions, and others sources are inadequate. Those who were exposed to the dust in any way should be monitored for as long as it takes to achieve a reasonable degree of certainty about the long-term effect of breathing in the pulverized remains of the trade center and everything—and everyone—it once held.

For the others—those who are not sick or whose illnesses, unfortunate though they may be, cannot be scientifically linked to the dust—no Super Bowl victory will mark the time they stop thinking of themselves as victims the way the people of New Orleans did early in 2010 (only to wake up a few months later with BP oil trashing their shores, reviving the wretched lucklessness of Katrina and proving how fleeting such artificial impulses can be). Ultimately, it is only within themselves that those consumed by ground zero's afterclap will find the power to clear away the distortions and rebuild perceptions of their own world. Taking nothing away from their hard work and sacrifices at ground zero, it may be necessary to accept that "What else could it be?" is not a valid medical diagnosis or a convincing legal argument. As the years since the attacks pile up, figuring out who is to blame becomes less important than trying to bring it all to an end and, in so doing, rid ourselves once and for all of the mistrust and confusion that were so tragically embodied in the dust.

Endnotes

[1] Both the 2008 and 2009 annual reports are available at www.nyc.gov/html/doh/wtc/html/studies/medgroup.shtml.

[2] World Trade Center Medical Working Group of New York City, *2009 Annual Report on 9/11 Health*, 24 September 2009.

[3] Personal interview, 30 July 2009.

[4] See http://frwebgate.access.gpo.gov/cgi-bin/getdoc.cgi?dbname=111_cong_bills&docid=f:h847ih.txt.pdf.

Epilogue

On the eve of the most bitterly contested trial in recent New York history, both sides in the massive ground zero lawsuit blinked. On a Thursday afternoon in early March 2010, lawyers announced that they had reached the comprehensive type of global settlement that Judge Alvin Hellerstein had been advocating so earnestly for so many years. The 70-page draft agreement that Hellerstein had alluded to in his courtroom a few months earlier, much to the surprise of lawyers, had morphed into 95 pages of excruciatingly detailed compromise, followed by an entire alphabet of exhibits detailing an elaborate scheme for putting a price on sickness without determining fault.

With New York City straining for a way to bring this sorrowful chapter to a peaceful end, the proposal was instantly acclaimed. In a hastily organized round-robin of news conferences and interviews, lawyers for the plaintiffs, the defense, and the captive insurance company recognized the document as an imperfect solution, but one they believed addressed basic issues of fairness that would finally allow injured responders to receive the compensation they justly deserved. The draft deal triggered a citywide catharsis, finally bleeding off some of the bile that had soured New Yorkers since the earliest conflicts over safety and the meaning of the dust.

The good feelings didn't last long and largely evaporated when the dollar figures in the deal were examined more closely. In the years since David Worby had filed the first lawsuit on behalf of Det. John Walcott in 2004, the $1 billion that Congress had dedicated to insuring the city and its contractors had remained firmly fixed at the center of the litigation, and the draft settlement maintained that singular focus. The aggregate worth of the proposal, with all contingencies included, came to $657 million, leaving the captive insurance company with a reserve of around $350 million to cover future lawsuits. Despite having spent $200 million on the city's defense since 2004, the captive fund still contained the original $1 billion, plus an additional $100 million, because some of the contractors' private insurance companies had been forced to cover defense costs. The captive also had accrued interest on its holdings without making major payouts.

Both sides were exhausted after so many years of legal skirmishes and finally gave in. The city's immunity claim was still pending, but it made no sense to wait for Hellerstein to make tough decisions about the legal point he had skirted for years. And even though Worby and Paul Napoli had often told the court that the full $1 billion that Congress had put into the insurance fund was not enough, they had agreed to a far smaller amount just weeks after some of their benchmark cases began to fall apart under closer scrutiny. Had those cases gone to trial as scheduled on May 17, 2010, the first proceedings likely would have been Daubert hearings in which Hellerstein would have had to decide on the admissibility of the scientific evidence and expert witnesses that the plaintiffs planned to use to support their claims about the dust's toxicity. James Tyrrell and the city's legal team were prepared to aggressively challenge the plaintiff's science, which Hellerstein had said all along he expected to be inconclusive, and that could have weakened the responders' cases considerably.

Not only had Worby and Napoli agreed to a smaller settlement amount, but they were sticking to the full fee schedule they had written into their contracts years before. They were to receive a third or more of every individual award, which meant that they stood to rake in more than $200 million of the total settlement. They had written in sweeteners to encourage responders to accept the offer, including an unusual cancer insurance policy with the Metropolitan Life Insurance Company. This insurance was intended to cover the responders' fears of getting cancer in the future. Under the policy, they would receive up to $100,000 if they were diagnosed with leukemia, lymphoma, multiple myeloma, or certain other types of cancer before 2025. By writing the policy and agreeing to the terms of coverage over such a long period, Metropolitan seemed to be tipping its hand in the case. The potential liability of covering 10,000 plaintiffs exceeded $1 billion, whereas the company was being paid only $25 million. Apparently, Metropolitan had bet that this group of rescue and recovery workers did not face extraordinarily high risks of coming down with cancer, otherwise it wouldn't have stuck its neck out to write the policy.

The cancer policy also addressed the concerns of the city and its contractors about future liability. In order to be eligible for the insurance policy and to participate in the settlement itself, plaintiffs had to sign away their rights to sue for any injury—including cancer—that might arise in the future. Furthermore, the proposal would make it tough for new cases to be brought against the city because it required lawyers to first provide reasonable scientific evidence of a scientific link between illnesses and ground zero exposure, the kind of threshold criteria that Worby and Napoli never had to meet.

Settlements can draw a line under a dispute but they don't necessarily resolve anything. This agreement did not imply that the city had accepted blame for what happened, or that the responders had dropped their claims about the city's negligence. Neither science's questions about the relationship between dust and disease, nor the law's questions about who was at fault, were answered. Nor did this settlement prevent new plaintiffs from coming forward. The big price tag, and the captive's bountiful reserves, in fact may have attracted even more litigants. In just the first week after the draft settlement was announced, lawyers filed 600 new cases.

Once again it seemed that the mistrust which had haunted New York since 9/11 was spreading through the city's streets. While the lawyers praised the plan, rescue workers involved in the suit began to attack it. They complained of being pressured to opt in without knowing how much they would receive in compensation. They objected to the way the proposal excluded many diseases. They turned against their own lawyers when they realized that the Worby–Napoli team intended to take a third or more of the money. And many of the workers worried that accepting the terms of the settlement might preclude them from getting a better deal if the Zadroga bill were somehow approved in Washington. Just days after the draft settlement was announced, a House subcommittee approved the main provisions of the bill and moved it to the full committee. The New York congressional delegation worried that the settlement proposal would impede passage of the Zadroga bill, as representatives from other parts of the country questioned the need for it on top of the $657 million payout. But it turned out that the bill threatened the fate of settlement, as responders said they preferred to wait for the legislation to pass before signing. Under terms of the settlement, the 10,000 plaintiffs had 90 days to decide whether to accept the deal. The settlement wouldn't take effect unless at least 95 percent of them signed on.

Hellerstein said that because he had not been directly involved in the negotiations, he would temporarily stop the clock on the pending trials while he analyzed the settlement's fairness and transparency. He also took the unusual step of opening his courtroom to anyone who wanted to tell him how they felt about the proposal. He wanted to provide the same kind of forum that he had offered the families of dead firefighters who had tried to sue the city over the faulty radios a few years before.

On the day he threw open his courtroom to the public, Hellerstein listened to the tearful accounts of several plaintiffs—including John Walcott and Richard Volpe, Worby's first clients. When former New York City detective Candiace Baker told Hellerstein that she'd had five surgeries already for breast cancer, Hellerstein asked her "What do you think my ruling should be?" Baker was flustered; she didn't know how to answer. "Just be as sympathetic and compassionate as possible. That's all I can possibly ask." Another plaintiff, John Damato, said it would be good if the judge could get other defendants to join the settlement. Hellerstein responded, "A judge can't get anyone to settle. That's a matter of private conviction. All I can do is schedule trials and rule according to the merits."

Then Hellerstein did something that surprised even the most experienced attorneys who thought they'd seen everything. Reversing the normal decorum of a federal court, he rose slowly from his chair on the bench and addressed the lawyers and plaintiffs who remained seated before him.

"I have no formal notes," Hellerstein said in an even voice that reached to the back of the courtroom. Standing erect at the bench, he struck a pose of both humility and strength. "I speak, as it were, from the heart."

For much of the previous decade Hellerstein had presided over a multitude of ground zero cases, quietly listening to the families of the victims, to the wounded survivors, to the lawyers on all sides arguing fine points of law, as well as to emotional appeals to his humanity. Through it all he had tried to uphold what he understood were imperfect laws that often left innocent people feeling aggrieved, abused, and abandoned. He confessed that the years he had spent presiding over ground zero cases were the greatest burden, and the greatest challenge, of his life.

"From the beginning I've felt that these [cases] are special, that the people who responded on 9/11 were our heroes," he told those in the courtroom who sat in rapt attention to his words. "They cushioned the blow that was inflicted on our city, our state, our nation, and on each one of us as individuals." He looked over at Walcott sitting in the second row of benches and said he understood that many people had been worn down by the fight and were tired of the delays, but what he was going to say next probably would delay things even further. In his black robe he looked like a short, bespectacled preacher addressing his uneasy congregation. He raised his right hand and admitted that his efforts at reaching a fair settlement of the cases had, in essence, failed. "In my judgment," he said, "this settlement is not enough."

Some of the responders let out a short burst of nervous applause. No one was quite sure whether Hellerstein had invited such a reaction, or would use his power to eject whoever was responsible for the breach of etiquette. "No, I don't want that," he said. "I'm a judge. I'm not a negotiator. I'm giving my impressions." After all the time he had spent shepherding the massive docket of cases forward, Hellerstein made it clear that he had no intention of just sitting idly by as a settlement was put into effect.

While he had been sitting down, Hellerstein was a respected federal judge presiding over an enormously complex legal matter. But standing, he seemed to take on a far more public role, leaving behind the neutrality of the bench and taking up the cloak of advocacy. When he made the extraordinary offer to go to firehouses and meeting halls and personally explain the terms of the settlement, he stepped even further out of character. As Hellerstein became more animated, he turned more emotional. He had stinging criticism for nearly everyone involved in the litigation. He accused Tyrrell and the captive insurance company of defending the city with such rigor and aggressiveness that they left "no bridge unburned and no field unravaged." He charged the captive with fueling the extravagant defense. He complained that Napoli had given far too little scrutiny to claims of illness when he signed up clients, adding many simply because people said they were sick without subjecting them to any tests. But he defended Napoli's work and said it had been conducted at great expense. It would be unfair to expect the plaintiffs to pay such a large percentage of their awards to defray those costs, Hellerstein said. Instead, he also seemed to view the $1 billion plus captive fund as found money that ought to be spent. Just as the captive was going to pay the city's expenses, he said, so too should it pay the plaintiffs' fees. The unaccustomed sound of applause again arose inside courtroom's wood paneled walls.

"No, no. I don't want this. This is not a political speech," Hellerstein objected, gesturing subtly with his hands, so that he looked every bit a politician. It wasn't clear exactly what the judge's remarkable address was supposed to be, or what he would say next. He vowed to cap the plaintiffs' lawyers' fees at reasonable levels and submit the bills to the captive. He wanted the Talmudic draft to be simplified so that workers would know how much they would receive before they decided whether to participate. And Hellerstein wanted the captive to reconsider whether it legitimately needed to reserve so much of the $1 billion for future claims. He said that current needs might well be more important than future ones, and seemed to kick the can down the road, implying that if more money is needed, the city could go back to Congress.

Hellerstein's greatest concern as he promoted a settlement always had been to make sure that those who were most severely injured received the bulk of the compensation. He knew that with 10,000 plaintiffs in the pool, even large amounts of money would dwindle to modest individual payments unless he found a way to skim off cases that had little scientific backing. Hellerstein had so far said little about the science involved in linking the dust to disease. He told the courtroom that he was severely disappointed that the settlement had discarded the computerized database that he had compiled, with the great effort of the special masters, in favor of an entirely new severity chart. In the midst of all the hyperbole and misinformation surrounding the impact of the dust, the special masters' work had sharply delineated what was known about cause and what, lacking hard proof, was considered scientifically implausible.

Although it had not been made public, the special masters' analysis had brought a new perspective to the cases. They had shown that the number of rescue and recovery workers who were seriously ill was far lower than the tallies that Worby and Napoli had claimed. The database contained reports of 61 deaths, 110 heart attacks, and 807 instances of cancer. The most common cancer on the list was skin cancer (188), followed by lung cancer (107) and lymphoma (95). In all, the list covered 57 different types of cancers, including many rare types such as endocrine, vaginal, and penile cancers that had been reported by one or two plaintiffs in the years since 9/11 but that had little or no suspected linkage to the dust.

In addition, the special masters had reported that 2,918 plaintiffs had no illness or impairment that could be categorized on the severity chart. Some had not even submitted medical records to indicate that they had consulted a doctor or been tested about their condition. The special masters surmised that these plaintiffs might have declined to take the tests because they expected to rank quite low on them, which would have handicapped their chances of receiving compensation. Hellerstein finally came out that day in court and said what he had long suspected, and what he had hoped the special masters would have helped him establish—there were too many cases with too little evidence backing their claims. That raised the question of motivation, and that clearly upset Hellerstein.

"If there are discrepancies, I want to know about them. If people have been feeding information into our data bank that is not accurate or for which they wish to escape, I want to know about it. If there's been fraud, I want to know about it," Hellerstein said, looking out over the plaintiffs' lawyers seated in front of him, "and so does the United States attorney."

He also demanded transparency, accountability, and judicial control over the settlement process. Then, just about half an hour after he had stood up to address the court room, Hellerstein was finished. "That is the end of the program," he told the stunned lawyers. He thanked them, and quickly left.

Hellerstein's impassioned tirade blew up the settlement that had taken two years to draft, and left both sides bewildered and concerned. After weighing their options, the city and its contractors challenged Hellerstein's authority to interfere in the settlement, filing an appeal that bounced the matter back to the Second Circuit Court of Appeals. It had become clearer than ever that no matter what legal routes could be navigated, the city would continue to be burdened for the foreseeable future with the uncertainties of 9/11 and its afterclap. The judge's strong reaction would undoubtedly make it more difficult to reach the kind of consensus that a broad settlement requires, although few doubted that a settlement eventually would emerge. Some plaintiffs praised Hellerstein for literally standing up for them in court, yet they were left even more confused than ever about what would happen to them, and how long they would have to wait for help to arrive.

For a brief time, the draft settlement had seemed to offer a way out of the darkness. It did not answer the burning questions about the dust, but it did provide a framework for getting on with life in a city that had spent too long already in the shadows of that day at the dawn of the new millennium. Science hadn't upended the settlement. Neither had the law. It was scuttled because Hellerstein stood up and declared that the system had not worked. Nearly a decade after the towers fell, the courts had not proved liability on the part of the city or its contractors, and had not produced scientific evidence linking the dust to serious disease. Regardless, Hellerstein believed that the $1 billion ought to be spent. The fixes he demanded in essence created a successor to the original compensation fund, but one that would end up burning through as much as $400 million in legal fees to distribute the money. This outcome made it clear that putting up such a bounty may be the least effective way of providing help in the aftermath of a disaster. By avoiding the tough decisions, by winking at the law and bypassing the science, Hellerstein earnestly hoped to satisfy the public's concern that justice be done.

Shocked though they were by the judge's outburst, and frustrated by his interference, both sides realized that they had little choice but to stow away the rhetoric, roll up their sleeves, and get real. The city was well aware that the appeal process could last years, without any guarantees. And on the plaintiffs' side, it was clear that many responders shared the judge's concerns and would probably turn against the settlement. The lawyers set out to find amendments that would satisfy Hellerstein, protect the captive's reserves, and result in an offer that was appealing enough for 95 percent of the responders to accept.

Nearly three months went by before they came back with a plan that Hellerstein was willing to approve. All the major players had given up something, starting with the trial lawyers. The tempest of complaints about their fees led Napoli, Worby, and the other plaintiff lawyers to lower their take from the standard one-third to an exceptional one-quarter. This would still leave them with more than $150 million, but the pot for claimants grew by $55 million.

The captive insurance company agreed to increase the overall amount of compensation by another $50 million. And New York City kicked in the equivalent of about $20 million by allowing municipal employees to hold on to any workers compensation funds they may have received. Normally, the money would have to be repaid once a settlement is reached.

The final result was a package that satisfied Hellerstein's two primary concerns—more money for those who were injured most seriously, and a clear preference for those with illnesses plausibly related to ground zero—although both considerations would prove to be contentious. The new settlement could be worth as much as $712.5 million. The 2,500 workers with minor ailments or no injuries at all would only get a base award of $3,250, minus lawyer's fees and expenses. Although this group constituted 26 percent of the total plaintiffs, their recoveries would amount to just 1.6 percent of the settlement's payout. Another 2,500 workers fit into the next two categories of injury where compensation was somewhat greater, though still quite limited. The remaining 5,000 most seriously injured workers, and the families of some of those who had died, would receive the bulk of the money—about 94 percent of the total.

The new settlement provided far more detailed information about projected payouts and clearly laid out the different categories of injuries into which the participating plaintiffs would be placed. Under this scheme, a worker who developed serious asthma or a lung-scarring disease like sarcoidosis that has been shown by scientific studies to have a relationship to exposure would receive more compensation than someone who developed a heart condition or a solid tumor cancer, such as breast cancer, that so far had not been plausibly linked to the dust. John Walcott's leukemia was included on the list. Marty Fullam's polymyositis was not, but his fibrosis and the lung transplant operation would put him into a higher category.

A respected independent firm was selected to make the decisions about the severity of worker injuries and arrange the payouts so that all claims would be settled in the relatively short time-span of a single year, or just around the time of the tenth anniversary of the attack. Kenneth Feinberg, who ran the original 9/11 fund, was brought in as final arbiter to decide appeals and objections, and he promised to do so quickly and fairly. And Roy D. Simon, a legal ethics expert, was given a special task. He would oversee the plaintiffs' lawyers to make sure they communicate the terms of the settlement accurately and do not pressure anyone into accepting, an extra precaution that could prevent the kind of problems that have haunted Napoli and his lawyers since the big settlement was reached in the fen-phen case a decade ago.

Hellerstein, too, had compromised on the terms of the new settlement. He had dropped his demand that the captive pay the plaintiffs' legal fees. And he did not insist on raiding the captive's reserves. He got the transparency he demanded and the sense of fairness that he said was the "quintessence" of a judge's duties. The way Hellerstein saw it, those who were hurt the most deserved the most, especially if their illnesses could be linked to exposure. No definitive proofs were offered, nor were they requested. Causation was a given, providing the kind of presumptive proof that had long been sought.

However, a provision that was included in the deal suggested that all sides realized, but couldn't openly acknowledge, that a settlement would not settle all issues and the conflict was likely to continue. Anyone who opts out of the settlement to carry on the court fight, and anyone who files a new lawsuit, would first have to prove that there's a plausible connection between the injury and ground zero exposure. Had such a requirement been in place from the beginning, many of the 10,000 suits up for settlement never would have been accepted by the court.

When he held an emotional day-long fairness hearing on the amended settlement, Hellerstein listened patiently as injured workers—some tearful, some enraged—retold their ground zero stories. As they stood at the podium in the crowded courtroom, their entire woeful trajectory from worker to hero to victim to claimant took shape. It embarrassed some of them—big, burly guys who apologized for baring their troubles publicly as they were forced by illness and financial destitution to plead for help. Some tearfully thanked Hellerstein for standing up for them, but then revealed their anger, complaining that the new deal didn't do enough for their particular situation. Candiace Baker, the disabled detective who spoke out at the first hearing several months earlier, called the new deal "wonderful," but was obviously pained that her breast cancer would be worth far less than another responder's lung cancer. She asked for "compassionate equity for all who have suffered." Hellerstein sympathized with her, but said there simply wasn't enough money to do what she asked.

An iron worker who said he'd gone through several operations for an orthopedic injury grabbed the podium and glared at Hellerstein. "I don't want this offer. I want a settlement that's fair to me." Workers who had accepted money from Feinberg's 9/11 fund said it was unfair that they were being blocked from the settlement. Workers who filed their lawsuits after the court's deadline said they were being disqualified unfairly. Workers with mental injuries, or temporary blindness, or early menopause, or children with birth defects, all raged against the inequity of the deal that Hellerstein and the others were embracing.

At the same hearing, some workers showed how dead tired they were of the whole process that had dragged on for nine years and threatened to consume their whole lives, or what remained of them. They echoed Ken Feinberg, who spoke at the fairness hearing by way of a computer link from Washington because President Obama had just named him administrator of a $20 billion compensation fund for the BP oil spill in the Gulf of Mexico. "Perfect is the enemy of the good," he said, a sentiment shared by Hellerstein himself, who said he hoped that the workers would vote to approve the settlement "not because it is perfect, but because it is good. And that's the best you can do."

Responders had three months to decide whether to participate in the settlement, or plunge ahead with their lawsuits. For some, it was an easy decision. "It's time to do the right thing and put this behind everybody," said Perry Forgione, a retired F.B.I. agent who rushed down when the crumbled towers were still smoking. "This has gone on too long."

Others felt the new settlement offered them so little that they would lose nothing if they continued to fight in court. And some were willing to take a chance that the long-delayed Zadroga bill, which would reopen a compensation fund, could actually be passed by the Democrat-controlled Congress and signed into law by the president. Feinberg, Napoli, and Hellerstein warned that the legislation was anything but certain, and waiting for it could turn out to be an endless gambit without any guarantee of fairness, justice, or resolution. They hailed what seemed, at first blush, to be an end to this painful episode in the city's life, though they all realized that the confusion, anger, and resentment caused by the dust were likely to persist for a long, long time.

More important, the ground zero tragedy continued to lay out a blueprint for dealing with other disasters, including the oil spill that was wrecking lives and livelihoods along the Gulf coast. Some workers had fallen ill and, in a pattern that would be familiar to so many people in New York, concern grew that exposure to the oil and the dispersants used to break it up could cause illness and disease. Many of the same issues that have been fought over with such passion in Judge Hellerstein's courtroom are likely to plague the recovery of the Gulf for years to come unless the lessons of ground zero have been learned. Feinberg's appointment to both the ground zero settlement and the BP compensation fund tied the two events together in an extraordinary way. Beneath both lie the same fragile substrata of truth, honesty, common sense, and good judgment. In such difficult situations, there can be no room for arrogance, no way to correct wrongs with words, no escaping consequences by wishing them away, no means of getting at the truth by exaggerating the facts, and no hope of eliminating injustice without first clearing the way for justice.

INDEX

Symbols

$1 billion fund, 273
  lawsuits, 264-265
21 MC 100, 256-259
50-H hearings, 266
1975 fire at telephone company
  switching station, 90
1993 World Trade Center
  attack, 104
9/11 studies
  reliability, 217
  results of
      Mount Sinai studies, 223-225
      Mount Sinai study 2006,
        218-223

A

Abadie, James, 60, 268
accelerated latency, 246
advocacy, 305, 307
afterclap, 313, 315
Agency for Toxic Substances and
  Disease Registry, 154
Agent Orange, 274
air monitors, 77
air quality, 37, 39-40
Air Transportation Safety and
  System Stabilization Act, 256

air-monitoring equipment, 49
Airborne Visible/Infrared Imaging
  Spectrometer (AVIRIS), 22
alkalinity of dust, EPA reaction, 296
AMEC, 58
American Home Products, 249
anguish of families, 272
Anna (rescue dog), 129-131
anosmia, 305
apartments, decontaminating, 150
Armed Forces Institute of
  Pathology, 182
Army Corps of Engineers, 55
asbestos, 15, 19, 102, 296
  dust, 20
  exposure levels, 35
  mesothelioma, 102
  safety standards, 35-37
aspergillosis, 131
asthma, 158, 223
Asthmamoms.com, 146
AstraZeneca, Budesonide
  inhalers, 90
ATC Associates of New York, 70
Atlas, Sarah, 128-134, 275
Ausmus, David, 58, 72-74
autopsies
  guidelines for, 235
  of Zadroga, James, 229-231
AVIRIS (Airborne Visible/Infrared
  imaging Spectrometer), 22

In an increasingly competitive world, it is quality
of thinking that gives an edge—an idea that opens new
doors, a technique that solves a problem, or an insight
that simply helps make sense of it all.

We work with leading authors in the various arenas
of business and finance to bring cutting-edge thinking
and best-learning practices to a global market.

It is our goal to create world-class print publications
and electronic products that give readers
knowledge and understanding that can then be
applied, whether studying or at work.

To find out more about our business
products, you can visit us at www.ftpress.com.